PHP

20 Lessons to Successful Web Development

About the Author

Robin Nixon is a prolific author on programming and web development (as well as psychology and motivation), with his books having been translated into numerous foreign languages and frequently topping both the U.S. and international computer book charts. He has worked with computers and technology all his life, and began writing about the subject about 35 years ago.

He has authored hundreds of articles, and over two dozen books, and is a popular video and online instructor, with thousands of students taking his courses. Robin is also an accomplished programmer, developer, and entrepreneur, with several successful Internet startups to his name, from which he has learned a wealth of programming hints and tips, which he enjoys passing on in his expanding range of web development books, including the following titles:

- *HTML5: 20 Lessons to Successful Web Development* (McGraw-Hill Education, 2015)
- *JavaScript: 20 Lessons to Successful Web Development* (McGraw-Hill Education, 2015)
- *CSS & CSS3: 20 Lessons to Successful Web Development* (McGraw-Hill Education, 2015)
- *Learning PHP, MySQL, JavaScript, CSS & HTML5* (O'Reilly, 2014)
- *Web Developer's Cookbook* (McGraw-Hill Education, 2012)
- *HTML5 for iOS and Android* (McGraw-Hill Education, 2010)

About the Technical Editor

Albert Wiersch has been writing software since the Commodore VIC-20 and Commodore 64 days in the early 1980s. He holds a Bachelor of Science degree in computer science engineering and an MBA from the University of Texas at Arlington. Albert currently develops and sells software that helps web developers, educators, students, businesses, and government agencies check their HTML and CSS documents and their websites for quality problems, including many SEO (search engine optimization), mobility, and accessibility issues, with discounts made available to students. His website is *HTMLValidator.com*.

PHP

20 Lessons to Successful Web Development

Robin Nixon

New York   Chicago   San Francisco
Athens   London   Madrid   Mexico City
Milan   New Delhi   Singapore   Sydney   Toronto

Library of Congress Cataloging-in-Publication Data

Nixon, Robin, 1961–
  PHP: 20 lessons to successful web development / Robin Nixon.
    pages cm
  ISBN 978-0-07-184987-6 (alk. paper)
  1. PHP (Computer program language) 2. Internet programming. 3. Web site development.
I. Title.
  QA76.73.P224.N5935   2015
  006.7'6—dc23   2014045720

McGraw-Hill Education books are available at special quantity discounts to use as premiums and sales promotions, or for use in corporate training programs. To contact a representative, please visit the Contact Us pages at www.mhprofessional.com.

PHP: 20 Lessons to Successful Web Development

1234567890 DOC DOC 1098765

ISBN   978-0-07-184987-6
MHID   0-07-184987-4

Sponsoring Editor Brandi Shailer	**Copy Editor** Bart Reed	**Illustration** Cenveo Publisher Services
Editorial Supervisor Patty Mon	**Proofreader** Claire Splan	**Art Director, Cover** Jeff Weeks
Project Manager Kritika Kaushik, Cenveo® Publisher Services	**Indexer** Ted Laux	**Cover Designer** Jeff Weeks
Acquisitions Coordinator Amanda Russell	**Production Supervisor** Jean Bodeaux	
Technical Editor Albert Wiersch	**Composition** Cenveo Publisher Services	

To Julie

Contents at a Glance

Contents

x Contents

Acknowledgments

Once again I would like to thank the amazing team at McGraw-Hill Education, with whom it is always a real pleasure to work on new book projects. In particular, I would like to thank my Sponsoring Editor Brandi Shailer, Amanda Russell for overseeing the project's development, Editorial Supervisor Patty Mon, Production Supervisor Jean Bodeaux, Copy Editor Bart Reed, and Jeff Weeks for the excellent cover design. Thanks also goes again to Albert Wiersch (whom I have had the pleasure of working with on a number of occasions) for his meticulous eye for detail during technical review.

Introduction

Why This Book?

The concept for this book grew out of Robin's extremely popular online courses, in which thousands of students are enrolled. From their feedback, it became evident that the reason for this popularity was that students love the way the material is broken up into easy-to-digest lessons, each of which can be completed in an hour or less. They also like the no-nonsense, jargon-free, and friendly writing style.

Now, working together, Robin and McGraw-Hill Education have further revised, updated, and developed his PHP course into this book, which not only will teach you everything you need to learn in 20 lessons (of less than an hour each), but also includes a detailed video walkthrough for each lesson, comprising over 5.5 hours of footage in total.

Watch the video after reading the lesson to reinforce key concepts, or use the video as a primer to working through each print lesson. Together, these course materials make learning PHP easier than it has ever been, and are the ideal way for you to add these essential skills to your web development toolkit.

Access the videos by going to mhprofessional.com/nixonphp/.

Who Should Read This Book

Each lesson is laid out in a straightforward and logical manner, with plenty of examples written using simple and clear PHP. Before moving onto each subsequent lesson, you have the opportunity to test your new knowledge with a set of 10 questions about the material you have just learned. You can also work along with every lesson by watching its accompanying video tutorial.

Even if you've never programmed before, you will still learn everything you need from this book, because the principles behind how programming works are fully explained, and no prior knowledge is ever assumed. Between the lessons, the self-test questions, and the videos, this course will ensure that you learn the language thoroughly and quickly.

To save you typing them in, all the example files from the book are saved in a freely downloadable zip file available at the companion website: *20lessons.com*.

What This Book Covers

This book covers every aspect of PHP, starting with basic syntax and language rules, such as where and how you include PHP in your web documents. You will also learn about numeric and string variables, arrays and objects, and how to assign, manipulate, and read values. More advanced techniques, such as using hashes to index into associative arrays and accessing multidimensional arrays, are also made easy.

How to loop code and control program flow with conditional statements is explained in plain English, as well as how to create and use functions and methods, in either a procedural or object-oriented manner. Important techniques such as managing cookies and local storage as well as controlling background Ajax communications are all revealed in simple, short examples.

By the time you finish the book's 20 lessons, you'll have a thorough grounding in PHP, and will be able to use it to dynamically enhance your web pages.

How to Use This Book

This book has been written in a logical order so that each lesson builds on information learned in the previous ones. You should begin at Lesson 1 and then work sequentially through the book, proceeding to the next lesson only when you can correctly answer the self-test questions in the previous one.

Lessons should take you less than an hour to finish, including viewing the accompanying video walkthrough provided with each one. With over 5.5 hours of video in total, that's an average of 16 minutes dedicated to each lesson.

How Is This Book Organized?

This book takes you right from the basics through to advanced techniques, and includes the following lessons.

In Part I, Introduction to PHP; Incorporating PHP Into a Web Page; Learning PHP Language Syntax; Using Constants and Superglobals; Working with Arithmetic Operators; Applying Comparison and Logical Operators; Creating Arrays; Managing Multidimensional Arrays; Calling Array Functions; Advanced Array Manipulation; Controlling Program Flow; and Looping Sections of Code.

In Part II, the lessons include: Writing Functions; Manipulating objects; Handling Errors and Expressions; Building Web Forms; Maintaining Security; Accessing Cookies and Files; Advanced File Handling; and Authentication, Sessions and Ajax.

PART I

PHP Basics

1

Introduction to PHP

 To view the accompanying video for this lesson, please visit mhprofessional.com/ nixonphp/.

PHP is a free scripting language that is provided on most Linux, Unix, and BSD systems, or it can easily be installed on them. It is also freely available on both Microsoft Windows PCs and Apple Mac OS X computers. Therefore, no matter what platform you develop with, there is a version of PHP available for you.

The lessons in this book are aimed squarely at people who have learned basic HTML (and perhaps a little CSS) but are interested in doing more. For example, you may wish to create more dynamic systems, provide form processing of user-supplied data, support Ajax functionality, and more. During the course of these lessons, you'll be shown how to do all these things and much more using PHP.

As you progress, it is never assumed that you know anything about a solution, and you are taken through each example, step by step, with the explanations included, so there is minimal need to look up anything elsewhere. All the examples' files from the lessons are in a free ZIP archive, which you can download at the *20lessons.com* website.

A Little History

The PHP programming language was written by Rasmus Lerdorf, and it was originally crafted from a set of Perl scripts he combined into what he called his "Personal Home Page" tools, hence the name PHP. He used these scripts to display data such as his résumé as well as store and report analytics such as his web page activity, among other things. Having started his project in 1994, Lerdorf refined it by rewriting all the scripts in C, compiling them, and then releasing the result to a Usenet group in 1995. The syntax of PHP was similar to Perl because it was loosely based on that used in the C programming language, and it had much of the same functionality that PHP provides today, with access to variables, form handling, and embedded HTML.

The Usenet upload was received with enthusiasm, and soon a team of developers had assembled who spent the next couple of years extending, improving, and testing PHP until they felt it was ready for wider publication in 1997, particularly once Zeev Suraski and Andi Gutmans (a pair of Israeli developers) had rewritten the main parser, making it significantly faster and more powerful. They also changed the full name of the program to *PHP: Hypertext Processor*.

Soon after, the Israeli developers started work on rewriting the core engine of PHP, which was called Zend (presumably a contraction of Zeev and Andi), the same name as a company they founded in Israel. For a while Zend offered a superb introductory solution for beginning programs in the form of their free Community Edition server. However, this is no longer available. Therefore, until you know whether you'll need all the extra features of a premium product, I generally recommend you begin with installing the free XAMPP suite (see "Installing a PHP Server," later in the lesson).

Info for Programmers

If you can already program in another language such as C or Java, for example, you'll find yourself at home with PHP, and here are a few things you should know about the language that will make your learning process even quicker. If you are not a programmer, you may skip to the next section because these terms will be explained in later lessons.

To begin with, PHP supports much of the structured programming syntax used in C, such as `if()` statements, `while()` and `for()` loops, `switch()` statements, and so on. Also, like in C, each statement must be terminated with a semicolon.

PHP is a scripting language, so it's not compiled until runtime. Also, as with other scripting languages, it uses dynamic typing, in which types (integer, string, array, and so on) are associated with values rather than variables. Values are interpreted as integers, floating point, strings, or other types according to the way in which they are used within an expression. This makes PHP easy to use because you don't have to declare the type of a variable. However, it can result in unexpected errors in certain instances, unless you force the variable type in a process known as *casting*.

Being scripted, PHP code can be placed within HTML tags to add functionality to basic HTML web pages. In fact, you can have as many segments of PHP as you like in a web document, or simply include PHP program files. Unlike in C and Java, though, all variables in PHP must be prefaced with a $ symbol, and omitting this symbol is the cause of most syntax errors encountered by beginners to PHP—so make sure you use it.

PHP supports object-oriented programming (OOP) and offers private and protected member variables and methods, along with abstract classes, final classes, abstract methods, and final methods. It also uses a standard way of declaring constructors and destructors, similar to that of other object-oriented languages such as C++, and it has a standard exception handling model.

Why Is PHP so Popular?

There are three main reasons for PHP's popularity. First of all, PHP integrates seamlessly with HTML. Even if you know next to no programming, it's very easy to rename your *.html* files to *.php*, and they will automatically become PHP programs, albeit ones that display themselves as an HTML page.

But then, whenever you need a little dynamic functionality, you can drop in a quick line of PHP code, such as the following snippet, for example, which will display the day of the week (like "Wednesday"):

```
<?php echo date("l"); ?>
```

Second, it's easy to learn. With a few simple PHP functions under your belt, almost without knowing it, you're already a PHP programmer. Add in `for()` loops and a couple of other constructs, and you can very quickly start making your own dynamic websites.

Third, there's excellent support from the PHP programming community; just type **help PHP** into Google, and you'll be presented with a staggering 1.4 billion search results.

Downloading and Installing Web Browsers

If you are going to test your PHP programs thoroughly, you will need to see how they run on all the different browsers currently in use. Following is a list of the five major web browsers and their Internet download locations. The web pages at these URLs are smart and offer up the correct version to download according to your operating system, if available:

- **Apple Safari**   *apple.com/safari*
- **Google Chrome**   *google.com/chrome*
- **Microsoft Internet Explorer**   *microsoft.com/ie*
- **Mozilla Firefox**   *mozilla.com/firefox*
- **Opera**   *opera.com/download*

Even though Safari and Chrome (and now Opera) are built on the same Webkit rendering engine, to ensure your programs work as intended, you should install as many of these browsers on your computer as you can, because they all have their own particular quirks and differences.

Unfortunately, not all browsers are available on all hardware configurations, because development of Internet Explorer for the Mac was halted many years ago (when it reached version 5), but you can install all other main browsers on OS X. Also, if you're running any version of Windows from XP onward, you will be able to install all the latest browsers, except for the latest version of Safari, because Apple stopped updating Safari for Windows (also at version 5) in about 2012 (seems like a bit of tit-for-tat going on here between Apple and Microsoft).

Your best option on a Mac is to either perform a dual install of Windows alongside OS X or ensure you have access to a Windows PC. After all, unless you intend to only develop for Mac computers, people using a Windows operating system will represent two-thirds of your users. And developers using Windows systems really need to obtain access to a Mac for testing purposes.

As for Linux, not only does it not have access to Internet Explorer, there is no version of Safari either, although all the other browsers do come in Linux flavors. And, as with OS X, although various solutions exist that incorporate Wine for running Internet Explorer, they only seem to work with some distributions and not others. Therefore, it can be a bit of a minefield trying to find a bulletproof way for you to run Windows browsers on Linux.

What it all comes down to is that, as a developer, you need access to as wide a range of platforms on which to test your web pages as you can get your hands on—and not just from the point of view of different browsers and hardware, because you also must take into consideration differing graphics cards and processor speeds (which can be critical where performance is demanded) as well as, depending on the application, various alternative types of input.

Note   Don't forget that nowadays you also need to check your projects on iOS and Android phones and tablets, as well as Windows Phone devices. And be prepared for some extra coding, because phones and tablets work quite differently from desktops and laptops, mainly due to the emphasis on touch for input.

Choosing a Program Editor

Long gone are the days of relying on a simple text editor for coding, because software for writing program code has progressed by leaps and bounds in recent years, with text editors having been replaced by powerful program editors that highlight your syntax using different colors and can quickly locate things for you such as matching (and missing) brackets and braces, and so on.

Following is a list of free program editors (including the platforms they run on and their download URLs). These will all do a great job of helping you to write code quickly and efficiently. Which one you choose is largely down to personal preference—in my case, I have settled on Notepad++, which is shown in Figure 1-1.

Free Program Editor	Platform	URL
Bluefish	Linux/Mac	*bluefish.openoffice.nl*
Cream	Linux/Windows	*cream.sourceforge.net*
Editra	Linux/Mac/Windows	*editra.org*
Free HTML Editor	Windows	*coffeecup.com/free-editor*
jEdit	Linux/Mac/Window	*jedit.org*
Notepad++	Windows	*notepad-plus.sourceforge.net*

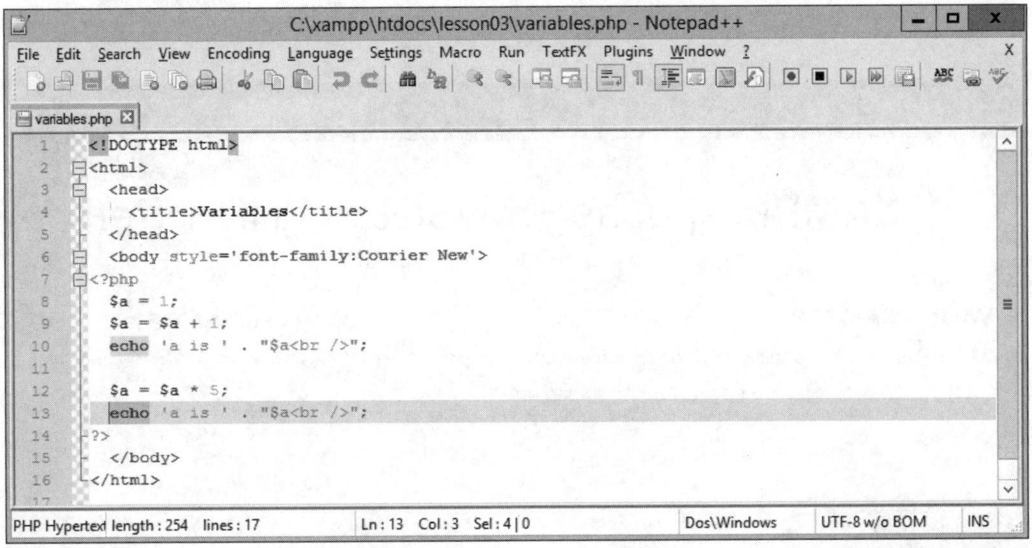

The Notepad++ window titled "C:\xampp\htdocs\lesson03\variables.php - Notepad++" shows the following code in the editor tab "variables.php":

```
1   <!DOCTYPE html>
2   <html>
3     <head>
4       <title>Variables</title>
5     </head>
6     <body style='font-family:Courier New'>
7   <?php
8       $a = 1;
9       $a = $a + 1;
10      echo 'a is ' . "$a<br />";
11
12      $a = $a * 5;
13      echo 'a is ' . "$a<br />";
14  ?>
15    </body>
16  </html>
17
```

Status bar: PHP Hypertext length : 254   lines : 17   Ln : 13   Col : 3   Sel : 4 | 0   Dos\Windows   UTF-8 w/o BOM   INS

FIGURE 1-1   Editing a PHP file in Notepad++

When using a program editor, you will usually find that by moving the cursor to different parts of a program, you can highlight sections of the code. For example, placing the cursor next to any bracket in Notepad++ automatically highlights the matching one.

Program editors also commonly support multiple tabs, folding away sections of code that aren't being worked on, multiple views into the same document, search and replace across multiple documents, and so on—all features that you will miss once you grow used to using them.

Installing a PHP Server

If you wish to test your code on a local development computer before uploading it to a web server elsewhere, you'll need to install a web server and PHP processor. This means you can instantly try out any code changes you make without having to upload them to a server first, thus speeding up the development process.

Installing a PHP web server is relatively simple because there's a great suite of server software called XAMPP that includes a PHP processor, Apache Web Server, MySQL database, and even a Perl processor (should you need access to one). You can download an installer for all of Windows, OS X, and Linux from *apachefriends.org*, as shown in Figure 1-2.

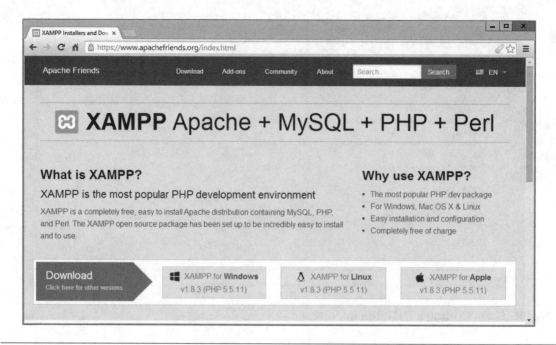

FIGURE 1-2   You can download XAMPP right from the website's main page.

Installation is quite straightforward. Simply follow the various prompts and (unless you have a good reason to choose otherwise) accept the default options given to you during setup.

Note On a Linux computer the chances are that you already may have all of PHP, Apache and MySQL already installed, and you might well be able to do without XAMPP. But if not, or if you're unsure, go ahead and install XAMPP.

The place where you will store all your PHP files (and from where they will run) is known as the server's *document root,* and you will need to know where this is. Following is a list of default locations for document root that XAMPP creates on different operating systems. If you keep your various HTML, JavaScript, and PHP files in that folder (and subfolders), they can all be served up by the Apache Web Server:

- **Windows**   C:/xampp/htdocs
- **Mac OS X**   /Applications/XAMPP/htdocs
- **Linux**   /opt/lampp/htdocs/

For further assistance on setting up XAMPP on your computer, visit one of the following FAQ pages:

- **Windows** apachefriends.org/faq_windows.html
- **Mac OS X** apachefriends.org/faq_osx.html
- **Linux** apachefriends.org/faq_linux.html

Summary

With all that preamble and introduction out of the way, you should be ready to start out on the lessons, beginning with the following one, which explains how to incorporate PHP code in your web pages.

Self-Test Questions

Test how much you have learned in this lesson with these questions. If you don't know an answer, go back and reread the relevant section until your knowledge is complete. You can find the answers in the appendix.

1. What are the three major platforms on which PHP is available?

2. Is PHP a compiled or scripted language?

3. How many sections of PHP can you include in an HTML document?

4. Which character must be placed in front of all PHP variables?

5. Does PHP support object-oriented programming (OOP)?

6. What file extension should you give to PHP documents?

7. What are the five main browsers with which you should test your PHP programs?

8. With which software can you write and edit PHP programs?

9. How can you install a PHP server on your computer?

10. From where are PHP programs stored and run on your computer?

Incorporating PHP into a Web Page

 To view the accompanying video for this lesson, please visit mhprofessional.com/nixonphp/.

The whole point of PHP is that it is designed to offer dynamic functionality to what previously were static web pages. Therefore, PHP code is generally embedded within the web page to which it applies. This can be in the form of the direct code itself or by means of a statement that tells the browser the location of a file containing some PHP to load in and execute. This external file may be on the same or a different web server.

Additionally, the location within a web page at which you insert the PHP (or link to a PHP file) becomes the location where any output from the PHP will be inserted. Therefore, for this and other reasons, where you place your PHP can be important. So I'll begin this course by looking at how and where you should include PHP in your web pages.

Where to Place the PHP Code

It can make a difference where you place your PHP code. For example, if you wish default output to go straight into the current document's body, you may choose to place your PHP somewhere directly within the <body> and </body> tags. On the other hand, if you wish to be able to output HTML within the head of a document, you might choose to place your PHP code within the <head> and </head> tags. Or you might place *all* your HTML output within a PHP script, outputting it from built-in functions.

In the Document Head

To insert your PHP within the head of a document, you must place < ?php and ? > tags where the script is to go, like this (highlighted in bold):

```
<html>
  <head>
    <title>Page Title</title>
    <?php
      // Your PHP goes here
    ?>
  </head>
  <body>
    The document body goes here
  </body>
</html>
```

In the Document Body

To insert your PHP within the body of a document, you must place < ?php and ? > tags where the script is to go, as shown here (highlighted in bold text) and in Figure 2-1, where some PHP commands are placed within a document's body in code being viewed in a program editor:

```
<html>
  <head>
    <title>Page Title</title>
  </head>
  <body>
    The document body goes here
    <?php
      // Your PHP goes here
    ?>
  </body>
</html>
```

Including PHP Files

If you wish to keep your PHP code separate from your document contents (something you are likely to want to do once your PHP starts to become any length other than small), you can place it in its own file (usually with the file extension *.php*) and,

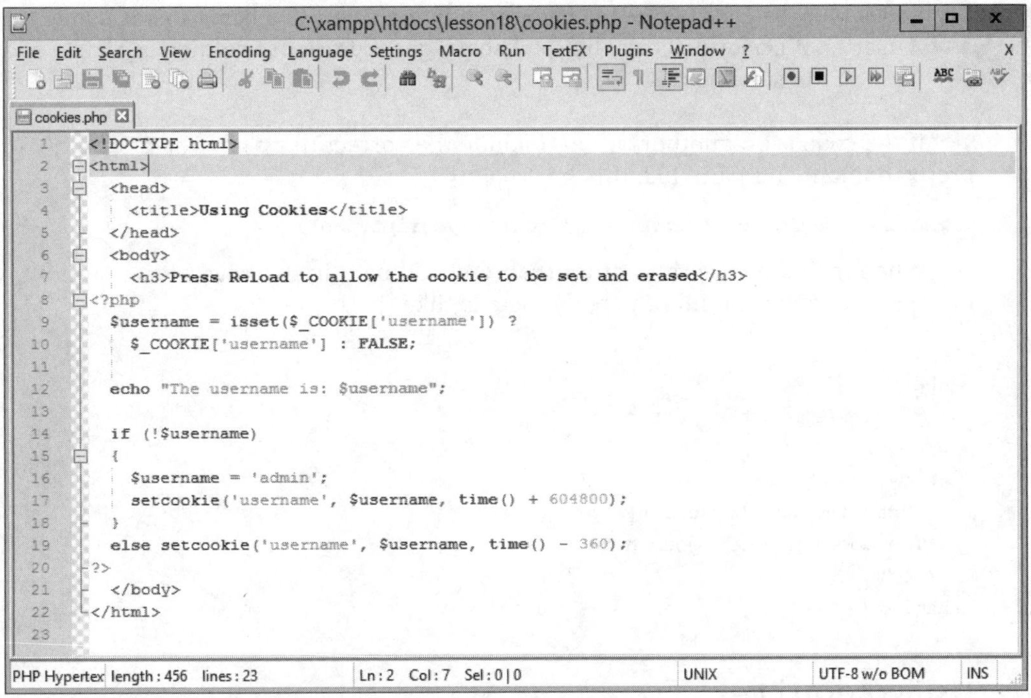

```
                C:\xampp\htdocs\lesson18\cookies.php - Notepad++         _ □ X
File  Edit  Search  View  Encoding  Language  Settings  Macro  Run  TextFX  Plugins  Window  ?         X

cookies.php

  1    <!DOCTYPE html>
  2    <html>
  3      <head>
  4        <title>Using Cookies</title>
  5      </head>
  6      <body>
  7        <h3>Press Reload to allow the cookie to be set and erased</h3>
  8    <?php
  9      $username = isset($_COOKIE['username']) ?
 10        $_COOKIE['username'] : FALSE;
 11
 12      echo "The username is: $username";
 13
 14      if (!$username)
 15      {
 16        $username = 'admin';
 17        setcookie('username', $username, time() + 604800);
 18      }
 19      else setcookie('username', $username, time() - 360);
 20    ?>
 21      </body>
 22    </html>
 23

PHP Hypertex  length : 456   lines : 23        Ln : 2  Col : 7  Sel : 0 | 0        UNIX        UTF-8 w/o BOM    INS
```

FIGURE 2-1   PHP embedded in an HTML document

instead of inserting lines of code between `<?php` and `?>` tags, you would simply place an `include` statement, like this (highlighted in bold):

```
<html>
  <head>
    <title>Page Title</title>
    <?php
      include 'myscript.php';
    ?>
  </head>
  <body>
    The document body goes here
  </body>
</html>
```

If the script file is not in the current directory, you must include the path along with the filename, like this:

```
<?php include 'pathtofolder/myscript.php'; ?>
```

If the code is on another server, include the correct `http://` (or `https://`) prefix, domain and path, like this:

```
<?php include 'http://server.com/folder/myscript.php'; ?>
```

When including a script, rather than embedding it in the head of a document, you may choose to place it into the body instead, like this:

```
<html>
  <head>
    <title>Page Title</title>
  </head>
  <body>
    <?php include 'myscript.php'; ?>
    The document body goes here
  </body>
</html>
```

Using `require`

When you issue an `include` statement, if the file to include is not found, no error will be displayed. However, because the file is not included, your page may not display correctly. To cater to this possibility, you can use the alternative `require` statement, which will issue an error if the file is not found, like this:

```
<?php require 'myscript.php'; ?>
```

Using `include_once` and `require_once`

Sometimes you wish to have a script included *only once* in a web page, and you can do this by adding the suffix `_once` to either the `include` or `require` statement, like this:

```
<?php include_once 'myscript.php'; ?>
<?php require_once 'myscript.php'; ?>
```

In either case, if the file has already been included into the current document, the statement will be ignored so that the file is not included again. Otherwise, the file will be included if it exists. If the file doesn't exist, no error will be given if you use `include_once`, but you will receive an error when using `require_once`.

Using Comments

Before looking at the PHP language and its syntax in the following lesson, I want to first introduce the commenting feature. Using comments, you can add text to a PHP program that explains what it does. This will help you later when you are debugging, and is especially helpful when other people have to maintain code that you write.

There are two ways to create a comment in PHP, the first of which is to preface it with two slashes, as follows:

```
// This is a comment
```

You can also place a comment after a PHP statement, like the following, which assigns a value to a variable (remember that PHP variables begin with a $ symbol):

```
$anumber = 42; // Assigns 42 to $anumber
```

Alternatively, if you wish to temporarily prevent a line of code from executing, you can insert a comment marker before it, and the statement will be completely ignored, like this:

```
// $anumber = 42;
```

Sometimes you need to be able to comment out more than a single line of text. In this case, you can use the multiline form of commenting, where you start the comment with /* and end it with */, like this:

```
/* This is a multiline
   set of comments, which
   can appear over any
   number of lines     */
```

 As well as supporting extensive documentation, this form of commenting lets you temporarily comment out complete blocks of code by simply placing the start and end comment tags as required—something that can be extremely helpful when debugging.

Using Semicolons

You must add a semicolon after every PHP statement, and you can place more than one statement on a single line, as long as you separate the statements with a semicolon. For example, the three following lines of code are all valid syntax:

```
$a = 1;
$b = 2;
$a = 1; $b = 2;
```

However, none of the following are valid because PHP will not know how to make sense of anything due to the omission of semicolons:

```
$a = 1
$b = 2
$a = 1 $b = 2
```

 Think of the semicolon as acting like a command that tells PHP it has reached the end of a statement and can now process it. You do not, however, have to place semicolons at the end of lines that are commented out.

Summary

Now you know how and where to put PHP in your web pages and have a basic understanding of how to create a PHP statement or comment. In the following lesson, I'll begin to explain the syntax of the language.

Self-Test Questions

Test how much you have learned in this lesson with these questions. If you don't know an answer, go back and reread the relevant section until your knowledge is complete. You can find the answers in the appendix.

1. Where in a document can you place sections of PHP code?

2. How can you include a file of PHP instructions into a document?

3. How can you prevent an external PHP file from being included multiple times?

4. How can you ensure that an external PHP file is included (issuing an error if this is not possible)?

5. How can you ensure that a PHP file is included *and* that it doesn't get included more than once?

6. How can you create a single-line comment in PHP?

7. How can you create a multiline comment in PHP?

8. What must you place after each PHP instruction to indicate it is complete?

9. Is this line of code legal PHP?

   ```
   $items = 120; $selection = 7;
   ```

10. Will this line of PHP code work?

    ```
    $items = 120 $selection = 7;
    ```

LESSON 3

Learning PHP Language Syntax

To view the accompanying video for this lesson, please visit mhprofessional.com/
nixonphp/.

I've already discussed some of the syntax used by the PHP language, such as how
to comment out sections of code and how semicolons must be used after each
statement. But what is meant by *syntax*? Well, it's a set of rules that define how to
correctly structure a PHP program.

In this lesson, I'll outline the major syntax issues so that when you start programming,
you'll introduce the minimum of errors, so please forgive me if there's a little overlap with
earlier lessons.

Case Sensitivity

PHP is what is known as a *case-sensitive language,* which means that it distinguishes
between the use of the uppercase and lowercase letters (that is, a-z and A-Z). For example,
the variable $MyVariable is quite different from $myvariable (variables being
special names used to stand in for values such as numbers or strings of characters,
which is explained a little further on).

PHP will treat these as two totally different variables, so you need to be careful
when choosing your variable names. Generally, I observe the following guidelines so that
I can more easily go back and understand code I have written some time in the past:

- All global variables that are accessible anywhere in a program are set to all uppercase,
  such as $HIGHSCORE.
- Temporary variables used in loops are single lowercase letters, such as $j.

This is the formatting that I use, but you may choose to apply different upper- and
lowercase rules here, or you can simply stick to all lowercase—it's entirely up to you.

Whitespace

Any spaces and tabs are known as *whitespace*, and any combination of these is usually treated by PHP as if it were a single space. The exception is when they are placed inside quotation marks, in which case they form part of a string, and all the characters are used.

Newline and carriage return characters are also treated as whitespace by PHP (unless within quotes). For example, the statement $a = $b + $c; is valid on a single line, but you may also format it in the following manner, which illustrates one reason for PHP requiring semicolons (to allow you to split long statements across multiple lines):

```
$a = $b
+ $c;
```

Variables

A *variable* in any programming language is simply a container for a value. For example, imagine that you have a few empty plastic pots into which you can place items (see Figure 3-1). Think of these as a metaphor for variables, in that you can take a small piece of paper and write the number 42 (for example) on it and insert it into one of the pots. If you then take a marker pen and write $MyVariable on the pot, it is just like a PHP variable being set using this line of code:

```
$MyVariable = 42;
```

FIGURE 3-1   An empty pot and blank piece of paper

Figure 3-2 shows the pot now labeled and the paper written on. You can now manipulate this variable in a variety of ways. For example, you can add another value to it, like this:

```
$MyVariable = $MyVariable + 13;
```

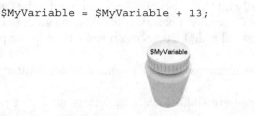

FIGURE 3-2   The pot has been labeled and the paper written on.

This has the effect of adding 13 to the value of 42 already stored in the variable so that the result is 55, the new value held in the variable. This is analogous to taking the piece of paper with the number 42 written on it out of the pot labeled $MyVariable, noting the value, adding 13 to it, and then replacing that piece of paper with another on which you have written the number 55 (see Figure 3-3), which you then place back into the pot.

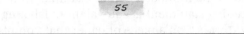

FIGURE 3-3   **A new slip of paper with the number 55 on it**

Likewise, you might issue the following command, which will multiply the current value in the variable (55) by 3:

```
$MyVariable = $MyVariable * 3;
```

Again, this is equivalent to taking the paper from the pot, performing the multiplication, and placing a new piece of paper with the result of 165 (see Figure 3-4) back into the pot. This way, any time that value needs to be referenced (looked up), the pot can simply be opened and the slip of paper inside then read.

165

FIGURE 3-4   **Another piece of paper, this time with the number 165 on it**

Variable Naming

A number of rules govern how you use the PHP programming language. For instance, variables must begin with a $ symbol, which should be followed by either an uppercase or lowercase letter (a-z or A-Z) or an underscore (the _ character).

After the first letter or underscore, variables can contain uppercase or lowercase letters, digits (0-9), or underscores. Variables may not contain any mathematical operators (such as + or *), punctuation (such as ! or &), or spaces.

String Variables

When a variable is used to store a number (as in the preceding examples), it's known as a *numeric variable.* However, it's also possible to store text in a variable, in which case the variable is called a *string variable* (because sequences of characters are called *strings* in programming languages).

Examples of strings include the name "Bill Smith", the sequence of characters "A23bQ%j", and even the characters "123", which in this case comprise a string of digits (because "123" is in quotes), not the number 123.

In the same way you can store a number in a variable, you can store a string, and you use the same method of assignment, like this:

```
$Name = "Mary Jones";
```

Notice the use of double quotation marks around this string. These are what tell PHP that the value is a string, and this is how you can assign the string `"123"` to a variable, as opposed to the number `123`, for example. In terms of the pot and paper metaphor, the preceding statement is equivalent to labeling a new pot as `$Name` and writing `"Mary Jones"` on a piece of paper that you place in it, as shown in Figure 3-5.

FIGURE 3-5   This pot is labeled $Name and contains a string value.

Obviously, you can't perform arithmetic on strings (without first converting them to numbers—and only if possible), but there are other actions you can take, such as shortening them, adding more characters to the front, middle, or end, extracting a portion of a string, and more. For example, you can concatenate two strings together (attach one to the other) using the . (dot) operator, like this:

```
$Singer = "Elvis";
$Singer = $Singer . " Presley";
```

The result of these two statements is to concatenate the string `"Elvis"` (first assigned to and then read from the variable `$Singer`) with the string `" Presley"` and place the resulting string back into the variable `$Singer`.

Using Quotation Marks in Strings

You have seen the use of the double quote character to indicate the start and end of a string, but you may also use the single quote if you prefer, like this:

```
$Dinner = 'Fish and Chips';
```

The end result is almost identical, whichever type of quotation marks you use, but there is a subtle difference explained a little further on, in the section "Embedding Variables within a String."

There is a good reason why you may choose one type of quote instead of the other, and that's when you need to include a particular quotation mark within a string.

For example, suppose you needed to store the string `"Isn't the weather fine?"`. As it stands, using double quotation marks works just fine, but what would happen if you surrounded the string with single quotation marks instead, like this: `'Isn't the weather fine?'`?

In this case, you would get a syntax error because PHP would see only the string `'Isn'` and then some gibberish following it, like this: `t the weather fine?'`. Then again, what about the string `'Jane said, "Hello"'`? This time, using single quotes around the string works. However, because of the double quotes within it, if you were to surround the string with double quotes, like this, `"Jane said, "Hello""`, PHP would see one string (`"Jane said, "`), what appears as some gibberish (`Hello`), and another string with nothing in it (`""`). It would give up at all this and generate an error.

Placing a pair of quotes together with nothing between them (like `""` or `''`) results in what is called the *empty string*. It is commonly used for erasing or initializing the value of a string variable.

Using Heredoc Strings

There's another way you can create a string in PHP that removes the need to surround it in quotation marks of any kind, and that's to use the *heredoc syntax*, like this:

```
$tobeornottobe = <<<_EOT
  To be, or not to be, that is the question:
  Whether 'tis Nobler in the mind to suffer
  The Slings and Arrows of outrageous Fortune,
  Or to take Arms against a Sea of troubles,
  And by opposing end them: to die, to sleep
_EOT;
```

Heredoc text behaves just like a double-quoted string, but without needing the double quotes. This means that no quotes of either type in a heredoc need to be escaped (but the escape codes listed in the following section can still be used).

The value `_EOT` is an identifier that marks the start and end of a heredoc string, and it follows the same naming rules for any PHP label. However, a convention for heredocs is to preface them with an underscore and to use only capital letters, so I generally use `_EOT` (for End Of Text) so I can always find all my heredoc strings with a quick search.

You must be careful when using a heredoc because the exact token following the `<<<` must appear at the *start* of the line following the heredoc text. It must also end with a semicolon, and there must not be any spaces or tabs before or after the semicolon. If there is no semicolon, or if the heredoc identifier is indented, or if spaces or tabs appear before or after the semicolon, then the heredoc will fall through to the end of the script (and therefore be unterminated), thus resulting in nasty errors.

Escaping Characters

Escape characters help you overcome other potential pitfalls. For example, consider occasions when you might require both types of quotes to be included within a string, like this: `"Mark said, "I can't wait""`? As it stands, this string will cause a syntax error, but you can easily fix it using the escape character, which is simply a backslash, like this: `"Mark said, \"I can't wait\""`.

What the escape character does is tell PHP to ignore the \ character and to use the character following it as a string element (character), and not a string container (better known as a delimiter).

You may escape either of the quotation marks inside a string to ensure they are used only as string elements, and you can also use escape characters to insert other characters that you cannot easily type in, such as tabs and newlines, as follows:

- `\'`   single quote
- `\"`   double quote
- `\\`   backslash
- `\b`   backspace
- `\f`   form feed
- `\n`   newline
- `\r`   carriage return
- `\t`   tab

Embedding Variables Within a String

One of PHP's more powerful features is the ability to embed a variable name inside a string, which will then be replaced with the variable's value. For example, the following code creates two variables and then embeds them in a string variable:

```
$profession = "writer";
$name       = "Robin";
$string     = "My name is $name and I am a $profession";
```

The result is that `$string` will now contain the value `"My name is Robin and I am a writer"`. To embed variables within strings, the strings must be surrounded with double quotes. If you use single quotes, the exact contents of the string will be used and no variable values will be substituted.

For example, the following results in `$string` only containing the value `'My name is $name and I am $age'`, without any variable substitution:

```
$age    = "969";
$name   = "Methuselah";
$string = 'My name is $name and I am $age';
```

You may also place variables within heredoc strings, because they behave like double-quoted strings.

Now you see another reason for PHP requiring that variables begin with a $ symbol—it supports the ability to embed them in strings.

Variable Typing and Casting

In PHP, unlike some other programming languages, a variable can change its type automatically. For example, a string can become a number, and vice versa, according to the way in which the variable is referenced. For example, take the following assignment in which the variable $MyVar is given the string value of "12345":

```
$MyVar = "12345";
```

Although the string is created from a group of all digits, it is a string. However, PHP is smart enough to understand that sometimes a string can be a number. For example, in the following assignment, it converts the string value in $MyVar to a number prior to applying the subtraction, and then the resulting value (which is now the number 12000) is stored back in $MyVar, which has now become a numeric variable:

```
$MyVar = $MyVar - 345;
```

Likewise, a number can be automatically converted to a string, as in the following two lines. Here, the numeric variable $Time is set to the value 6 and then the string " O'clock" is appended to the number, which is first turned into a string (using the . symbol, which is the string concatenation operator) to make this string concatenation possible:

```
$Time = 6;
$Time = $Time . " O'clock";
```

The result is that $Time is now a string variable with the value "6 O'clock".

Because of this changing of variables from one type to another (known as *automatic type casting*), it is not actually correct to think of PHP variables in terms of type, so I will no longer do so. Instead, you should consider only their contents and how PHP will interpret them.

However, sometimes it is necessary for you to force the type of a variable, and you can do this with PHP's cast operators, as follows:

- **(int)** or **(integer)**   Cast to an integer
- **(bool)** or **(boolean)**   Cast to a Boolean value
- **(float)** or **(double)** or **(real)**   Cast to a floating point number
- **(string)**   Cast to a string
- **(array)**   Cast to an array
- **(object)**   Cast to an object
- **(unset)**   Cast to NULL (since PHP 5)

For example, consider the following statement and ask yourself what you think PHP should do with it:

```
$MyVar = (int) "12345";
```

The answer is that the string value is turned into an integer before being assigned to the variable. Likewise, you can use a cast like the following to turn a number into a string:

```
$MyVar = (string) 12345;
```

Alternatively, you can use the facility to embed a variable within a double-quoted string (or heredoc) to turn it into a string, like this:

```
$MyNum = 12345;
$MyVar = "$MyNum";
```

 Generally, the occasions on which you will find it beneficial to use casting are when you're dealing with values over which you have less control, such as user input that you are processing.

Summary

You will now have a good grounding in how variables work, so in the following lesson I'll show you some other types of variables known as constants as well as some handy system variables called superglobals.

Self-Test Questions

Test how much you have learned in this lesson with these questions. If you don't know an answer, go back and reread the relevant section until your knowledge is complete. You can find the answers in the appendix.

1. Is PHP case sensitive or case insensitive?

2. What are spaces, tabs, linefeeds, and some other nonalphanumeric/punctuation characters collectively known as?

3. What does PHP do with whitespace?

4. What is a numeric variable?

5. What is a string variable?

6. How can you include quotation marks in a string that are of the same type that enclose the string (and also include special characters in a string)?

7. What is a heredoc string?

8. Do PHP variables permanently retain the type they are initially assigned?

9. How can you force PHP to store a certain type of value in a variable?

10. How can you easily use a variable's value within a string without first breaking the string up into smaller parts?

4

Using Constants and Superglobals

To view the accompanying video for this lesson, please visit mhprofessional.com/nixonphp/.

When developing with PHP, you often need to work with values that never change. When doing so, the convention is to create constants to make this absolutely clear to other people who may maintain your code. It also assists you because constants cannot have their values changed, so some potential bugs can be avoided through using them.

Indeed, PHP itself comes with a wide range of constants, ready-assigned useful values, as well as a number of what are known as *superglobals*. In this lesson, I show you some of these superglobals and how to use them, and also offer a quick peek "under the hood" of the PHP engine to give you an insight into the rich set of information on tap for your programs.

Using Constants

Constants are similar to variables in that they store values to be accessed later. However, these values remain constant once defined (as you might expect) and cannot be changed. You define a constant like this:

```
define('SITE_NAME', 'ACME Products Web Store');
```

Then, to read the contents of the variable, you just refer to it like a regular variable (without preceding it with a dollar symbol):

```
echo SITE_NAME;
```

Another use for constants could be to support moving your code between different platforms. For example, when you use the XAMPP server on Linux, the document root will generally be in a different place for OS X compared to Windows. Therefore, if you need your program to be aware of this location, you could perhaps write some code such as the following, to set the constant DOC_ROOT to the correct value:

```
switch($platform) // Must be one of 'win', 'mac', or 'lin'
{
  case 'win': define('DOC_ROOT', 'C:/xampp/htdocs');              break;
  case 'mac': define('DOC_ROOT', '/Applications/XAMPP/htdocs'); break;
  case 'lin': define('DOC_ROOT', '/opt/lampp/htdocs');           break;
}
```

 You will learn about using the switch() and case statements in Lesson 11, but you should already be able to get the idea of how this works.

You can then use the constant later on as if it were a variable (but without the $ symbol in front of it), like this:

```
echo 'Document root is: ' . DOC_ROOT;
```

Predefined Constants

As well as supporting user-defined constants, PHP predefines a number of its own, some of which are exposed by the main engine for external use by PHP programs, such as the following *magic constants,* which start and end with two underscore characters:

- **__LINE__**   The current line number within the file.
- **__FILE__**   The path and filename of the current file. If this is used inside an include, the name of the included file is returned. __FILE__ always contains an absolute path with symbolic links resolved.
- **__DIR__**   The directory of the current file. If this is used inside an include, the directory of the included file is returned. This is equivalent to dirname (__FILE__). The directory name does not have a trailing slash unless it is the root directory.
- **__FUNCTION__**   Returns the function name as it was declared in a case-sensitive string.
- **__CLASS__**   Returns the class name as it was declared.
- **__METHOD__**   Returns the method name as it was declared.
- **__NAMESPACE__**   The name of the current namespace as defined at compile time.

One way you can use some of these variables is to help with your debugging by displaying information in strategic parts of a program, such as this:

```
echo "This is line " . __LINE__ . " of file " . __FILE__;
```

In this case, the current program line in the current file (including the path) being executed is output to the web browser.

The `echo` and `print` Commands

Having just used the echo command in the previous example, I should now explain it. The echo command can be used in a number of different ways to output text from the server to your browser. Simply place a variable or literal value (such as a string or number) after the echo command, and the contents of the variable or the literal value will be output to the browser.

You can also use the print command, which is quite similar to echo, except that print always returns the value 1, which means it can be used in expressions, whereas echo returns void and fails if placed in an expression. Also, the echo command is usually the faster of the two, and it can take multiple values separated by commas, whereas print accepts only a single value.

Here's an example to output whether the value of a variable is TRUE or FALSE using print, something you could not perform in the same manner with echo (because print is being used within an expression):

```
($var == TRUE) ? print "true" : print "false";
```

As you will learn in a Lesson 5, the question mark is being used here as the *ternary operator,* to test the expression that precedes it. Whichever command is on the left of the following colon is executed if $var == TRUE evaluates to TRUE, whereas the command on the right is executed if $var == TRUE evaluates to FALSE.

Superglobal Variables

Starting with PHP 4.1.0, several predefined variables are available. These are known as *superglobal variables,* which means they are accessible absolutely everywhere in a PHP program. These superglobals contain lots of useful information about the currently running program and its environment, as follows:

- **`$GLOBALS[]`**   An associative array containing references to all variables that are currently defined in the global scope of the script. The variable names are the keys of the array. See Lesson 7 for more details on array keys, and see Lesson 13 for how to use the $GLOBALS[] array.
- **`$_SERVER[]`**   An array containing information such as headers, paths, and script locations. The entries in this array are created by the web server, and there is no guarantee that every web server will provide any or all of these. See Lesson 18 for details.
- **`$_GET[]`**   An associative array of variables passed to the current script via the HTTP Get method. See Lesson 16 for details.
- **`$_POST[]`**   An associative array of variables passed to the current script via the HTTP Post method. See Lesson 16 for details.
- **`$_FILES[]`**   An associative array of items uploaded to the current script via the HTTP Post method. See Lesson 17 for details.
- **`$_COOKIE[]`**   An associative array of variables passed to the current script via HTTP Cookies. See Lesson 18 for details.

- **$_SESSION[]**   An associative array containing session variables available to the current script. See Lesson 20 for details.
- **$_REQUEST[]**   An associative array that by default contains the contents of $_GET[], $_POST[], and $_COOKIE[].
- **$_ENV[]**   An associative array of variables passed to the current script via the environment method.

Among the various pieces of information supplied by superglobal variables is the URL of the page that referred the user to the current web page. To illustrate how you use the superglobals, this referring page information can be accessed like this:

```
$came_from = $_SERVER['HTTP_REFERER'];
```

If the user came from another (referring) page, and the user's browser supplies the referring page (some browsers may not provide this information), then the URL will be saved in $came_from. Otherwise, if the user came straight to your web page (for example, by typing its URL directly into the browser), or if the user's browser does not supply the referring URL, then $came_from will simply be set to an empty string.

As another example, the $_GET[] and $_POST[] arrays contain any data sent to the script from a web form as key/value pairs (explained in Lesson 16). Therefore, if a key with the name username was posted, you could retrieve and display its value from the superglobal array like this:

```
echo $_POST['username'];
```

Superglobals and Security

A word of caution is in order before you start using superglobal variables, because they are often used by hackers trying to find exploits to break into your website. What they do is load up $_POST[], $_GET[], or other superglobals with malicious code they hope you will not predefine, such as Unix or MySQL commands.

Therefore, you should always sanitize these variables before using them. As you will learn more about in Lesson 17, one way to do this is via the PHP htmlentities() function. What it does is convert certain characters into HTML entities. For example, the less-than and greater-than characters (< and >) are transformed into the strings < and > so that they are rendered harmless.

Therefore, the following is a much better way to access an array such as $_GET[] (and other superglobals):

```
$message = htmlentities($_GET['message']);
```

Note   Although sanitizing input at the earliest possible opportunity is the safest means of handling user data, you must remember that the data has been sanitized in all the code that processes it. For example, remember that there will be no < characters, only $lt; entities. Should you wish to convert the string back at some point, you can do so with the html_entity_decode() function.

Other PHP Variables

Figure 4-1 shows the result of using the `phpinfo()` function to display an incredibly in-depth amount of information about a PHP installation. In this instance, a value of 32 was passed to the function to list only the PHP variables in use, but without a number passed, you will be presented with everything—meaning page after page of information.

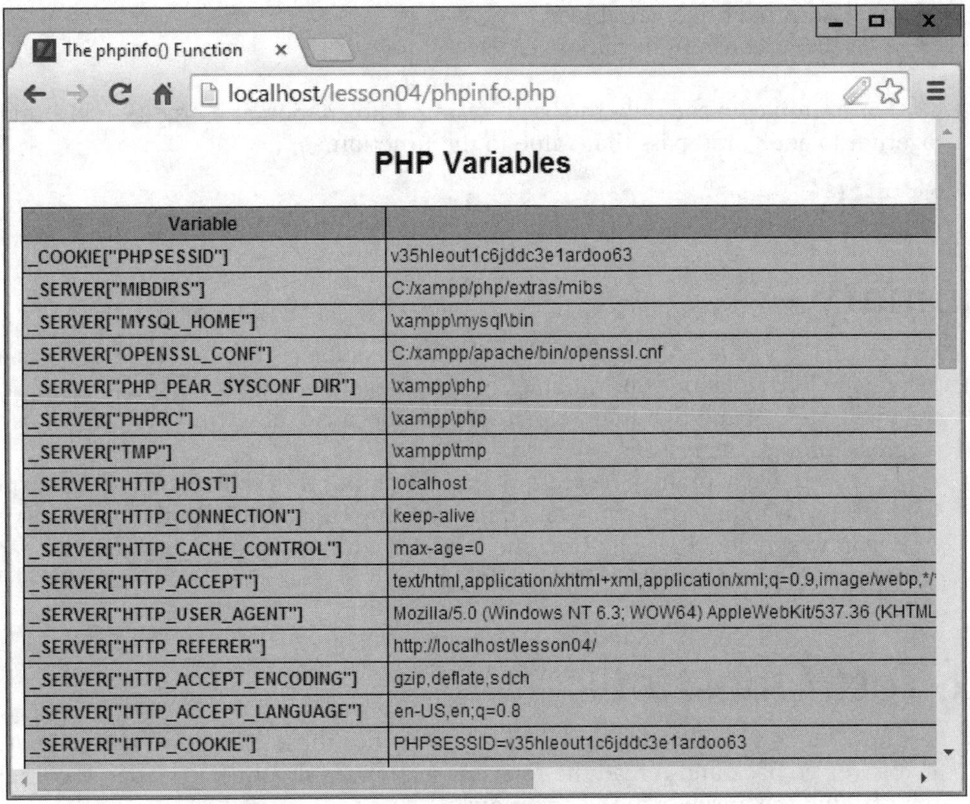

PHP Variables

Variable	
_COOKIE["PHPSESSID"]	v35hleout1c6jddc3e1ardoo63
_SERVER["MIBDIRS"]	C:/xampp/php/extras/mibs
_SERVER["MYSQL_HOME"]	\xampp\mysql\bin
_SERVER["OPENSSL_CONF"]	C:/xampp/apache/bin/openssl.cnf
_SERVER["PHP_PEAR_SYSCONF_DIR"]	\xampp\php
_SERVER["PHPRC"]	\xampp\php
_SERVER["TMP"]	\xampp\tmp
_SERVER["HTTP_HOST"]	localhost
_SERVER["HTTP_CONNECTION"]	keep-alive
_SERVER["HTTP_CACHE_CONTROL"]	max-age=0
_SERVER["HTTP_ACCEPT"]	text/html,application/xhtml+xml,application/xml;q=0.9,image/webp,*/
_SERVER["HTTP_USER_AGENT"]	Mozilla/5.0 (Windows NT 6.3; WOW64) AppleWebKit/537.36 (KHTML
_SERVER["HTTP_REFERER"]	http://localhost/lesson04/
_SERVER["HTTP_ACCEPT_ENCODING"]	gzip,deflate,sdch
_SERVER["HTTP_ACCEPT_LANGUAGE"]	en-US,en;q=0.8
_SERVER["HTTP_COOKIE"]	PHPSESSID=v35hleout1c6jddc3e1ardoo63

FIGURE 4-1   Using `phpinfo()` to display information about a PHP installation

This is a great way to see what's going on "under the hood," but should never be left open for public viewing on a production server, due to its potential to reveal weaknesses a hacker could exploit. I recommend a rummage through the output of `phpinfo()` whenever you think something strange seems to be going on; it could reveal something unusual about the server setup.

The values supported by `phpinfo()` follow; simply add the numbers together for the items you wish displayed, or don't supply an argument to see them all:

- **1**   Basic system information
- **2**   PHP credits
- **4**   Current local and master values for PHP directives
- **8**   Loaded modules and their respective settings
- **16**   Environment variable information
- **32**   All predefined variables
- **64**   PHP license information

For example, to see only the basic system information and credits, add 1 and 2 together to get 3, and pass that value to the function:

```
phpinfo(3);
```

Summary

Don't worry if you are not clear about some of the subjects covered here, such as arrays (which are like collections of variables grouped together) and functions (sections of code you can call and that may return a value), because they will be explained as you progress through the lessons.

However, we actually covered quite a lot of ground in this lesson, which explained some of the simpler PHP syntax and data-handling capabilities. In the following lesson, we'll start to see how these items come together with arithmetic operators to enable you to start creating simple PHP expressions.

Self-Test Questions

Test how much you have learned in this lesson with these questions. If you don't know an answer, go back and reread the relevant section until your knowledge is complete. You can find the answers in the appendix.

1. What is a PHP constant?

2. How do you define a constant in PHP?

3. What are predefined constants?

4. What is the difference between the `print` and `echo` commands?

5. Is this a valid PHP statement? `($var == TRUE) ? echo "true" : echo "false";`

6. Which superglobal arrays handle information sent to a PHP program via forms sent using Get and Post methods?

7. Which superglobal array contains cookie data?

8. With what PHP statement would you display the URL of a page from which a user was referred to the current one?

9. How can you sanitize input and other data by replacing characters in HTML tags with entities so that the browser displays tag names as text (rather than acting on them)?

10. With which command can you get PHP to display its configuration information as well as the current environment and script?

5

Working with Arithmetic Operators

 To view the accompanying video for this lesson, please visit mhprofessional.com/nixonphp/.

In the previous lesson, you saw a few examples of operators in action, such as the + operator used for addition, the . operator for concatenating strings together, the − operator used for subtraction, and the = operator used for assigning values.

But PHP supports many more operators than that, such as *, /, and more. It also includes functions you can draw on for more advanced expression evaluation, such as sin(), sqrt(), and many others. In this lesson, I'll explain all of these, how they work, and how to use them.

This is an important lesson because it covers much of the foundation of how PHP works, so even if you have programmed before using another language, I recommend you read this lesson thoroughly, because there are a number of things PHP handles in a unique manner.

Arithmetic Operators

The arithmetic operators in PHP are the ones that allow you to create numeric expressions, and there are more than simply addition, subtraction, multiplication, and division, as shown in Table 5-1.

You can try these operators out for yourself by loading the file *math_operators.php* from the companion archive into a browser, which should look like Figure 5-1. Try changing the various values and operators applied, and check the results you get.

TABLE 5-1 The Arithmetic Operators

Operator	Description	Example	Result
+	Addition	3 + 11	14
-	Subtraction	9 - 4	5
-	Negation (subtraction from 0)	-17	-17
*	Multiplication	3 * 4	12
**	Exponentiation (PHP 5.6+ like pow())	8 ** 2	64
/	Division	21 / 7	3
%	Modulus (remainder after division)	21 % 8	5
++	Increment	$a = 5; ++$a	($a equals) 6
--	Decrement	$a = 5; --$a	($a equals) 4

Note Because they perform arithmetic operations, I have included the ++ and -- operators as honorary members of Table 5-1, even though, technically, they are not arithmetic operators (because they can only be used to modify variable values). Normally, they are just known as the increment and decrement operators (see the following section).

The first four of these operators should be very clear to you, so I'll only explain the last three, starting with the modulus operator, %.

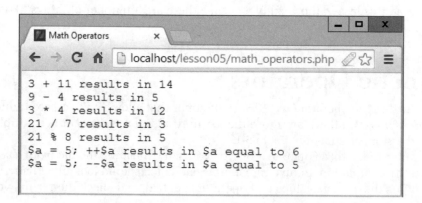

FIGURE 5-1 The arithmetic operators in use

Modulus

What the modulus operator returns is simply the remainder after calculating a division. For example, the modulus of 12 and 4, calculated using the expression 12 % 4, is 0, because 4 goes into 12 an exact number of times, so there is no remainder.

On the other hand, the modulus of 24 and 5 (calculated as 24 % 5) is 4, because 5 goes into 24 four times (5 × 4 is 20), leaving a remainder of 4, the modulus of the expression.

Exponentiation

In PHP 5.6 the ** operator was introduced, which raises a value to the power given. For example: 8 ** 2 is 8 to the power 2, or 8 squared (which is 64).

As you will learn in Lesson 13, this is equivalent to using the pow() function, like this:

```
echo pow(8, 2);
```

Incrementing and Decrementing Variables

Now let's look at the increment and decrement operators. These come in tremendously handy because without them, you would have to write expressions like this:

```
$a = $a + 1;
```

This is cumbersome when you only want to increment (or decrement) a value by 1. Therefore, the creators of PHP allow you to use the following syntax instead:

```
++$a;
```

I'm sure you will agree this is much shorter and sweeter. It also comes with fringe benefits too, because the increment and decrement operators can be used within flow control commands such as if() statements (which I explain in full detail in Lesson 11, but will give you a taste of here).

Consider the following code, which assumes that $Time contains a 24-hour time value between 0 and 23, and which is set up to trigger once an hour, on the hour (using code not shown here, but which is assumed to be in place):

```
$Time = $Time + 1;
echo "The time is $Time";

if ($Time < 12) echo('AM');
else            echo('PM');
```

This code first increments the value in $Time by 1, because this code has been called on the hour. Because it's now one hour since the last time it was called, $Time must be updated. Then the next line displays the time in the browser, prefaced by the string 'The time is '.

After that, an `if()` statement is reached that tests the variable $Time to see whether it currently has a value of less than 12. If so, it must still be the morning; therefore, the string `'AM'` is output. Otherwise, it's the afternoon, so `'PM'` is displayed—fairly straightforward stuff.

 This is a simple version of the `if()` statement in that it has only a single statement after the `if()`, and there is also only a single one after `else`. Therefore, no curly braces are used to enclose the action statements. See Lesson 11 for more details on using `if()` and `else` with multistatement actions.

However, good programmers always like to write the tightest and cleanest code possible in order to minimize the potential for bugs (although over-optimization can also introduce bugs!). Therefore, the following code is considered better programming practice because it removes an entire line of code, like this (with the incremented variable and operator highlighted):

```
echo 'The time is ' . ++$Time;

if ($Time < 12) echo 'AM';
else            echo 'PM';
```

To be even more succinct, we can use the ternary operator:

```
echo 'The time is ' . ++$Time;

echo ($Time < 12) ? 'AM' : 'PM';
```

 Of course, once $Time reaches the value of 23, when incremented the next time it needs to be reset to a value of 0. Here's where the modulus assignment operator (see "Assignment Operators," a little later on) can come in handy. By adding the statement `$Time %= 24;` after `++$Time;`, we ensure it always has a value between 0 and 23.

Pre-incrementing

What has occurred in the previous example is an instance of *pre-incrementing* the variable $Time. In other words, before the value in $Time is used, it is incremented. Only after this incrementing is the current value in $Time used for displaying in the echo statement.

In Figure 5-2, these lines of code have been called three times, with an original starting value for $Time of 9 (using the *file inc_and_dec.php* from the companion archive).

Post-incrementing

You may also place the ++ increment operator after a variable name, in which case it is known as *post-incrementing*. When you do this, the value in the variable being

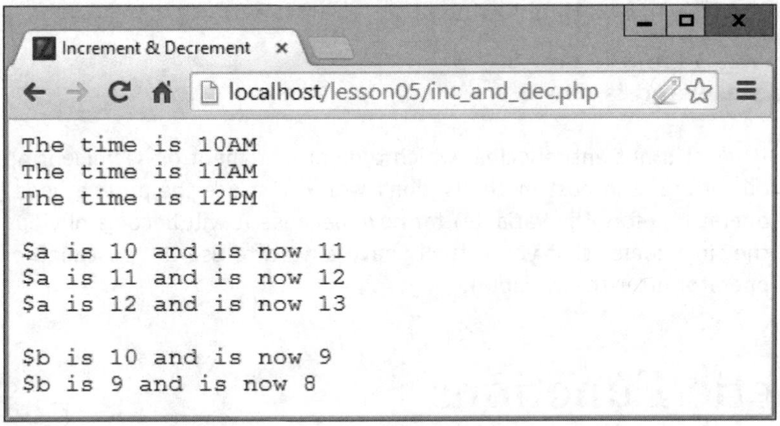

FIGURE 5-2   Using the increment operator

incremented is looked up *before* the increment, and that value is used by the code accessing it. Only *after* this value has been looked up and used in the expression is the variable incremented.

The following code illustrates this type of incrementing by displaying both the before and after values in the variable $a (with instances of the variable and increment operator highlighted):

```
echo '$a was ' . $a++ . ' and is now ' . $a;
```

Working through this statement from left to right, we see that first the string '$a was ' is output and then $a++ is displayed. This results in the current value of $a being displayed, and only then is $a incremented. After this, the string ' and is now ' is output, followed by the new value in $a, which now contains the incremented value from the earlier increment operation. Therefore, if $a has an initial value of 10, the following is displayed:

$a was 10 and is now 11

Pre- and Post-decrementing

You can use the decrement operator in exactly the same way as the increment operator, and it can either be placed before a variable for pre-incrementing or after for post-decrementing. Following are two examples that both display the same result but achieve it using pre-decrementing for the first and post-decrementing for the second (with instances of the variable and decrement operator highlighted):

```
echo '$b was ' . $b   . ' and is now ' . --$b . '<br>';
echo '$b was ' . $b-- . ' and is now ' .   $b;
```

Here, if $b has an initial value of 10, the following is displayed:

$b was 10 and is now 9
$b was 9 and is now 8

 If it's still not entirely clear which type of increment or decrement operator to use out of pre- and post-methods, don't worry; just use the pre-methods (with the operator before the variable) for now, because it will become obvious to you when the time comes that you actually have a need to use the post-method (with the operator after the variable).

Arithmetic Functions

To accompany the arithmetic operators, PHP comes with a math library of functions you can call on, among which are the following:

- **abs($a)**   Returns $a as zero or a positive number
- **acos($a)**   Returns the arc cosine of $a
- **asin($a)**   Returns the arc sine of $a
- **atan($a)**   Returns the arc tangent of $a
- **atan2($a, $b)**   Returns the arc tangent of $a / $b in radians
- **ceil($a)**   Rounds up to return the integer closest to $a
- **cos($a)**   Returns the cosine of $a
- **exp($a)**   Returns the exponent of $a (E to the power $a)
- **floor($a)**   Rounds down to return the integer closest to $a
- **log($a)**   Returns the log of $a base E
- **max($a,$b)**   Returns the maximum of $a and $b
- **min($a,$b)**   Returns the minimum of $a and $b
- **pow($a,$b)**   Returns $a to the power $b
- **rand($a,$b)**   Returns a random number between $a and $b, inclusive
- **round($a)**   Rounds up or down to return the integer closest to $a
- **sin($a)**   Returns the sine of $a
- **sqrt($a)**   Returns the square root of $a
- **tan($a)**   Returns the tangent of $a

You should be familiar with most of these; for example, to return the square root of 64, you would use the following:

```
sqrt(64); // Returns 8
```

However, a couple need a little more explaining, such as abs(). This takes any value (negative, zero, or positive), and if it is negative, turns it into a positive value, like this:

```
abs(27); // Returns 27
abs(0);  // Returns 0
abs(-5); // Returns 5
```

The other function possibly needing extra explanation is rand(). This returns a statistically random number (although not truly random) between (and including) the two values supplied. For example, if you wish to emulate a 12-sided dice, you might call it this way:

```
rand(1, 12); // Returns a number between 1 and 12
```

Many other math functions are available in PHP, and you can see the whole list at php.net/manual/en/ref.math.php.

Assignment Operators

Like many other languages, PHP tries to help you out by offering more efficient ways to achieve results. One of these ways is by letting you combine assignment and arithmetic operators together into six different types of assignment operator. This typically saves lines of code and makes your programs easier for you to write—and for others to understand.

Table 5-2 lists the assignment operators available, provides examples of them in use, and shows the result of doing so when the variable $a already contains the value 21.

TABLE 5-2 The Assignment Operators ($a Is Assumed to Have the Initial Value 21)

Operator	Description	Example	Result in $a
=	Simple assignment	$a = 42	42
+=	With addition	$a += 5	26
-=	With subtraction	$a -= 2	19
*=	With multiplication	$a *= 3	63
/=	With division	$a /= 10	2.1
%=	With modulus	$a %= 4	1

You can see the result of using the expressions in this table in Figure 5-3, created with the sample file *assignment_operators.php* from the accompanying archive.

For example, instead of using $a = $a + 5, you can use the more compact $a += 5. And you can use assignment operators in conjunction with other expressions and variables, as with the following example, which results in $a having a value of 15 (10 + (25 / 5)):

```
$a  = 10;
$b  = 25;
$a += ($b / 5);
```

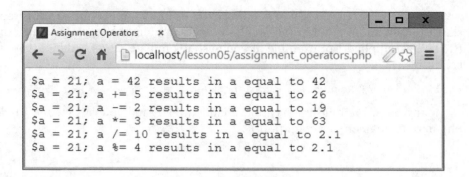

FIGURE 5-3   Using the various assignment operators

Summary

In this lesson, you have learned how to use arithmetic operators and functions, how to pre- and post- increment and decrement variables by values of 1 or more, and how to combine assignment and arithmetic operators to create more condensed code. In the next lesson, we'll continue our exploration of operators with comparison and logical operators.

Self-Test Questions

Test how much you have learned in this lesson with these questions. If you don't know an answer, go back and reread the relevant section until your knowledge is complete. You can find the answers in the appendix.

1. What are the four basic arithmetic operators and the symbols used for them in PHP?

2. Which operators are used for incrementing and decrementing variables?

3. What is the difference between pre- and post-incrementing and decrementing?

4. What is the modulus operator symbol, and what does it do?

5. With which function can you return a number as a non-negative value, regardless of whether it is positive or negative?

6. Given a numeric variable called $v that may have a negative, zero, or positive value, which math function out of min() or max() can be used (and how) to replace any negative value with 0, but leave a positive value untouched?

7. How can you obtain a pseudo-random number between 1 and 100, inclusive?

8. How can you combine the mathematical addition operator with the assignment operator to create a shorter expression than, for example, $a = $a + 23;?

9. If $a has the value 58, what will the expression $a /= 2; evaluate to?

10. How can you set the variable $n to contain the remainder after dividing it by 11?

6

Applying Comparison and Logical Operators

 To view the accompanying video for this lesson, please visit mhprofessional.com/ nixonphp/.

Continuing our exploration of operators, this lesson covers how to use comparison operators, creating statements using logic operators, and the precedence and associativity of operators. Don't worry, though, these are just fancy terms for some very simple operations.

For example, as you will soon learn, *comparison* is where you test whether a value is or isn't equal to another (or is greater than or less than), the *precedence of operators* refers to which operators get to be applied before which others, and *associativity* states the direction in which parts of a statement are evaluated (either right to left or left to right).

Comparison Operators

One of the most important processes that happens in a program is comparison. For example, possibly the most frequent type of construct used goes along the lines of *if this, then do that*. The job of comparison operators is to figure out the *this* part, and there are eight of them, as listed in Table 6-1.

Figure 6-1 shows several different comparison operators used on different values and the results obtained. This example uses the file comparison_operators.php, which is available in the companion archive.

If you haven't programmed before, some of these operators may seem a little confusing, especially seeing as we are taught as children that = is the equal-to operator. However, in programming languages such as PHP, = is used as an assignment operator.

41

TABLE 6-1   The Comparison Operators

Operator	Description	Example	Result
==	Equal to	1 == 1	TRUE
===	Equal in value and type	1 === '1'	FALSE
!=	Not equal to	1 != 2	TRUE
!==	Not equal in value and type	1 !== '1'	TRUE
>	Greater than	1 > 2	FALSE
<	Less than	1 < 2	TRUE
>=	Greater than or equal to	1 >= 1	TRUE
<=	Less than or equal to	2 <= 1	FALSE

Code would become harder to read (and the writers of programming languages would have a much harder time figuring out its meaning) if the = symbol were also used to make comparisons. Therefore, the == operator is used for comparisons instead, like this:

```
if ($a == 12) // Do something
```

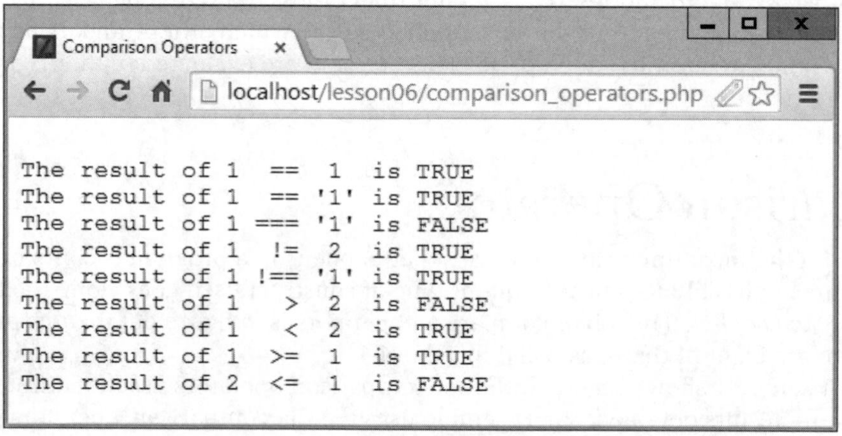

FIGURE 6-1   A selection of comparison operators in use

In PHP, however, the types of variables are loosely defined, and it's quite normal, for example, to ask whether 1 is the same as '1', because the string '1' can be used either as a string or as a number, depending on the context. Therefore, the following expression will return the value TRUE:

```
if (1 == '1') // Results in the value TRUE
```

Note   PHP uses the internal values of TRUE and FALSE to represent the result of making comparisons such as the preceding, and you can use the keywords TRUE and FALSE in your programming to check for these values.

Let's continue through the list of comparison operators. When you wish to determine whether two values are the same value *and* also of the same type, you can use the === operator, like this:

```
if (1 === '1') // Results in the value FALSE
```

Similarly, you can test whether values are *not* equal (but not comparing the type) using the != operator, like this:

```
if (1 != 2)   // Results in the value TRUE
if (1 != '1') // Results in the value FALSE
```

And if you wish to check whether two values are not equal in *both* value and type, you use the !== operator, like this:

```
if (1 !== '1') // Results in the value TRUE
```

The remaining comparison operators test whether one value is greater than, less than, greater than or equal to, or less than or equal to another, like this:

```
if (1 > 2)  // Results in the value FALSE
if (1 < 2)  // Results in the value TRUE
if (1 >= 1) // Results in the value TRUE
if (2 <= 1) // Results in the value FALSE
```

Logical Operators

PHP supports three logical operators with which you can extend your *if this* parts of code even further, as listed in Table 6-2.

Figure 6-2, created using the file logical_operators.php from the companion archive, shows these operators being used in expressions.

The && operator (known as the And operator) allows you to test for multiple conditions being TRUE, saving you from having to write multiple lines of code by combining them into a single expression. You can also use the and operator in the same way, like this:

```
if ($a == 4 &&  $b == 7) // Do this
if ($a == 5 and $b == 8) // Do that
```

TABLE 6-2 The Logical Operators

Operator	Description	Example	Result
&&	And	1 == 1 && 2 == 2	TRUE
and	And	1 == 1 and 2 == 2	TRUE
||	Or	1 == 1 || 2 == 3	TRUE
or	Or	1 == 1 or 2 == 3	TRUE
xor	Exclusive Or	1 == 1 xor 2 == 2	FALSE
!	Not	!(1 == 1)	FALSE

In this example, the statement following the first if () (just a comment in this instance) will be executed only if $a has a value of 4 and also $b has a value of 7. Next, we test whether at least one value is TRUE using either the || or the or operator, like this:

```
if ($a == 4 || $b == 7) // Do this
if ($a == 5 or $b == 8) // Do that
```

Here, if either $a has the value 4 or $b has the value 7, then the statement after the first if () will be executed, so only one of the expressions on either side of || needs to evaluate to TRUE.

 The and and or operators have a different precedence compared to && and ||. Along with the xor operator (detailed next), they have the lowest precedence, excluding the comma operator. So be careful because, for example, $a && $b || $c is equivalent to ($a && $b) || $c, but $a and $b || $c is equivalent to $a and ($b || $c). Note the different positions of the implied parentheses here (see "Operator Precedence," later in this lesson).

```
Logical Operators          ×

← → C ⌂  localhost/lesson06/logical_operators.php  ✎ ☆  ≡

The result of   1 == 1 &&  2 == 2 is TRUE
The result of   1 == 1 ||  2 == 3 is TRUE
The result of   1 == 1 xor 2 == 2 is FALSE
The result of !(1 == 1)           is FALSE
```

FIGURE 6-2 Using logical operators

Exclusive Or

Then there is the Exclusive Or operator, xor, which is TRUE if either part (but not both) of the two halves of an expression is TRUE, or FALSE if they both are TRUE or both are FALSE. To better understand this, imagine you need to clean the kitchen floor and you have two containers of cleaning chemicals. One contains ammonia and one contains bleach. Now, as you know, it's dangerous to mix both these chemicals together because they produce a toxic gas, so we definitely don't want to use them *both* on the floor.

We can create an analogue of this using PHP code, like so:

```
$a = TRUE;      // Use Ammonia
$b = FALSE;     // Don't use Bleach

if ($a xor $b) // If TRUE clean the floor
```

This code states that if only $a is TRUE or only $b is TRUE, then go ahead and clean the floor. But if both are FALSE the floor is not to be cleaned because no chemical has been selected. And if both are TRUE the floor also is not to be cleaned because it is dangerous to use both chemicals at once.

Boolean Negation

Lastly, you can negate (or invert) any expression's result using the ! symbol (known as the *Not* operator) by placing it in front of the expression (generally placing the expression within parentheses too, so that the ! doesn't apply only to a part of the expression), like this:

```
if (!(++$Lives > $MaxLives)) // Carry on playing
```

In this example, if the variable $Lives is incremented and its new value is not greater than the number of lives allowed (as stored in the value in $MaxLives), the result of the expression is FALSE. Then the ! operator negates this to turn that value into TRUE. Therefore, the statement after the if () will be executed because the player still has at least one life remaining.

On the other hand, if $Lives increments to a value greater than $MaxLives, the expression evaluates to TRUE, which is negated to FALSE, and so the code after the if () is not executed. Thus, the expression equates to the semi-English sentence, "Use up a life; then, if all lives have not yet been used, execute the code supplied."

 When an expression can only return either a TRUE or FALSE value, it is known as a Boolean expression. When combined with and, or, &&, ||, and !, such expressions are said to use Boolean logic. Boolean negation is different from when you place a subtraction operator in front of an expression to invert it from a positive to a negative value, or vice versa, because the ! operator turns a FALSE result into a TRUE one, and a TRUE result into a FALSE one.

The Ternary Operator

Ever on the lookout for ways to make program code simpler and more compact, program language developers also came up with a thing called the *ternary operator,* which allows you to combine "If this, then do that thing; otherwise, do another thing" logic into a single expression, like this:

```
echo $Lives > $MaxLives ? 'Game over' : 'Keep playing';
```

The way the ternary operator works is that you provide an expression that can return either TRUE or FALSE (a Boolean expression). Following this you put a ? character, after which you place the two options, separated with a : character, as follows:

```
expression ? do this : do that;
```

For example, another ternary expression might go like the following, which sets the string variable $AmPm to either AM or PM, according to the numeric value in the variable $Hour:

```
$AmPm = $Hour < 12 ? 'AM' : 'PM';
```

Bitwise Operators

There is a type of operator supported by PHP that (as a beginner to programming) you are most unlikely to use, due to it being quite advanced, and that's the bitwise operator. This type of operator acts on the individual 0 and 1 bits that make up binary numbers, and it can be quite tricky to use.

The bitwise operators are &, |, ^, ~, <<, and >>. In order, they support Bitwise And, Or, Exclusive Or, Not, left-shift, and right-shift on binary numbers. The bitwise operators can also be combined with the = assignment operator to make a whole new collection of bitwise assignment operators.

However, this isn't an advanced tutorial, so I won't go into how you use these operators—you already have enough new stuff to learn as it is. But if you're curious, you can check out the following web page, which covers them in some detail: php.net/manual/en/language.operators.bitwise.php.

Operator Precedence

In PHP, some operators are given a higher precedence than others. For example, multiplication has a higher precedence than addition, so in the following expression the multiplication will occur *before* the addition, even though the addition appears first:

```
$MyVar = 3 + 4 * 5;
```

The result of this expression is 23 (4 * 5 is 20, and 3 + 20 is 23). But if there were no operator precedence (with the expression executed simply from left to right), it would evaluate to 35 (3 + 4 is 7, and 7 * 5 is 35).

Providing precedence to operators obviates the need for parentheses in many circumstances, because the only way to make the preceding expression come out to 23 without operator precedence would be to insert parentheses as follows:

```
$MyVar = 3 + (4 * 5);
```

With this concept in mind, the creators of PHP have divided all the operators up into varying levels of precedence according to how "important" they are (in that multiplication and division are considered more "important" than addition and subtraction, due to their greater ability to handle large numbers).

Therefore, unless you intend to use parentheses in all your expressions to ensure the correct precedence (which would make your code much harder to write, and for others to understand, due to multiple levels of parentheses), you need to know these precedencies, which are listed in Table 6-3.

TABLE 6-3   Operator Precedence (1 Is Highest)

Precedence	Operators	Precedence	Operators
1	clone new	12	&
2	() []	13	^
3	++ --	14	|
4	~ - (int) (float) (string) (array) (object) (bool) @	15	&&
5	instanceof	16	||
6	!	17	? :
7	* / %	18	= += -= *= /= .= %= &= |= ^= <<= >>= =>
8	+ - .	19	and
9	<< >>	20	xor
10	< <= > >=	21	or
11	== != === !== <>	22	,

All you need to learn from this table, though, is which operators have higher precedence than others, where 1 is the highest and 22 is the lowest precedence. So where an operator has lower precedence but you need to elevate it, all you need to do is apply parentheses in the right places for the operators within them to have raised precedence.

Operator Associativity

PHP operators also have an attribute known as *associativity,* which is the direction in which they should be evaluated. For example, the assignment operators all have right-to-left associativity because you are assigning the value on the right to the variable on the left, like this:

```
$MyVar = 0;
```

Because of this right-to-left associativity, you can string assignments together, setting more than one variable at a time to a given value, like this:

```
$MyVar = $ThatVar = $OtherVar = 0;
```

This works because associativity of assignments starts at the right and continues in a leftward direction. In this instance, $OtherVar is first assigned the value 0. Then $ThatVar is assigned the value in $OtherVar, and finally $MyVar is assigned the value in $ThatVar.

On the other hand, some operators have left-to-right associativity, such as the || (or) operator, for example. You see, because of left-to-right associativity, the process of executing PHP can be speeded up, as demonstrated in the following example:

```
if ($ThisVar == 1 || $ThatVar == 1) // Do this
```

When PHP encounters the || operator, it knows to check the left side first. So, if $ThisVar has a value of 1, there is no need to look up the value of $ThatVar, because as long as one or the other expression on either side of the || operator evaluates to TRUE, the entire || expression evaluates to TRUE, and if the left half has evaluated to TRUE, then so has the whole || expression. In cases such as this, the PHP interpreter will eagerly skip the evaluation of the second half of the expression, knowing it is running in an optimized fashion.

Knowing whether operators have right-to-left or left-to-right associativity can really help your programming. For example, if you are using a left-to-right associative operator such as ||, you can line up all your expressions left to right from the most likely to be TRUE to the least likely. Therefore, it's worth taking a moment to familiarize yourself with the contents of Table 6-4 so that you will know which operators have what associativity.

TABLE 6-4 Operator Associativity

Associativity	Operators
Non-associative	`clone new ++ -- instanceof < <= > >= <> == != === !==`
Right-to-left associativity	`~ - (int) (float) (string) (array) (object) (bool) @` `! = += -= *= /= .= %= &= |= ^= <<= >>= =>`
Left-to-right associativity	`() [] * / % + - . << >> & ^	&& || ?: and xor or ,`

Summary

This lesson has brought you up to scratch with all you need to know about using operators, so now you're ready to start looking at some of PHP's more complex and interesting objects in the following lessons on using arrays—a slightly more complex (or perhaps I should say, more organized) form of data storage than variables.

Self-Test Questions

Test how much you have learned in this lesson with these questions. If you don't know an answer, go back and reread the relevant section until your knowledge is complete. You can find the answers in the appendix.

1. With which operator can you test whether two values evaluate to the same result?

2. How can you test whether two values evaluate to the same result *and* are both of the same type?

3. What are the results of these expressions: a) TRUE xor TRUE, b) TRUE xor FALSE, c) FALSE xor TRUE, and d) FALSE xor FALSE?

4. What is the result of ! (23 === '23')?

5. What single expression might you use to set the variable $bulb to the value 1 when the variable $daypart has the value 'night', and 0 when it doesn't?

6. To what value will PHP evaluate the expression 5 * 4 + 3 / 2 + 1?

7. How can you force PHP to evaluate the expression 1 + 2 / 3 * 4 – 5 from left to right?

8. Do the math operators (+, -, *, and /) have right-to-left or left-to-right associativity?

9. Do the assignment operators have right-to-left or left-to-right associativity?

10. When using the || operator, why is it a good idea to place the most likely to be TRUE expression on the left?

Creating Arrays

To view the accompanying video for this lesson, please visit mhprofessional.com/nixonphp/.

PHP is capable of managing data in a more powerful manner than simply via variables. One example of this is PHP arrays, which you can think of as collections of variables grouped together. For example, a good metaphor for an array might be a filing cabinet, with each drawer representing a different variable, as shown in Figure 7-1.

With the filing cabinet, as with the small pot metaphor in Lesson 3, to assign a value you should imagine writing it down on a piece of paper, placing it in the relevant drawer, and then closing the drawer. To read back a value, you open the drawer, take out the paper, read its value, return the paper, and close the drawer. The only difference between the cabinet and the pots is that the drawers of the filing cabinet (representing an array) are all in sequential order, whereas a collection of pots (representing variables) are stored in no particular order.

Although PHP arrays can be any size (up to the available memory in your computer), for the sake of simplicity I have only shown 10 elements in the figure. You can access each of the elements in an array numerically, starting with element 0 (the top drawer of the cabinet). This index number is important, because you might think that logically the number 1 would be the best starting point, but that isn't how PHP arrays are accessed—you should always remember that the first element is the zeroth.

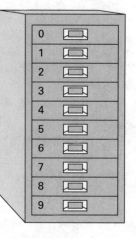

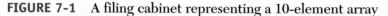

FIGURE 7-1 A filing cabinet representing a 10-element array

Array Names

The rules for naming arrays are exactly the same as those for naming variables. Array names must begin with a $ symbol, followed by either an uppercase or lowercase letter (a-z or A-Z) or the _ symbol. No other character may begin an array name.

Array names may not contain any mathematical operators (such as + or *), punctuation (such as ! or &), or spaces, but after the first character they may include the digits 0-9, any upper- or lowercase letters (a-z or A-Z), and the _ symbol.

Creating an Array

To create an array, you can declare it in advance (although you don't have to) to initialize it, like this:

```
$MyArray = array();
```

This array object contains no data but is ready for data to be assigned to its elements.

Assigning Values to an Array Element

You can populate arrays with data (in a similar manner to assigning values to variables), like this:

```
$MyArray[0] = 23;
$MyArray[1] = 67.35;
```

Here, the integer 23 is assigned to element 0 (the top drawer of the cabinet), whereas the floating point number 67.35 is assigned to the element at index 1 (the second drawer down, because they begin at 0). In fact, you can assign any legal value to an array element, including strings, objects, and even other arrays (which is discussed in the following lesson), like this:

```
$MyArray[3] = "Hello world";
$MyArray[4] = $OtherArray;
```

You are not restricted to assigning values in order, so you can go right in and assign values to any elements, like this:

```
$MyArray[9] = "Good morning";
$MyArray[7] = 3.1415927;
```

If you don't need your data stored in any particular array elements, you can instead insert values at the end of an array by omitting the element number. Therefore, the previous six assignments could be made like this (which would automatically use the indexes 0 through 5):

```
$MyArray[] = 23;
$MyArray[] = 67.35;
$MyArray[] = "Hello world";
$MyArray[] = $OtherArray;
$MyArray[] = "Good morning";
$MyArray[] = 3.1415927;
```

Using Indexes

The element number we have been using for storing a particular value is known as the array *index,* and you can use integer (as shown so far) or variable values as indexes. For example, the following first creates a variable and assigns it a numeric value, which is then used to assign another value to the array:

```
$MyIndex           = 123;
$MyArray[$MyIndex] = "Good evening";
```

This has the effect of assigning the string value "Good evening" to the element with an index of 123 in $MyArray[].

Retrieving Values

Once an array has been created and it has been populated with data, to retrieve a value from an array you simply refer to it, like this:

```
echo $MyArray[0];
```

This will fetch the value stored in the zeroth element of $MyArray[] (or the top drawer of the filing cabinet metaphor) and then pass it to echo to display it in the browser. You can, likewise, return a value using a variable, like this:

```
$MyIndex = 713;
echo $MyArray[$MyIndex];
```

Whatever value is stored in element 713 of the array will then be displayed in the browser.

 Note The preceding two examples (and many of the following ones) assume you have already created an array.

There are other ways you can use array values, such as assigning them to other variables or other array elements, or using them in expressions. For example, the following code assigns the value 23 to an array element, which is then looked up and used in an expression, in which 50 is added to it and the result (73) is displayed in the browser:

```
$MyArray[7] = 23;
echo $MyArray[7] + 50;
```

Or, for example, you may wish to display a value in a JavaScript alert window using code such as the following, which results in your browser looking like Figure 7-2 (although the style of the window varies by browser):

```
$MyArray[7] = 23;
echo '<script>alert(' . ($MyArray[7] + 50) . ')</script>';
```

Message from webp... X

⚠ 73

OK

FIGURE 7-2 Displaying a value in an alert window

Using Array Elements as Indexes

You can even go a step further and use the value stored in an array element as an index into another (or the same) array, like this:

```
$OtherArray[0]          = 77;
$MyArray[$OtherArray[0]] = "I love the movie Inception";
```

Here, the zeroth element of `$OtherArray[]` is assigned the integer value of 77. Once assigned, this element is used as the index into `$MyArray[]` (rather like the movie *Inception*, with arrays within arrays). However, this is quite complex programming, and you are unlikely to use these types of indexes as a beginner to PHP.

 The fact that you can use any valid integer value (including values in variables, array elements, and those returned by functions) means that you can use mathematical equations to iterate through arrays. For example, as you will discover in Lesson 9, it is easy to create code that runs in a loop to process each element of an array in turn.

Other Ways of Creating Arrays

You have already seen the following type of declaration for creating a PHP array:

```
$MyArray = array();
```

However, there are also a couple of other methods you can use, which also have the effect of simplifying your code, by allowing you to populate the array with some data at the same time. The first method is as follows:

```
$MyArray = array(123, "Hello there", 3.21);
```

Here, the array `$MyArray[]` is created and its first three elements immediately populated with three different values: an integer, a string, and a floating point number. This is equivalent to the following (much longer) code:

```
$MyArray    = array();
$MyArray[0] = 123;
$MyArray[1] = "Hello there";
$MyArray[2] = 3.21;
```

 Once you have created an array, if you need to apply any more values to elements within it, you must use the standard form of assigning values. If you reuse the short form of combined array creation and value assignment, it will simply reset the array to the values in the assignment.

Using Associative Arrays

Using numeric indexes is all well and good when you only have a few elements in an array to cope with. But once an array starts to hold meaningful amounts of data, using numbers to access its elements can be highly confusing. Thankfully, PHP provides a great solution to this by supporting the use of names to associate with array elements, in much the same way that variables have names.

Let's use PHP's associative arrays to store the ages of the players in a mixed, under 11, five-a-side soccer team. Here, the array is initialized and then the age of each player is assigned to an element in the array using the players' names:

```
$SoccerTeam = array();
$SoccerTeam['Andy']  = 10;
$SoccerTeam['Brian'] = 8;
$SoccerTeam['Cathy'] = 9;
$SoccerTeam['David'] = 10;
$SoccerTeam['Ellen'] = 9;
```

Having been assigned, these values can now easily be looked up by name, like this, which displays Cathy's age in the browser:

```
echo $SoccerTeam['Cathy'];
```

Keys, Values, and Hash Tables

When you use associative arrays, you are actually creating a collection of key and value pairs. The name you assign to an array element is known as the *key*, whereas the value you provide to the element is the *value*.

In other languages (such as JavaScript), this type of data structure is known as a *hash table*. When an object (such as a string) is used as a key for a value, this is called a *hash value*, and the data structure is the hash table.

Other Ways of Creating an Associative Array

If you wish, you can use a short form of creating and populating an associative array, like this:

```
$SoccerTeam = array(
   'Andy'  => 10,
   'Brian' => 8,
   'Cathy' => 9,
   'David' => 10,
   'Ellen' => 9
);
```

I'm sure you'll agree this is much simpler and easier to use, once you know that this type of code structure causes the creation of an array. But you may prefer to stick with the longer form until you are completely happy with using arrays. Also, I have chosen to be liberal with newlines here for reasons of clarity, but if you wish, you can run all these five sub-statements into a single line, like this:

```
$SoccerTeam = array('Andy' => 10, 'Brian' => 8, 'Cathy' => 9,
 'David' => 0, 'Ellen' => 9 );
```

As with standard variables and arrays, you are not restricted to only storing numbers in associative arrays, because you can assign any valid value, including integers, floating point numbers, strings, and even other arrays and objects. The following illustrates a couple of these:

```
$MyInfo = array(
  'Name'       => 'Bill Gates',
  'DOB'        => 1955,
  'Occupation' => 'Philanthropist',
  'Children'   => 3,
  'Worth'      => 79000000000
);
```

In the preceding example, both strings and numbers have been assigned to the array elements. You can read back any value simply by referring to it, like this, which displays the value in Occupation (namely Philanthropist) in the browser:

```
echo $MyInfo['Occupation'];
```

Summary

By now, you should be very comfortable with PHP arrays and will be beginning to see how they can make excellent structures for handling your data. If you are still a little hesitant, though, load the file *arrays.htm* (from the matching folder in the accompanying archive for this lesson) and play with the examples in it until you are sure you've got the hang of things. It's short and sweet and looks like Figure 7-3 when run.

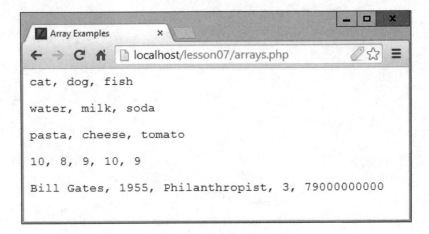

FIGURE 7-3   **A number of different array creation and accessing examples**

In the following lesson, I'll show you how there's actually a lot more to arrays than you've so far seen, and we'll begin to make some reasonably complex data objects.

Self-Test Questions

Test how much you have learned in this lesson with these questions. If you don't know an answer, go back and reread the relevant section until your knowledge is complete. You can find the answers in the appendix.

1. Which characters are allowed in PHP array names?

2. What types of values can be stored in an array element?

3. How can you create an unpopulated array?

4. How can you assign a value to specific elements in a numeric array.

5. How can you create and populate an array with a single instruction?

6. How can you add elements to a numeric array without specifying an index location?

7. How can you retrieve a value from a numeric array?

8. How can you reference a numeric array element using a variable?

9. How would you create and populate a new associative array to hold the names and phone numbers of three contacts?

10. How can you retrieve a value from an associative array?

8

Managing Multidimensional Arrays

To view the accompanying video for this lesson, please visit mhprofessional.com/nixonphp/.

Let me start by totally contradicting the title of this lesson and stating that there's actually no such thing as multidimensional arrays in PHP. But before you start scratching your head and wondering whether I've drunk too many cups of tea, let me say that you can *simulate* multidimensional arrays in PHP by assigning new arrays as the values for elements of an existing array.

But what exactly do I mean by *multidimensional* in the first place? Well, in the same way that a string of characters is a collection of individual letters, numbers, and other characters—which you can imagine being like a string of pearls, with each pearl occupying its right location, and the correct pearls on either side, all in the right order—an array is like a collection of variables all stored in their right locations.

In the previous lesson I used the metaphor of a filing cabinet for an array of 10 elements. If you imagine for a moment that each drawer in this filing cabinet is like *Doctor Who*'s Tardis (his time and space machine) in that it is much bigger on the inside than it is on the outside, then you should be able to also imagine being able to place another 10-drawer filing cabinet in each of the drawers of the original one! Figure 8-1 should help make this clearer.

Remember that these particular filing cabinets are not bound by the normal rules of space and time, so the small cabinets can contain just as much as the large one.

In fact, the cabinets are capable of holding an infinite amount of data, limited only by the restraints of the computer or server running PHP. I have simply drawn the secondary filing cabinets much smaller so that they fit into the figure.

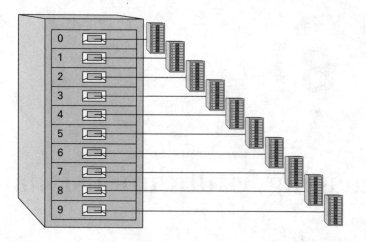

FIGURE 8-1   Representing a two-dimensional array with filing cabinets

Creating a Two-Dimensional Array

Let's see how we can use the ability of an array element being able to store another entire array to our advantage by considering a 10 times multiplication table, just like those often found on the classroom walls of school children (see Figure 8-2).

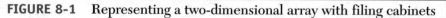

	1	2	3	4	5	6	7	8	9	10
1	1	2	3	4	5	6	7	8	9	10
2	2	4	6	8	10	12	14	16	18	20
3	3	6	9	12	15	18	21	24	27	30
4	4	8	12	16	20	24	28	32	36	40
5	5	10	15	20	25	30	35	40	45	50
6	6	12	18	24	30	36	42	48	54	60
7	7	14	21	28	35	42	49	56	63	70
8	8	16	24	32	40	48	56	64	72	80
9	9	18	27	36	45	54	63	72	81	90
10	10	20	30	40	50	60	70	80	90	100

FIGURE 8-2   A 10 times multiplication table

Each of the columns (or each of the rows) can be considered a one-dimensional array. For example, the first row could be created using the following code:

```
$MyTable0    = array();
$MyTable0[0] = 1;
$MyTable0[1] = 2;
```

```
$MyTable0[2]  =  3;
$MyTable0[3]  =  4;
$MyTable0[4]  =  5;
$MyTable0[5]  =  6;
$MyTable0[6]  =  7;
$MyTable0[7]  =  8;
$MyTable0[8]  =  9;
$MyTable0[9]  =  10;
```

Or, more succinctly:

```
$MyTable0 = array(1, 2, 3, 4, 5, 6, 7, 8, 9, 10);
```

Similarly, the second row could be created like this:

```
$MyTable1 = array(2, 4, 6, 8, 10, 12, 14, 16, 18, 20);
```

You can then continue like this for the remaining rows, so that you end up with the following set of statements:

```
$MyTable0 = array( 1,  2,  3,  4,  5,  6,  7,  8,  9, 10);
$MyTable1 = array( 2,  4,  6,  8, 10, 12, 14, 16, 18, 20);
$MyTable2 = array( 3,  6,  9, 12, 15, 18, 21, 24, 27, 30);
$MyTable3 = array( 4,  8, 12, 16, 20, 24, 28, 32, 36, 40);
$MyTable4 = array( 5, 10, 15, 20, 25, 30, 35, 40, 45, 50);
$MyTable5 = array( 6, 12, 18, 24, 30, 36, 42, 48, 54, 60);
$MyTable6 = array( 7, 14, 21, 28, 35, 42, 49, 56, 63, 70);
$MyTable7 = array( 8, 16, 24, 32, 40, 48, 56, 64, 72, 80);
$MyTable8 = array( 9, 18, 27, 36, 45, 54, 63, 72, 81, 90);
$MyTable9 = array(10, 20, 30, 40, 50, 60, 70, 80, 90,100);
```

At this point we now have one array for each row in the times table. With these now created, it is now possible to build a two-dimensional table by creating just one more table, a master table, like this:

```
$MasterTable     = array();
$MasterTable[0] = $MyTable0;
$MasterTable[1] = $MyTable1;
$MasterTable[2] = $MyTable2;
$MasterTable[3] = $MyTable3;
$MasterTable[4] = $MyTable4;
$MasterTable[5] = $MyTable5;
$MasterTable[6] = $MyTable6;
$MasterTable[7] = $MyTable7;
$MasterTable[8] = $MyTable8;
$MasterTable[9] = $MyTable9;
```

Alternatively, we can use the shorter form:

```
$MasterTable = array
(
    $MyTable0,
    $MyTable1,
    $MyTable2,
    $MyTable3,
    $MyTable4,
    $MyTable5,
    $MyTable6,
    $MyTable7,
    $MyTable8,
    $MyTable9
);
```

Note I have chosen to split this up into multiple lines for clarity, but you can equally include all the preceding in a single statement on one line, as follows:

```
$MasterTable = array ( $MyTable0, $MyTable1, $MyTable2, $MyTable3,
    $MyTable4, $MyTable5, $MyTable6, $MyTable7, $MyTable8, $MyTable9 );
```

Accessing a Two-Dimensional Array

Let's now look at how this relates to the filing cabinets in Figure 8-1 in terms of code. To recap, there's a main array called `$MasterTable[]`, with each of its elements containing another array, named sequentially `$MyTable0[]` through `$MyTable9[]`.

As you will recall from the previous lesson, accessing an array is as simple as the following, which outputs the value in the array held at a numeric index of 23 (which will be element 24 because arrays start from 0):

```
echo $SomeArray[23];
```

But what should you do when the value stored in an array element is another array? The answer is simple and elegant—you just add another pair of square brackets following the first pair and then place another index value into that new array between them, like this:

```
echo $MasterTable[0][0];
```

This statement displays the contents of the first element of the array that is stored in the first element of `$MasterTable[]`. Notice that there is no need to reference the sub-array by name (*sub-array* being the term I use for referring to arrays within arrays).

Likewise, if you wish to display the value held in the seventh element of the array stored in the third element of `$MasterTable[]`, you would use code such as this (remembering that array indexes start at 0 not 1, so the seventh and third elements will be 6 and 2, respectively):

```
echo $MasterTable[2][6];
```

In terms of the times table in Figure 8-2, this is equivalent to first moving to the third row down and then seventh column across, at which point you can see that the value shown is 21, as you will quickly see if you look at the source of *timestable.htm* (available in the companion archive):

```
<!DOCTYPE html>
<html>
  <head>
    <title>Two-Dimensional Array Example</title>
  </head>
  <body>
<?php
    $MyTable0 = array( 1,  2,  3,  4,  5,  6,  7,  8,  9, 10);
    $MyTable1 = array( 2,  4,  6,  8, 10, 12, 14, 16, 18, 20);
    $MyTable2 = array( 3,  6,  9, 12, 15, 18, 21, 24, 27, 30);
    $MyTable3 = array( 4,  8, 12, 16, 20, 24, 28, 32, 36, 40);
    $MyTable4 = array( 5, 10, 15, 20, 25, 30, 35, 40, 45, 50);
    $MyTable5 = array( 6, 12, 18, 24, 30, 36, 42, 48, 54, 60);
    $MyTable6 = array( 7, 14, 21, 28, 35, 42, 49, 56, 63, 70);
    $MyTable7 = array( 8, 16, 24, 32, 40, 48, 56, 64, 72, 80);
    $MyTable8 = array( 9, 18, 27, 36, 45, 54, 63, 72, 81, 90);
    $MyTable9 = array(10, 20, 30, 40, 50, 60, 70, 80, 90,100);

    $MasterTable = array(
      $MyTable0, $MyTable1, $MyTable2, $MyTable3, $MyTable4,
      $MyTable5, $MyTable6, $MyTable7, $MyTable8, $MyTable9);

    echo 'The value at location 2,6 is ' . $MasterTable[2][6];
?>
  </body>
</html>
```

Note   This code is equivalent to the filing cabinets in Figure 8-1, in that the $MasterTable[] array represents the large cabinet, while the $MyTable0[] array is the top small cabinet, and $MyTable9[] is the bottom small cabinet, as shown in Figure 8-3.

If you now take all the small filing cabinets and stack them up alongside each other, you will see how they represent the $MasterTable[] array, as shown in Figure 8-4. For all intents and purposes, we can forget about the main array (other than for using its name to index into the sub-arrays) and think only in terms of the 10 sub-arrays, and how to access each drawer using pairs of indexes.

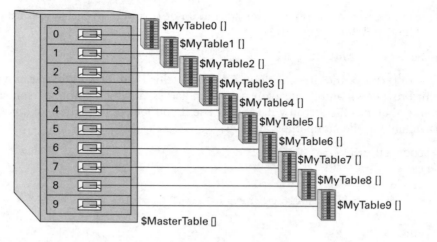

FIGURE 8-3 The relationship between the cabinets and arrays

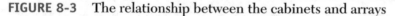

FIGURE 8-4 The small filing cabinets are now lined up alongside each other.

The first index goes down the drawers of the main cabinet, and the second one goes along the cabinets. Therefore, array index [3] [7] points to the fourth drawer down, and the eighth cabinet along.

Note If it helps to better visualize the rows and columns of such a two-dimensional array, imagine rotating the sub-cabinets counterclockwise by 90 degrees, so that they are laying flat, and then stacked on top of each other. It's starting to stretch the metaphor, but it may help to match up the drawers and array coordinates in your mind.

A More Practical Example

Obviously, a multiplication table is a trivial thing to re-create on a computer because it can be achieved with a couple of simple loops. So let's look instead at a more interesting example: that of a board for a game of Othello (also known as Reversi).

As you may know, there are 64 squares on an Othello board, laid out in an 8×8 grid, and two players take turns laying a counter of their color in such a way that one (or more) of their opponent's counters becomes sandwiched. These sandwiched counters are then turned over to reveal the opposite color underneath, and thus become the property of the current player.

Using a computer to represent an Othello board is simple using nested arrays, as in the following example, where a set game position is being assigned, with 'W' representing white counters and 'B' representing black counters:

```
$Row0 = array('-', '-', '-', '-', '-', '-', '-', '-');
$Row1 = array('-', '-', '-', '-', '-', '-', '-', '-');
$Row2 = array('-', '-', 'W', '-', 'B', '-', '-', '-');
$Row3 = array('-', '-', 'B', 'W', 'B', '-', '-', '-');
$Row4 = array('-', '-', 'B', 'B', 'B', 'W', '-', '-');
$Row5 = array('-', '-', 'B', '-', 'W', '-', '-', '-');
$Row6 = array('-', '-', '-', 'W', '-', '-', '-', '-');
$Row7 = array('-', '-', '-', '-', '-', '-', '-', '-');
```

The board can now be created by assigning these sub-arrays to a master array, like this:

```
$Board = array($Row0, $Row1, $Row2, $Row3, $Row4, $Row5, $Row6, $Row7);
```

It's now white's turn to play, and there are a few possible locations next to black counters that can be sandwiched, but let's assume that white elects to place the next counter at the location six down and four across.

Remembering that numeric arrays start at an index of 0, we can see that the possible index locations are [0] [0] through [7] [7], with [0] [0] being the top-left corner and [7] [7] the bottom-right corner. Therefore, to play at six positions down and four across, the array element to access is $Board[5] [3].

When this white counter is placed, it will sandwich the black one immediately above it (at location [4] [3]), and so we must make two changes to the array, as follows:

```
$Board[5] [3] = 'W';
$Board[4] [3] = 'W';
```

Figure 8-5 shows the *othello.php* example file (available in the companion archive), in which the before and after board positions are shown, as created by the preceding code.

Note   If you wish, you may continue adding arrays within other arrays until you run out of computer memory. All you do is place new arrays inside existing ones to add an extra dimension. For example, if you were to create additional sub-sub-arrays for each of the sub-array elements (a total of 64 new arrays), you could form eight complete Othello boards in a three-dimensional array, representing an 8×8×8 cube—now that would be an interesting game!

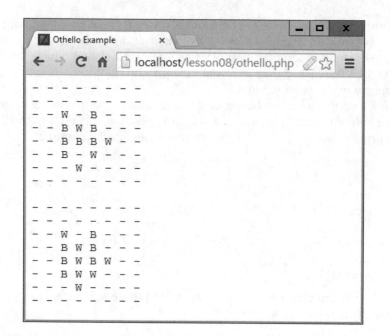

FIGURE 8-5 Modifying a two-dimensional game board array

Multidimensional Associative Arrays

As you might expect, just as with numeric arrays, you can create multidimensional associative arrays. Let me explain why you might want to do this by considering a small online store that sells toys for six different age ranges of children, as follows:

- Babies
- Toddlers
- Age 3–5
- Age 5–8
- Age 8–12
- Teenagers

These categories can be easily mapped into an associative array (as I'll show you in a minute), but let's first create some subcategories for each of the main ones, such as these:

- Babies
  - Rattle
  - Bear
  - Pacifier

- Toddlers
  - Wooden Bricks
  - Xylophone
  - Play Dough
- Age 3–5
  - Slide
  - Tricycle
  - Crayons
- Age 5–8
  - Dolly
  - Bicycle
  - Guitar
- Age 8–12
  - Tablet Computer
  - Remote Control Car
  - Frisbee
- Teenagers
  - MP3 Player
  - Game Console
  - TV/DVD Combo

Clearly these subcategories can also be mapped to associative arrays, but before we do that we have to go even deeper (yet more undertones of *Inception*) because a web store needs things such as pricing information and product availability, like this:

- Price
- Stock Level

Creating the Multidimensional Array

Armed with these details, we're now ready to start building the arrays needed by assigning values to the price and stock level of each product being sold to an associative array for each product, as follows:

```
$Rattle    = array('Price' =>   4.99, 'Stock' => 3 );
$Bear      = array('Price' =>   6.99, 'Stock' => 2 );
$Pacifier  = array('Price' =>   1.99, 'Stock' => 9 );
$Bricks    = array('Price' =>   5.99, 'Stock' => 1 );
$Xylophone = array('Price' =>  12.99, 'Stock' => 2 );
$PlayDough = array('Price' =>   8.49, 'Stock' => 7 );
$Slide     = array('Price' =>  99.99, 'Stock' => 1 );
$Tricycle  = array('Price' =>  79.99, 'Stock' => 1 );
$Crayons   = array('Price' =>   3.79, 'Stock' => 5 );
$Dolly     = array('Price' =>  14.99, 'Stock' => 3 );
```

```
$Bicycle   = array('Price' =>  89.99, 'Stock' => 2 );
$Guitar    = array('Price' =>  49.00, 'Stock' => 1 );
$TabletPC  = array('Price' => 149.99, 'Stock' => 1 );
$RemoteCar = array('Price' =>  39.99, 'Stock' => 2 );
$Frisbee   = array('Price' =>   7.99, 'Stock' => 6 );
$MP3Player = array('Price' => 179.99, 'Stock' => 1 );
$Console   = array('Price' => 199.99, 'Stock' => 2 );
$TVAndDVD  = array('Price' =>  99.99, 'Stock' => 1 );
```

Now that these basic data structures are complete, it's possible to group the products into the age range arrays, like this (note that the words in quotes are the keys and those after the => operators are the values, which are the names of the associative arrays previously created):

```
$Babies    = array('Rattle'            => $Rattle,
                   'Bear'              => $Bear,
                   'Pacifier'          => $Pacifier);
$Toddlers  = array('Wooden Bricks'     => $Bricks,
                   'Xylophone'         => $Xylophone,
                   'Play Dough'        => $PlayDough);
$Age3_5    = array('Slide'             => $Slide,
                   'Tricycle'          => $Tricycle,
                   'Crayons'           => $Crayons);
$Age5_8    = array('Dolly'             => $Dolly,
                   'Bicycle'           => $Bicycle,
                   'Guitar'            => $Guitar);
$Age8_12   = array('Tablet PC'         => $TabletPC,
                   'Remote Control Car' => $RemoteCar,
                   'Frisbee'           => $Frisbee);
$Teenagers = array('MP3 Player'        => $MP3Player,
                   'Game Console'      => $Console,
                   'TV/DVD Combo'      => $TVAndDVD);
```

 Note I used an underscore character between the digits in these age range arrays because the dash is a disallowed character in variable and array names (because it can be confused with the minus symbol). The dash is acceptable, however, when used as part of a quoted string for a key name.

Finally, the top array can be populated, like this (where the strings in quotes are the keys, and the values after the => operators are the names of the arrays just defined):

```
$Categories= array('Babies'    => $Babies,
                   'Toddlers'   => $Toddlers,
                   'Ages 3-5'   => $Age3_5,
                   'Ages 5-8'   => $Age5_8,
                   'Ages 8-12'  => $Age8_12,
                   'Teenagers'  => $Teenagers);
```

What has now been created is actually a three-dimensional array. The first dimension is the $Categories[] array, the second is each of the age range arrays, and the third is each of the product arrays containing the price and stock level.

 Note Remember that in each of these assignments the string on the left is the key and the item on the right is the value. In all but the innermost (or lowest) case, the value is the name of another array that has already been created. For the innermost case, the values are numeric values: the price and stock level.

Accessing the Arrays

You can now read and write to these stored values in the following manner, which returns the price of the slide, which is 99.99 (no currency type is specified in these examples, just values):

```
echo $Categories['Ages 3-5']['Slide']['Price'];
```

Alternatively, if you need to change a price on an item of inventory for any reason, such as the crayons, for example (currently 3.79), you can alter it in the following manner, which reduces the price by 0.20:

```
$Categories['Ages 3-5']['Crayons']['Price'] = 3.59;
```

Likewise, when you sell an item of stock, you can reduce the inventory level (the stock level) in a similar manner. The following decreases the stock level of game consoles by 1, using the pre-decrement operator:

```
--$Categories['Teenagers']['Game Console']['Stock'];
```

Obviously, the inventory for even the smallest online store is sure to be far greater than what's used in this example, and there are going to be many additional attributes for some toys, such as different sizes and colors, as well as images, descriptions, technical specifications, and other details about the product, all of which could easily be built into this multidimensional structure of arrays.

The file *toystore.php* in the companion archive contains all the preceding prepopulated arrays and the example statements that access them. You may wish to try experimenting with it to read from and write to other items of data within the array structure.

Summary

You may not realize it, but we've now covered a huge amount of territory in just eight lessons. With less than half the book completed, you are already becoming an accomplished PHP programmer. Hopefully, it's all making sense to you, and arrays are beginning to feel like second nature. Therefore, in the next lesson, we'll look at some fun we can have using the array-accessing functions provided with PHP.

Self-Test Questions

Test how much you have learned in this lesson with these questions. If you don't know an answer, go back and reread the relevant section until your knowledge is complete. You can find the answers in the appendix.

1. PHP doesn't support multidimensional arrays natively, so what is the process of emulating such a structure?

2. What kind of array structure would you create to hold the contents of a 3 × 3 Tic-Tac-Toe board?

3. Given the array $oxo, containing a 3 × 3 Tic-Tac-Toe board, how might you reference the element in the top-left corner? How about the bottom-right corner?

4. How can you pre-increment a numeric value stored in an associative array at `$PageClicks['homepage']`?

5. How can you post-decrement a numeric value stored in an associative array at `$PageClicks['homepage']['menu']`?

6. How might you populate an associative array called `$marbles` with three sizes of marbles (small, medium, and large), of which you have (in order) 17, 23, and 21 bags?

7. How might you create a similar array to the `$marbles` array in Question 6, but with each array element containing a sub-array (rather than a numeric value), suitable for storing additional information?

8. What is one way you could access the second-level array elements for the `$marbles` array in Question 7 to also store information for the marble colors (red, green, and blue), along with their matching stock quantities?

9. Assuming all the elements for the array in Question 8 have been assigned values for the three sizes, three colors, and stock quantities, how could you determine the stock level of medium-sized bags of blue marbles?

10. Given a value stored in an associative, two-dimensional array, at `$marbles['large']['red']`, how can you increment this value by 10 with a single statement?

9

Calling Array Functions

 To view the accompanying video for this lesson, please visit mhprofessional.com/
nixonphp/.

To make arrays even more powerful, PHP comes readymade with a selection of
handy functions for accessing and manipulating them. For example, you can join
arrays together, push new items onto an array (and pop them off again later), reverse
the data in an array, sort it alphabetically or numerically, and more.

In this lesson, we'll look at a small selection of these functions and how to use
them. If you would like to see the complete set of array functions, you can view the
documentation page at php.net/manual/en/ref.array.php.

Using `foreach()`

The first feature I'd like to introduce is `foreach()`, because with it you can iterate
through an array one element at a time, which we will need to do in the following
examples in order to see the results. To show how this iteration works, let's start with
a simple array:

```
$Cats = array('Long Hair', 'Short Hair', 'Dwarf',
              'Farm', 'Tabby', 'Tortoiseshell');
```

Now, let's use `foreach` to display all its elements, as follows (resulting in
Figure 9-1):

```
foreach($Cats as $cat)
{
  echo "$cat<br>";
}
```

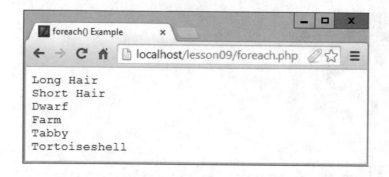

FIGURE 9-1   The contents of $Cats[] are displayed.

What's happening here is the as keyword creates a new variable called $cat, which takes on the value in each element of $Cats[] in turn, as the loop iterates through the array. Then the contents of the curly braces are executed once for each element in $Cats[] until there are no more elements left in the array to process.

Note   Here you see one of my programming styles, which is to often use the plural of a word for an array name and the singular for a single element in that array (as extracted by foreach(), for example). I also tend to make the singular variable all lowercase to further indicate that it is only a member of a larger object.

For reasons I will explain in Lesson 12, the curly braces can be omitted when there is only a single statement to be executed by such a loop. Therefore, for the sake of simplicity in the following examples, I will reduce this type of code to the much shorter following example:

```
foreach($Cats as $cat) echo "$cat<br>";
```

In an associative array, you can also use foreach() to extract both the key and the value for each element. For example, consider the soccer team array from Lesson 7:

```
$SoccerTeam = array(
   'Andy'  => 10,
   'Brian' => 8,
   'Cathy' => 9,
   'David' => 10,
   'Ellen' => 9
);
```

Using foreach(), you can extract all this data as follows:

```
foreach($SoccerTeam as $player => $age)
  echo "$player is $age years old<br>";
```

In this example, each time around the loop, $player is given the key for the current element, and $age is set to the value for that element. Now that there's an easy way to display the contents of an array, we can start to look at the array functions provided by PHP and see how to use them. You can try both of these examples for yourself by loading the *foreach.php* example from the companion archive into your browser.

Using `array_merge()`

Using the `array_merge()` function, you can return a new array created by joining two other arrays together. The two original arrays are not changed in any way by this function; only the result of joining them together is returned.

To see how this works, let's create a second array to go with the `$Cats[]` array created a little earlier, as follows:

```
$Dogs = array('Pit Bull', 'Spaniel', 'Terrier',
              'Beagle', 'Shepherd', 'Bulldog');
```

With both arrays now created, we can run the `array_merge()` function on them, like this:

```
$Pets = array_merge($Cats, $Dogs);
```

And now to see the result of this operation, we can issue the following statement:

```
foreach($Pets as $pet) echo "$pet<br>";
```

The code to create these two arrays and the preceding pair of statements can be found in the *array_merge.php* file in the companion archive. As you can see in Figure 9-2, the result is that the new array `$Pets[]` now contains all elements from both the `$Cats[]` and `$Dogs[]` arrays, in order.

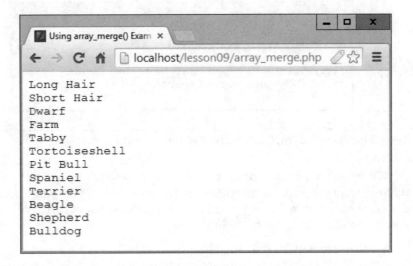

FIGURE 9-2   The two arrays have been merged.

For a similar result, but with the contents of the `$Dogs[]` array before the `$Cats[]`, you could equally have issued this statement:

```
$Pets = array_merge($Dogs, $Cats);
```

In fact, you could omit the creation of the `$Pets[]` array altogether and simply iterate through the result of the `array_merge()` call, like this:

```
foreach(array_merge($Cats, $Dogs) as $pet)
  echo "$pet<br>";
```

Using `implode()`

Sometimes you may wish to turn all the elements in an array into a string, and this is easy to do using the `implode()` function. For example, let's take the case of the `$Cats[]` array, as follows:

```
echo implode(' and ', $Cats);
```

This statement calls the `implode()` function, passing it the string `' and '`, which is used as a separator, to be inserted between each element, as shown in Figure 9-3. You may use any string as the element separator, or none at all, as in the following three examples:

```
echo implode($Cats);
echo implode('',   $Cats);
echo implode(',',  $Cats);
```

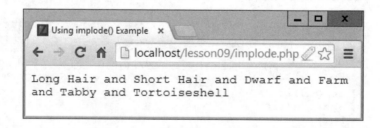

FIGURE 9-3   The result of imploding array elements into a string

When nothing or an empty string (`' '`) is passed to `implode()` as its first argument, no separator is inserted between element values, whereas a comma or any other value passed to it is used as the separator. So, in turn, the three previous statements display in the following ways:

Long HairShort HairDwarfFarmTabbyTortoiseshell
Long HairShort HairDwarfFarmTabbyTortoiseshell
Long Hair,Short Hair,Dwarf,Farm,Tabby,Tortoiseshell

PHP also supports the alias (a different name for the same function) of `join()`, which works in an identical manner to `implode()` and is included for greater compatibility with other languages such as JavaScript.

The `array_walk()` Function

One very quick and easy way to process all the elements in an array is to pass the array to another function, via PHP's `array_walk()` function. For example, the following code creates an array populated with numbers and then applies the new `CalcRoot()` function to each element, all via a single call to the `array_walk()` function:

```php
$Nums = array(99, 16, 11, 66.5, 54, 23);
array_walk($Nums, 'CalcRoot');

function CalcRoot($item)
{
   echo "Root $item is " . sqrt($item) . '<br>';
}
```

What happens is that every item in the array is looked up and then passed as an argument to the function given to `array_walk()`. This process repeats until all items have been passed in turn to the supplied function. You can see the result of running this code (*array_walk.php* in the companion archive) in Figure 9-4.

 You will have noticed that the function `CalcRoot()` is not called in the normal fashion (for example, `echo CalcRoot(64);`). Rather, just the name of the function is passed as a quoted string. This is because *we* don't want to call the function at this particular point; we only want to tell `array_walk()` which function *it* should call, and `array_walk()` is smart enough to understand that the string value it is passed is the name of a function to be called.

```
Using array_walk()          ×

← → C ⌂   localhost/lesson09/array_walk.php

Root 99 is 9.9498743710662
Root 16 is 4
Root 11 is 3.3166247903554
Root 66.5 is 8.15475321515
Root 54 is 7.3484692283495
Root 23 is 4.7958315233127
```

FIGURE 9-4   Iterating through an array with `array_walk()`

Note Functions are so central to PHP programming that some of these examples need to use them before I get a chance to explain how they work. Still, I'm sure you get the gist for now, and everything you need to know about using and creating functions (such as `CalcRoot()` in this example) is explained in Lesson 13.

Using `array_push()`

There are a couple of good reasons for using the `array_push()` function. First, you can add a new element to the end of an array without knowing how many items already exist in that array. For example, normally you would need to know the current array length and then use that value to add extra values, like this (using the `$Cats[]` array once more):

```
$Cats        = array('Long Hair', 'Short Hair', 'Dwarf',
                      'Farm', 'Tabby', 'Tortoiseshell');
$len         = sizeof($Cats);
$Cats[$len]  = 'Siamese';
```

The new variable `$len` is used to hold the length of the array (the number of elements it contains). In this instance, the value will be 6, for elements 0 through 5. Therefore, the value in `$len`, being 6, is suitable to use as an index into the next available element, and so that is what it is used for—the value 6 points to the seventh element because element indexes start at 0. In fact, if the variable `$len` is not to be used anywhere else, it's actually superfluous, so you could replace the final two lines of the preceding example with this single statement:

```
$Cats[sizeof($Cats)]  = 'Siamese';
```

However, it is much simpler to let PHP keep track of array lengths and simply tell it to add a new element to the `$Cats[]` array, like this:

```
array_push($Cats, 'Siamese');
```

You can verify that the element has been added with the following `foreach()` loop (which results in Figure 9-5, the code for which is available as *array_push.php* in the companion archive):

```
foreach($Cats as $cat) echo "$cat<br>";
```

The second reason you might want to use `array_push()` is because it's a quick way of storing values in a sequence that then have to be recalled in the reverse order. For example, using `array_push()` you can keep adding elements to an array, like this:

```
array_push($MyArray, 'A');
array_push($MyArray, 'B');
array_push($MyArray, 'C');
```

Then, as you will see in the following description of `array_pop()`, you can also remove these elements from last to first, such that the value C will be taken off first, then B, then A, and so on.

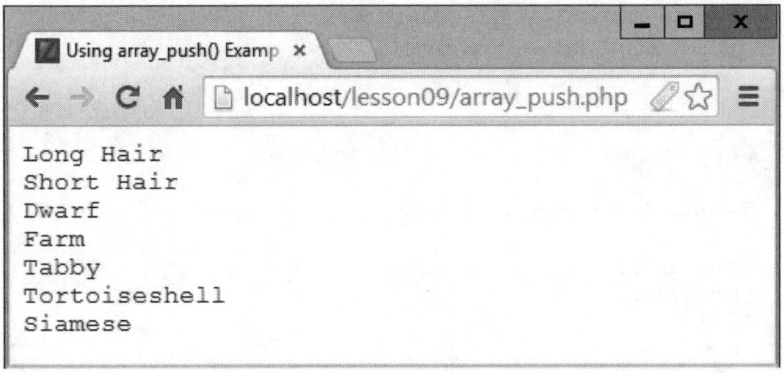

```
Using array_push() Examp  ×

← → C 🏠  🗋 localhost/lesson09/array_push.php  ✏️☆  ≡

Long Hair
Short Hair
Dwarf
Farm
Tabby
Tortoiseshell
Siamese
```

FIGURE 9-5   Pushing a new element onto an array

Using `array_pop()`

At its simplest, `array_pop()` enables you to remove the last element from an array (and in this instance discard the returned value), using code such as this:

```
array_pop($MyArray);
```

To remove the last element from an array and store it in a variable (for example), you use code such as this:

```
$MyVariable = array_pop($MyArray);
```

You can apply `array_pop()` to an existing array with values in it, which can have been assigned when the array was created, via a call to `array_push()` or in any other way. The `array_pop()` function then pulls the last item off the array (removing it from the array) and then returns that value. Looking again at the `$Cats[]` array, we can create a working example like this:

```
$Cats = array('Long Hair', 'Short Hair', 'Dwarf',
              'Farm', 'Tabby', 'Tortoiseshell');

echo 'Popping off the value ' . array_pop($Cats) . '<br><br>';
echo 'Remaining elements: <br><br>';

foreach($Cats as $cat) echo "$cat<br>";
```

The result of running this code (available as *array_pop.php* in the companion archive) is shown in Figure 9-6, where you can see that the value `Tortoiseshell` was popped off the array, and underneath all the remaining elements are displayed, confirming that the previous final element has now been removed.

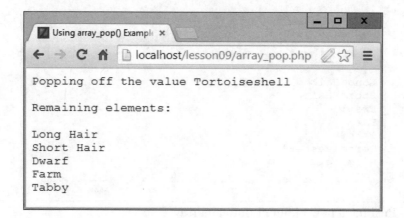

FIGURE 9-6   Popping an element off an array

Using `array_push()` and `array_pop()` Together

The `array_pop()` function is most commonly used with `array_push()` when writing code that uses recursion. Recursion is any section of code that calls itself and can then call itself again, and keep on doing so until the task of the code is complete (it's like *Inception* yet again!).

If this sounds complicated, consider a search algorithm for exploring a maze such as the one in Figure 9-7, in which the objective is to find your way from the starting point at a to the finish at y.

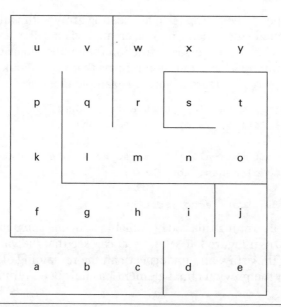

FIGURE 9-7   A simple 5×5 maze

You can clearly see the path to follow, but a computer is not so smart and will need to investigate the maze as if it were a rat, with walls higher than it can see over. A program to do this will easily find its way along the path a-b-c-h, but then it will encounter a choice of going either left to location (or cell) g or right to i.

Let's assume it chooses the latter after selecting a direction at random. The program will then follow the path i-d-e-j, only to encounter a dead end, requiring the program to return. Let's look at tracking this entire path so far using the array_push() function:

```
$Maze = array();
array_push($Maze, 'a');
array_push($Maze, 'b');
array_push($Maze, 'c');
array_push($Maze, 'h');
array_push($Maze, 'i');
array_push($Maze, 'd');
array_push($Maze, 'e');
array_push($Maze, 'j');
```

If you assume that there's also some extra code (not documented here) that knows which cells have and haven't been visited, the program can then use the simple method of popping each cell off the array until it reaches one where it can get to a cell not yet visited. Pseudo-code (the actions to take expressed in plain English) to do this might look like this:

```
While no unvisited cell is accessible...
   ...pop a location off the array
```

And the sequence of actions that would happen within the loop section of this code would be like this:

```
$Location = array_pop($Maze); // Returns 'j'
```

Because no unvisited cell can be reached from j (as determined by the code that we assume is there but not documented), the loop will go round again, and again, until an unvisited cell can be accessed, resulting in four additional calls to array_pop(), as follows:

```
$Location = array_pop($Maze); // Returns 'e'
$Location = array_pop($Maze); // Returns 'd'
$Location = array_pop($Maze); // Returns 'i'
$Location = array_pop($Maze); // Returns 'h'
```

Now, when the program finds it has popped the location h off the stack, it discovers there's a new cell it can go to, namely g, and so the process continues along the path g-f-k-p-u-v-q-l-m, at which point another choice of directions is encountered: either r or n.

To track this path, the program will push all the cells between g and m onto the array, and then (if direction n is chosen) also push the path n-o-t-s, at which point another dead end will be encountered.

Then, as before, the code will pop off all the cells in a loop until it reaches `m`, at which point the unvisited cell `r` is accessible and the final path out of the maze is discovered: `r-w-x-y`.

Note Recursion is quite complex programming, especially for beginners, which is why I have not documented the ancillary code you would use to take care of tracking the visited and unvisited cells. I simply wanted to offer a visual example of recursion that would explain what's going on, and show how to use `array_push()` and `array_pop()` together. But don't worry if you find any of it confusing, because you can safely move on with the lessons and come back here another time, when you find an actual need for these functions.

Using `array_reverse()`

When you want to reverse the order of elements in an array, you can call the `array_reverse()` function. To use the function, you call it like this:

```
$MyArray = array_reverse($MyArray);
```

Figure 9-8 shows this function being used to reverse the `$Cats[]` array from previous examples, the code for which is available as *array_reverse.php* in the companion archive.

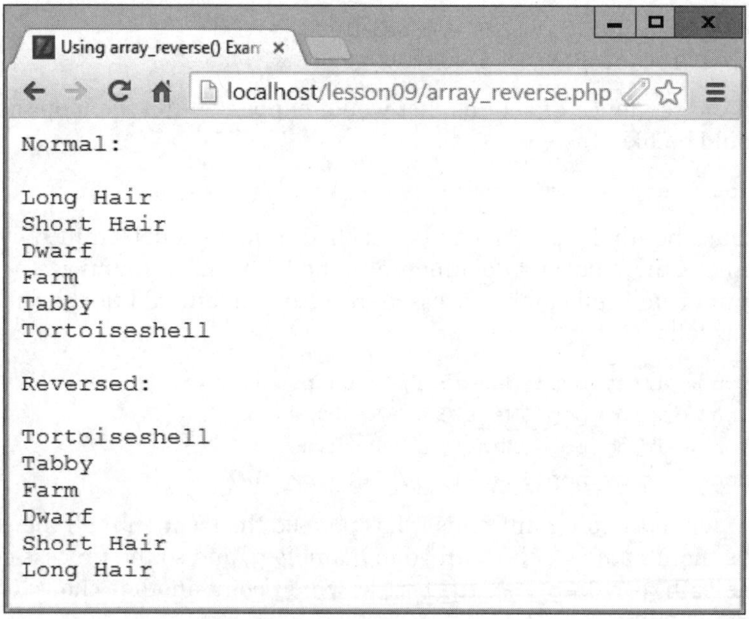

Using array_reverse() Exam
localhost/lesson09/array_reverse.php
Normal:
Long Hair
Short Hair
Dwarf
Farm
Tabby
Tortoiseshell
Reversed:
Tortoiseshell
Tabby
Farm
Dwarf
Short Hair
Long Hair

FIGURE 9-8 Array elements before and after reversing

Some languages (such as JavaScript) actually reverse the array when their version of the `array_reverse()` function is called, rather than simply returning a new, reversed array. This technique can save time in some circumstances, but it also requires additional code to store temporary arrays when you don't want that behavior. Fortunately, PHP doesn't alter the original array, so you don't have to concern yourself with saving a copy first should you need it.

The `array_flip()` Function

Lastly, in this lesson I'd like to show you the `array_flip()` function, which is quite interesting in that it returns a new array where all the key/value pairs are reversed, so that the keys become the values, and vice versa.

A good use of this could be, for example, to switch first and last names in a contact list to enable sorting by either name. Here's an example that creates a three-element array, displays its contents, and then displays a flipped version:

```
$Actors = array('Jack'   => 'Nicholson',
                'Marlon' => 'Brando',
                'Julia'  => 'Roberts');

echo 'Normal: <br><br>';
foreach($Actors as $key => $value) echo "$key $value<br>";

$Actors = array_flip($Actors);

echo '<br>Flipped: <br><br>';
foreach($Actors as $key => $value) echo "$key $value<br>";
```

The result of running this code (saved in the companion archive as *array_flip.php*) is shown in Figure 9-9.

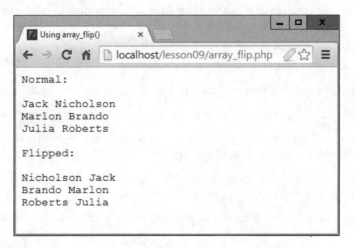

FIGURE 9-9 Flipping key and index values in an array

Even if any of the values in an array are numeric, they will still switch and become keys (and vice versa), because it is perfectly acceptable for both keys and values to be either numeric or string values. However, only integer or string values are accepted by the function; therefore, any other values encountered will not get flipped, but will cause a warning to be issued.

Summary

Arrays are a mainstay of any PHP programming that involves data processing, because they are so much easier to work with than individual and separate variables—so I hope you found this lesson easy going. With your newly acquired knowledge of PHP array functions (and how to use them), you are now ready to learn about more advanced array manipulation in the following lesson.

Self-Test Questions

Test how much you have learned in this lesson with these questions. If you don't know an answer, go back and reread the relevant section until your knowledge is complete. You can find the answers in the appendix.

1. With which function can you iterate through a numeric array to extract its values, and how?

2. With which function can you iterate through an associative array to extract the key/value pairs, and how?

3. With what statement could you merge together the arrays $Cars and $Trucks into a new array called $Vehicles?

4. With which statement can you combine all the elements of the array $Itinerary into a string using a separator string of ', '?

5. With what statement could you call the function process() on all elements of the array $info[]?

6. With which function can you add a new value to the end of an array?

7. How can you read and remove the last item in an array with a single statement?

8. When calling the array_push() function, does the value supplied get added to the start or to the end of the array?

9. When calling the array_pop() function, is the value removed from the start or from the end of the supplied array?

10. How can you switch all the keys in an array with their associated values?

10

Advanced Array Manipulation

To view the accompanying video for this lesson, please visit mhprofessional.com/nixonphp/.

Once you get the hang of using PHP arrays, you'll wonder how you managed without them. With arrays, you can group types of data together into logical collections, such as lists of inventory, members of organizations, contact details, and so on. You can then manipulate the data in useful ways, such as by sorting (in forward or reverse order) and by appending or inserting new items, removing entries, and even combining these operations.

In this lesson, you'll learn everything you need to know in order to process all types of data best handled collectively by numeric indexing, or keys and values.

Using FILO and FIFO Arrays

As you will recall from the array_push() discussion in the previous lesson, pushed values are added to the *end* of an array, such that when you come to pop them off again they are returned in reverse order. This is often referred to as a FILO (First In, Last Out) array. When an array is used this way, it is also sometimes called a *stack*.

There is also a FIFO (First In, First Out) stack, more commonly known as a *buffer*, which is typically used for handling events such as keyboard input, where the key-presses should be stored (buffered) until needed and must be returned in the order they were pressed.

 Note First In, Last Out (FILO) stacks are sometimes also known as Last In, First Out (LIFO) stacks or arrays, and First In, First Out (FIFO) buffers are also sometimes called Last In, Last Out (LILO) buffers, too. These alternative terms mean the same things and work in the same ways.

Buffering Using an Array

If you were to use the `array_push()` function to try and store keyboard input in a buffer, the letters of the word `Fred` (for example) would be inserted like this, with the start of the array at the left of the string shown in the comments, and the end of the array (onto which values are pushed and popped) at the right of the string:

```
array_push($Buffer, 'F'); // 'F'
array_push($Buffer, 'r'); // 'Fr'
array_push($Buffer, 'e'); // 'Fre'
array_push($Buffer, 'd'); // 'Fred'
```

However, when you then came to pop the values back out again, they would be returned in the inverse order from that in which they were entered (going from right to left), like this:

```
$char = array_pop($Buffer); // 'd'
$char = array_pop($Buffer); // 'e'
$char = array_pop($Buffer); // 'r'
$char = array_pop($Buffer); // 'F'
```

Unfortunately, this isn't the way a buffer needs to operate (because this example is operating as FILO instead of FIFO), but you can correct this by reversing the array contents when storing new elements, as with the following code (which assumes the buffer has already been populated with the first three letters of the word, in the correct order for calls to `array_pop()` to retrieve them):

```
// The buffer currently contains 'erF'

$Buffer = array_reverse($Buffer); // 'Fre'
array_push($Buffer, 'd');          // 'Fred'
$Buffer = array_reverse($Buffer); // 'derF'
```

How this works is that when a new letter is to be added to the buffer, the array is first reversed, so that when the `array_push()` function is called (even though the letter is pushed to the end of the array), it will be in the correct place (with the d next to the e).

Then, having pushed the new letter into the buffer, a second call to `array_reverse()` puts the array back into the correct order, such that the `array_pop()` function can be called to retrieve the contents (from right to left) in the right order, like this:

```
$char = array_pop($Buffer); // 'F'
$char = array_pop($Buffer); // 'r'
$char = array_pop($Buffer); // 'e'
$char = array_pop($Buffer); // 'd'
```

In summary, to make this trick work, you reverse an array before pushing to it, and then reverse it again afterward, which has the effect of pushing to the start (rather than the end) of an array—cumbersome and potentially slow, but workable.

Using `array_unshift()` and `array_shift()`

Although the previous (somewhat long-winded) code shows how to create and manage a buffer using the `array_push()` and `array_pop()` functions in conjunction with `array_reverse()`, you will be pleased to learn that you can create buffers much more easily by pushing values directly to the *start* of an array with the (curiously named) `array_unshift()` function, like this:

```
array_unshift($Buffer, 'F'); // 'F'
array_unshift($Buffer, 'r'); // 'rF'
array_unshift($Buffer, 'e'); // 'erF'
array_unshift($Buffer, 'd'); // 'derF'
```

The buffer now contains the letters in the inverse order to that in which they were added, and they are therefore arranged such that if you now call the `array_pop()` function, all the letters will be retrieved (from right to left) in the order in which they were added, like this:

```
$char = array_pop($Buffer); // 'F'
$char = array_pop($Buffer); // 'r'
$char = array_pop($Buffer); // 'e'
$char = array_pop($Buffer); // 'd'
```

You can also pop from the start of an array using the matching `array_shift()` function.

Using `sort()`

PHP comes with a handy `sort()` function to sort arrays alphabetically (and case-sensitively) in ascending order. This function is a little unusual in that it changes the actual array to which it is applied, unlike most other PHP array functions, which simply return a new array, leaving the original untouched.

To sort an array, simply call the `sort()` function, passing it the array to be sorted, as with this example, which uses the `$Cats[]` array:

```
$Cats = array('Long Hair', 'Short Hair', 'Dwarf',
              'Farm', 'Tabby', 'Tortoiseshell');
sort($Cats);
```

The result of issuing this `sort ()` call (the code for which is available as *sort.php* in the companion archive) is shown in Figure 10-1.

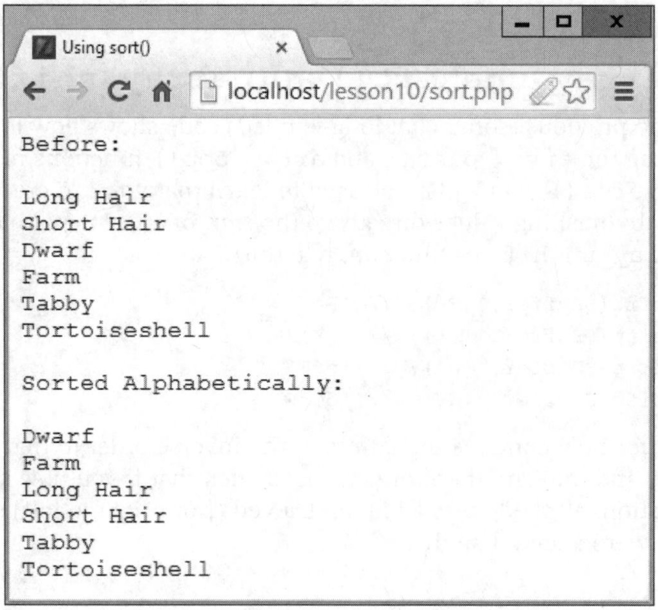

FIGURE 10-1   Sorting an array alphabetically

If all you require is an alphabetical sort in ascending order, then `sort ()` is just the function for you. However, should you need to sort an array numerically, you need to pass the specifier `SORT_NUMERIC` to the `sort ()` function, like this:

```
sort($NumericArray, SORT_NUMERIC);
```

Reversing a Sort

To obtain a reversed sort of any kind (alphabetic, numeric, and so on), all you need to do is pass the sorted array to the `array_reverse()` function, like this (as shown in Figure 10-2):

```
sort($Cats);
$Cats = array_reverse($Cats);
```

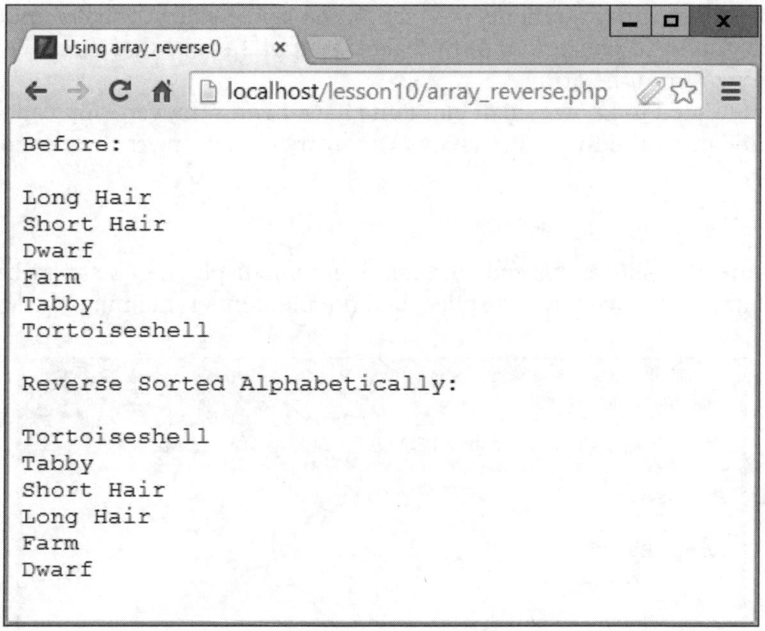

```
Before:

Long Hair
Short Hair
Dwarf
Farm
Tabby
Tortoiseshell

Reverse Sorted Alphabetically:

Tortoiseshell
Tabby
Short Hair
Long Hair
Farm
Dwarf
```

FIGURE 10-2   Sorting in reverse alphabetical order

Using `array_splice()`

The `array_splice()` function is tremendously powerful and can be used in a variety of different ways. It's the Swiss Army Knife of PHP array functions, because with it you can remove one or more elements from an array, or insert one or more into an array, and you can do either at any position within the array. What's more, you can remove and insert at the same time, providing a replace facility that can swap one or more elements with more, the same, or fewer elements.

Removing Elements from an Array

Let's look first at how to remove one or more elements from an array, starting with the `$Cats[]` array we've been using. In the following example, the `array_splice()` function is called with three arguments. The first is the array to splice, the second is the element index at which to perform the splice (starting from 0), and the third argument is the number of elements to be removed:

```php
$Cats = array('Long Hair', 'Short Hair', 'Dwarf',
              'Farm', 'Tabby', 'Tortoiseshell');
array_splice($Cats, 2, 3);
```

Therefore, with arguments of 2 and 3, the splice starts at the element index 2, which is the third one, and the third argument of 3 states that three elements are to be removed from the array.

If you need to know which elements have been removed, you can access the result of calling the function, which is an array containing the removed elements, like this:

```
$Removed = array_splice($Cats, 2, 3);
```

Figure 10-3 shows this code brought together, displaying the array before splicing, the elements removed by the splice, and the elements remaining afterward.

FIGURE 10-3   Removing elements from an array

Inserting Elements into an Array

Using a similar call to `array_splice()`, you can insert new values into the array, as in the following example, which adds two more breeds of cat starting at the third element:

```
array_splice($Cats, 2, 0, array('Siamese', 'Persian'));
```

Here, the first argument following the argument $Cats is the third element in the array, and the following argument of 0 tells array_splice() there are no elements to be removed.

After this there is an array containing two new elements, which tells array_splice() to insert these elements into the $Cats[] array, starting at the element at location 2 (the third one). You may place as many values as you like here to insert as many new elements as you need. The result of making this call is shown in Figure 10-4.

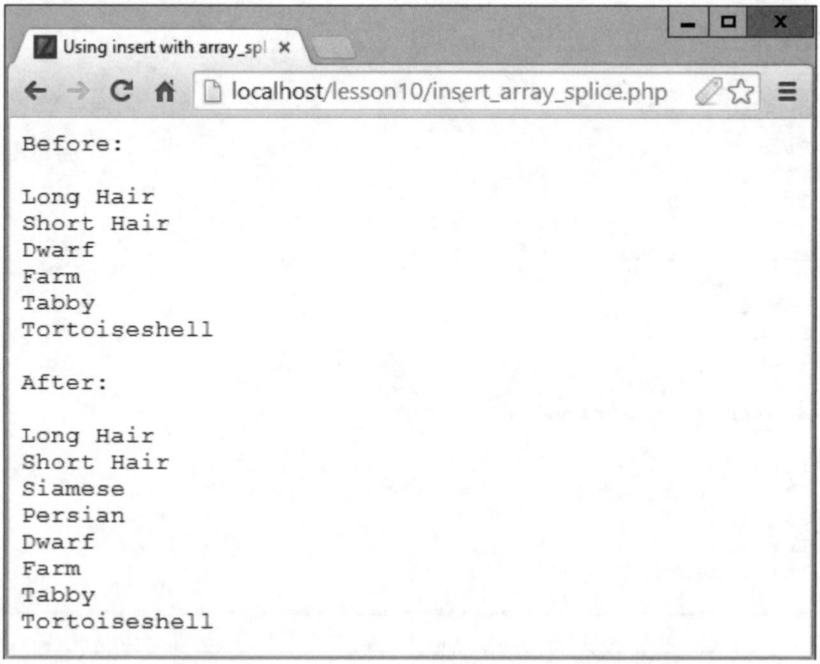

```
Using insert with array_spl ×

← → C ⌂  🗋 localhost/lesson10/insert_array_splice.php   ✎☆  ≡

Before:

Long Hair
Short Hair
Dwarf
Farm
Tabby
Tortoiseshell

After:

Long Hair
Short Hair
Siamese
Persian
Dwarf
Farm
Tabby
Tortoiseshell
```

FIGURE 10-4   Inserting values into an array

If there is only a single item to insert into an array with array_splice(), you do not need to embed it within an array() function, so the following statements are equivalent:

```
array_splice($Birds, 8, 0, array('Penguin'));
array_splice($Birds, 8, 0, 'Penguin');
```

Advanced Array Splicing

Finally, you can remove and insert elements at the same time using a call such as the following:

```
$Results = array_splice($Cats, 2, 3, array('Siamese', 'Persian'));
```

This statement tells `array_splice()` to use a splice index of 2 (the third element), at which location it must remove three elements, and then insert the new values supplied. The result of issuing this call is shown in Figure 10-5.

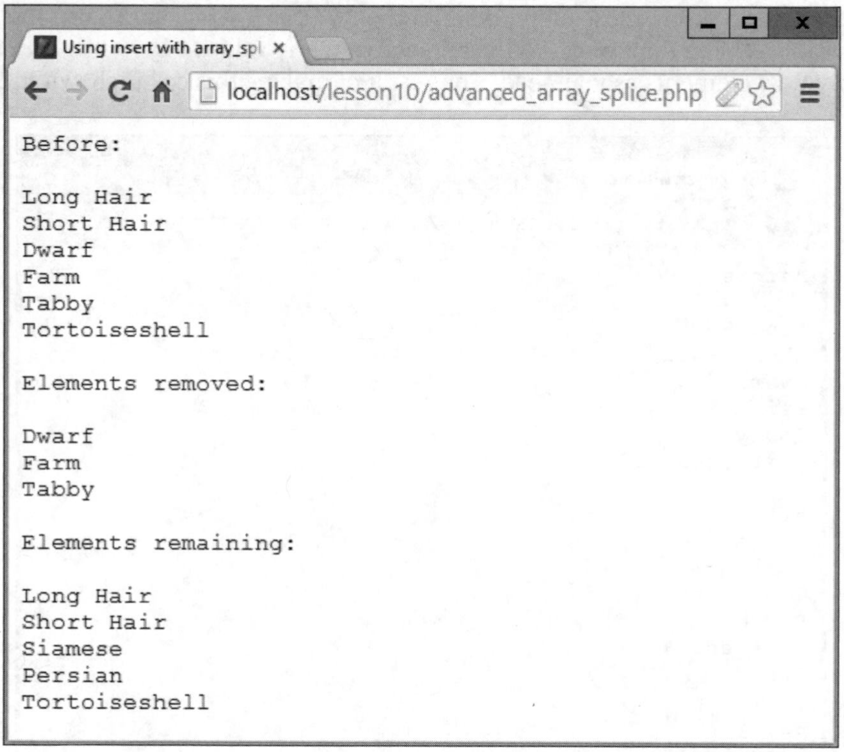
Using insert with array_spl
localhost/lesson10/advanced_array_splice.php
Before:
Long Hair
Short Hair
Dwarf
Farm
Tabby
Tortoiseshell
Elements removed:
Dwarf
Farm
Tabby
Elements remaining:
Long Hair
Short Hair
Siamese
Persian
Tortoiseshell

FIGURE 10-5 Removing items from and inserting them into an array

Example files are available in the companion archive demonstrating all three types of splicing. They are *array_splice.php*, *insert_array_splice.php* and *advanced_array_splice.php*.

Summary

You now know how to use all types of PHP arrays, whether single- or multidimensional, numeric, string, associative, or otherwise. Coupled with your earlier knowledge of variables and operators, you are now ready to really get down to power programming, beginning with the following lesson on controlling program flow.

Self-Test Questions

Test how much you have learned in this lesson with these questions. If you don't know an answer, go back and reread the relevant section until your knowledge is complete. You can find the answers in the appendix.

1. What does the term FILO stand for with arrays, and what is this type of array more commonly known as?

2. What does the term FIFO stand for with arrays, and what is this type of array more commonly known as?

3. With which function can you push a value to the start of an array?

4. With which function can you pop a value from the start of an array?

5. How can you sort the array $Recipes [] alphabetically?

6. How can you numerically sort the array $Temps []?

7. What should you do if you need to have access to the original order of an array after it has been sorted?

8. With what statement could you remove the elements at indexes 4 and 5 from the array $URLs [] (remember that array elements start at 0)?

9. With what statement could you insert the string google.com into the array $URLs [], starting at index 6?

10. With what statement could you store the string google.com in the array $URLs [], starting at index 3, overwriting the existing value?

Controlling Program Flow

To view the accompanying video for this lesson, please visit mhprofessional.com/
nixonphp/.

Having reached this second half of the course, you've actually already learned
a lot of PHP. You should understand how to incorporate PHP into a web page,
the syntax to use, how to handle numeric variables, strings, and arrays, and how to
use operators in expressions according to their associativity—and you've even learned
the basics of handling program flow control using the if() and else keywords.

In this lesson, you'll consolidate your knowledge of the latter so that you can
precisely control the flow of program execution.

The if() Construct

You've already seen the if() construct (more commonly referred to as a *statement*)
in use a few times, but only with single-line statements, so here's the full syntax of
an if() statement:

```
if (expression)
{
  // Execute this code, which can be one...
  // ...or more statements
}
```

In this example, *expression* can be any expression at all created using numbers,
strings, variables, objects, and operators. The result of the expression must be a Boolean
value that can be either TRUE or FALSE, such as $MyVar > 7, and so on.

The curly braces encapsulate the code that must be executed upon the expression
evaluating to TRUE, and there can be none, one, or many statements.

Omitting the Braces

To enable you to create short and simple if () statements without having to use braces, they are optional if only one statement is to be executed upon the expression being TRUE, like this:

```
if ($Time < 12) echo 'Good morning';
```

If the code to execute is quite long (so that it might wrap to the following line), you may wish to start it on the following line. However, if you do so, because no curly braces are being used to encapsulate the statement, it's best to indent the statement by a couple of spaces or a tab so that it's clear that it belongs to the if () statement, like this:

```
if ($Time < 12)
  echo 'Good morning. How are you today?';
```

Indeed, if you have a really long statement to execute, it can also be a good idea to split it over several lines at suitable points, like this:

```
if ($Time < 12)
  echo 'Good morning. Following is the list '  .
    'of all your appointments for today. The ' .
    'important ones are highlighted in bold';
```

Here, I have split the output into three parts by breaking it into strings, which are displayed one after the other using . operators. I also further indented the follow-on lines to clearly indicate that they belong to the echo command.

However, in my view, this has become a borderline case where you might be better advised to encapsulate the statement within curly braces, because this will ensure there is no ambiguity, and you won't have to worry about the wrapping of long lines diminishing the code readability, like this:

```
if ($Time < 12)
{
  echo 'Good morning. Following is the list of all your
appointments for today. The important ones are highlighted
in bold';
}
```

Some program editors will automatically indent wrapped around lines for you (based on the indent at the start of the line), thus making the code even more readable, and looking like this:

```
if ($Time < 12)
{
  echo 'Good morning. Following is the list of all your
    appointments for today. The important ones are highlighted
    in bold';
}
```

In this latter case, the program editor will treat all three lines of the statement as a single line, which they are. Don't try to format your code like this using newlines, though, because this will split it into multiple lines and cause errors—unless you also break the statement into parts, as detailed earlier.

Positioning of Braces

The reason you can lay out your code in a variety of ways is that PHP supports the use of tabs, spaces, and newlines as *whitespace* (which is ignored). Because of this, programmers can choose to place the curly braces wherever they like. As you have seen, when I use them, I generally place the opening and closing brace directly under the if() statement's first character, and then indent the encapsulated statements, like this:

```
if (expression)
{
  // Execute this code, which can be one...
  // ...or more statements
}
```

Other programmers, however, choose to place the opening curly brace immediately after the if(), like this:

```
if (expression) {
  // Execute this code, which can be one...
  // ...or more statements
}
```

Both of these (and other) types of layout (such as leaving the closing curly brace at the end of the final statement) are also perfectly acceptable.

There are also some less-used layouts preferred by other programmers, but the preceding tend to be the main two. I advocate the first type because (even though it requires an extra line feed for each opening brace) it makes the opening braces indent to the level of the closing ones, so that if you have several nested statements, you can more clearly determine that you have the right number of opening and closing braces, and that they are all in the right places. It also places more vertical whitespace between the expression and the statements that follow, which I find helpful. However, which system you use is entirely up to you (but it's a good idea to stay consistent and use only one system).

The **else** Statement

To accompany the if() statement there's the else keyword, which follows the same rules as if(), except the code following an else is executed only if the expression following the if() evaluates to FALSE. If the code comprises a single statement, it doesn't require encapsulating in curly braces, but if it has two or more statements, then braces are required.

You use the `else` keyword in conjunction with `if()`, like this:

```
if ($Age < 18)
{
  echo 'You are not an adult.';
}
else
{
  echo 'You are an adult.';
}
```

Because both of these keywords only include a single statement, you can safely omit the braces if you wish, like this:

```
if ($Age < 18)
  echo 'You are not an adult.';
else
  echo 'You are an adult.';
```

If there's room, you can even move the statements up to directly follow the keywords, like this:

```
if ($Age < 18) echo 'You are not an adult.');
else           echo 'You are an adult.';
```

 In this instance I opted to indent the second statement until it lined up underneath the first one. This helps make it clear what's going on at a glance if I were to come back to this code some months later. However, how you lay out your whitespace is entirely up to you.

Another convention regarding braces I recommend you consider using is that if one of the statements in an `if()` ... `else` construct uses braces, then so should the other, even if the other one only has a single statement. You can see the difference in the following (all valid) examples, and I think you'll find that Example 3 (with both sets of statements in braces) is the easiest to follow:

```
if ($Age < 18) // Example 1
{
  echo 'You are not an adult. ';
  echo 'Sorry, you cannot vote yet.';
}
else
  echo 'You are an adult.';


if ($Age < 18) // Example 2
  echo 'You are not an adult. ';
else
```

```
{
  echo 'You are an adult. ';
  echo 'You can vote.';
}

if ($Age < 18) // Example 3
{
  echo 'You are not an adult. ';
  echo 'Sorry, you cannot vote yet.';
}
else
{
 echo 'You are an adult.';
}
```

You don't *have* to follow this advice, but it will certainly make your debugging a lot easier if you do, and other programmers who may have to maintain your code will thank you for it.

The `elseif()` Construct

You can extend the power of if() ... else even further by also incorporating elseif() constructs (better known as *statements*). They provide a third option to the original if() statement, and you place them before the final else statement (if there is one). The following example illustrates how you might use this keyword:

```
if      ($Value < 0) echo 'Negative';
elseif ($Value > 0) echo 'Positive';
else                echo 'Zero';
```

 As with other examples, I have used whitespace liberally in the preceding code to line the statements up and make them easier to follow.

The elseif() statement follows the same rules as the if() and else statements with regard to using curly braces to encapsulate multiple statements (but not requiring them for single statements). However, I give the same recommendation as I did earlier that if even one of the parts of an if() ... elseif() ... else construct uses braces, then I advise you to use braces for all parts.

Of course, if you don't have any further test conditions to act upon, you don't have to use a concluding else after an if() ... elseif() construct (such as if you don't need to deal with the case of a zero value in the preceding example).

 The purpose of the else keyword is as a catch-all, to trap all possible values that remain and execute the statement(s) attached to it if none of the preceding statements in the clause are TRUE.

The `switch()` Statement

The `if()`, `elseif()`, and `else` statements are very powerful, and comprise much of PHP programming. But they are not the most efficient method of controlling program flow when there are more than three options to consider. For example, imagine there's an input field on a web page with the following string values from which the user must select their age range:

- 0–1
- 2–3
- 4–6
- 7–12
- 13–17
- 18+

Now, here's some code you might use to process the value returned by the input, as shown in Figure 11-1, in which a value of 13-17 has been preselected for the string variable $Age (using the *if_else.php* file from the companion archive):

```php
$Age = '13-17';

if ($Age == '0-1')
{
    echo 'You are a baby. ';
    echo 'How can you read this?';
}
else if ($Age == '2-3')
{
    echo 'You are a toddler.';
}
else if ($Age == '4-6')
{
    echo 'You are an infant. ';
    echo 'You go to nursery or school.';
}
else if ($Age == '7-12')
{
    echo 'You are a child.';
}
else if ($Age == '13-17')
{
    echo 'You are a teenager. ';
    echo 'You are old enough to use Facebook.';
}
else echo 'You are an adult.';
```

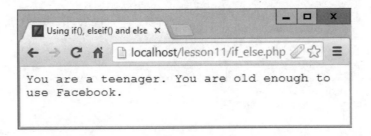

FIGURE 11-1   Using multiple `else if()` statements

In the UK, where I live, an *infant* is a child under the age of 6 or so, and generally will attend an "infant" school, so that's the term I use. North Americans, however, would probably refer to kindergartners.

Don't you think all those repeated `elseif()` statements are rather cumbersome, and the code feels somewhat heavier than it could be? Well, the answer is to restructure code such as this using a `switch()` statement in conjunction with the `case` and `break` keywords, like this (and as shown in Figure 11-2):

```
$Age = '4-6';

switch($Age)
{
   case '0-1':   echo 'You are a baby. ';
                 echo 'How can you read this?';
                 break;
   case '2-3':   echo 'You are a toddler.';
                 break;
   case '4-6':   echo 'You are an infant. ';
                 echo 'You go to nursery or school.';
                 break;
   case '7-12':  echo 'You are a child.';
                 break;
   case '13-17': echo 'You are a teenager. ';
                 echo 'You can use Facebook.';
                 break;
   default:      echo 'You are an adult.';
}
```

This was created using the *switch.php* file from the companion archive in which the string $Age is preassigned the value 4-6.

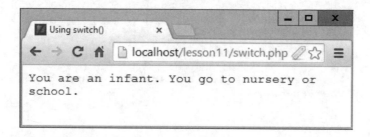

FIGURE 11-2   Using a `switch()` statement

I'm sure you'll agree that `switch()` statements are a lot clearer than sets of sprawling `elseif()`s. To use one, simply place the expression or variable to be tested in the parentheses following the `switch` keyword, and then within a pair of curly braces (which are required) provide a number of `case` statements and an optional `default` case.

Following each `case` keyword, place one possible value that the `switch` variable or expression might have. In this example, `$Age` can only have string values, but you can equally test for digits or floating point numbers, too. After the possible value, place a colon followed by the statements to execute if the value matches the `switch` variable or expression. In this example, it's one or more `echo` statements.

 Note how no curly braces are required to contain multiple statements. This is because once the code following the colon starts executing, it will keep on going, executing statement after statement (ignoring any following `case` tests), until the closing curly brace at the end of the `switch()` statement is encountered.

Using the `break` Keyword

Because program flow will continue to the end of a `switch()` statement (executing all the remaining statements regardless of any `case` keywords encountered), you must mark the end of a sequence of statements to be executed with a `break` keyword. This causes program flow to jump to just after the closing brace of the `switch()` statement.

 You will also encounter the `break` keyword in Lesson 12, where it is used to break to the end of looping structures of code.

Using the `default` Keyword

In the same way that the `else` keyword is a catch-all device for dealing with any other values not caught by `if()` or `elseif()` statements, you can use the `default` keyword within a `switch()` statement to catch any values not matched by the `case` statements.

In the previous example, because all possible values for $Age are tested for except 18+, then if none of the case statements match, $Age must contain the value 18+. Therefore, the default case is triggered and the statement following it writes the string You are an adult. to the browser.

> There is no break keyword after the default option in the preceding example because it is the final statement in the switch() statement. A break keyword is superfluous in this position, because it would only add extra, unnecessary code. There is, however, nothing stopping you from placing the default statement anywhere within a switch() statement (even at the start), but if you do so you must add a break keyword after the statements it executes. Otherwise, program flow will fall through to the following cases, rather than to the end of the switch() statement.

Allowing Fall-Through

Sometimes you may not want to use the break keyword because you wish to allow cases to "fall through" to other cases. For example, consider the case of wanting to choose the correct language to display on a multinational website. Using a simple input field (or even a geolocation program if you want to be really smart), you could return a string containing the user's country name, for example, perhaps out of the following:

- Australia
- Brazil
- France
- Germany
- Portugal
- Spain
- UK
- USA

Then, the code to process the country name in the variable $Country to a language to use in the variable $Language might look like this:

```
switch($Country)
{
  case 'Australia':
  case 'UK':
  case 'USA':
  default:          $Language = 'English';
                    break;
  case 'Brazil':
  case 'Portugal': $Language = 'Portuguese';
                    break;
```

```
   case 'France':    $Language = 'French';
                     break;
   case 'Germany':   $Language = 'German';
                     break;
   case 'Spain':     $Language = 'Spanish';
}
```

Only after the variable $Language has been assigned its value is the break keyword used. So if any of the countries Australia, UK, or USA are selected, then $Language is set to English, which is also selected for any other value not tested for by the cases in the switch() statement (because the default keyword is included within the fall-through group of cases).

A fall-through also occurs for Brazil and Portugal, both of which countries speak Portuguese, but the remaining countries have different languages and don't use any case fall-throughs. Note that there is no break keyword after the final statement as it is not needed, because the end of the switch() has already been reached.

 Because many people in the USA speak Spanish, if you wanted to cater for them, you could change the USA option to USA English, and then add USA Spanish as a fall-through to Spain—and while at it, you could also add Canada English as a fall-through to English, and Canada French as a fall-through to France, depending on your target locations.

Summary

This lesson concludes everything you need to know to write basic PHP programs. You can now handle data in various ways, including variables and arrays; you are able to use complex operators and expressions; and you can now direct the flow of your programs. In the next lesson, we'll start to look at more advanced aspects of PHP, beginning with putting together various types of looping constructs.

Self-Test Questions

Test how much you have learned in this lesson with these questions. If you don't know an answer, go back and reread the relevant section until your knowledge is complete. You can find the answers in the appendix.

1. What is the basic PHP construct for testing whether an expression evaluates to TRUE?

2. Within which pair of characters must you enclose if() statements when there is more than one?

3. What statement can you use to take action if the result of an if() condition is FALSE?

4. When an if() expression evaluates to FALSE, how can you then test another expression?

5. How many if(), elseif(), and else statements can you use in a sequence of conditions?

6. In an if() ... elseif() ... else construct, what is a good rule of thumb to apply to how statements should be encapsulated with curly braces?

7. When there is more than one elseif() statement in a sequence of conditions, what can be a better construct to use instead of if() ... elseif() ... else?

8. Which keyword is used to test each individual condition in a switch() statement?

9. What keyword is used to signify the end of a sequence of statements following a case keyword?

10. In a switch() statement, which keyword is the equivalent of the else section, as used with an if() construct?

Looping Sections of Code

▶ To view the accompanying video for this lesson, please visit mhprofessional.com/nixonphp/.

In the previous lesson, you learned all about program flow control, branching, and using if(), else, and switch() statements. These are perfect for altering the program flow according to values and expressions, but not so good when you need to repetitively execute a process, such as processing a document a word at a time to find typographical errors.

This is the type of situation where PHP's looping statements come into their own. With them, you form a loop around a core group of statements and then keep the loop circulating until (or unless) one or more conditions are met, such as when the end of the document is reached (in the case of a spelling checker).

More than that, the different loop types supported also enable you to preassign values to variables used in the loop, or only enter into a loop if a certain expression is satisfied.

Using **while()** Loops

The while() loop provides the simplest type of PHP loop. In English what it does is something like this: "While such-and-such is true, keep doing so-and-so, until such-and-such is no longer true, or forever if such-and-such is always true." Here's an example that will display the 10 times table (as shown in Figure 12-1):

```
$j = 0;

while ($j++ < 10)
{
  echo "$j times 10 is " . $j * 10 . '<br>';
}
```

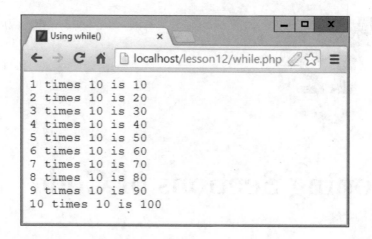

FIGURE 12-1 Using while() to calculate the 10 times table

The code used for this and the other examples in this lesson is available in the files *while.php*, *do_while.php*. *for.php*, *break.php*, and *continue.php* in the companion archive, freely downloadable from *20lessons.com*.

The Example in Detail

This code starts by initializing the variable $j to 0. This variable is used to decide when to loop (and when to stop looping) and also for calculating the times table. Then, the while() statement tests for $j having a value of less than 10. The first time around its value is 0, so the expression evaluates to TRUE. Note also that $j is post-incremented after making the test by using the ++ increment operator. This means that the second time around the loop, $j will represent a value of 1 in the expression and then be incremented to 2:

```
while ($j++ < 10)
```

Inside the braces is a single statement that prints the value in $j, some text, and then the result of multiplying $j by 10. Because $j was post-incremented after the test at the start of the loop, it now has a value of 1, so the sentence 1 times 10 is 10 is output to the browser:

```
echo "$j times 10 is " . $j * 10 . '<br>';
```

After the echo statement is executed, the end of the loop is reached and program flow returns to the start of the loop once more, where $j is once again tested for having a value less than 10.

This time around it now has a value of 1, so that satisfies the test, and then $j is post-incremented, giving it a value of 2. Because $j now has a value of 2, the sentence 2 times 10 is 20 is output to the browser, and the loop goes round another time.

This process continues until $j has a value of 10, and the test at the start of the loop therefore no longer results in TRUE, so program execution jumps to just after the closing brace of the while() statement.

 Note   Because there is only a single statement inside this loop, just as with for() statements, you can omit the curly braces if you wish, as follows:

```
while ($j++ < 10)
    echo "$j times 10 is " . $j * 10 . '<br>';
```

Using do ... while() Loops

With a while() loop, if the test at the start is not satisfied, program execution will not flow into the loop. Sometimes, however, you want program flow to go around a loop at least once, in which case it's necessary to perform the loop test after each iteration.

For example, suppose you wish to calculate the factorial of the number 10 (sometimes displayed mathematically as 10!). This involves multiplying all the numbers from 1 to 10 together, like this: $10 \times 9 \times 8 \times 7 \times 6 \times 5 \times 4 \times 3 \times 2 \times 1$.

Using a loop to do this is an efficient method of calculating this value, particularly because once the loop has been built, it can be used to calculate the factorial of any number. And one thing we know for sure about this loop is that it will execute at least once. Therefore, a do ... while() structure may be best suited, and one way you can achieve that is like this:

```
$j = 10;
$f = 1;

do
{
   $f *= $j--;
} while ($j > 0);

echo '10! is ' . $f;
```

One of the neat things about this loop is that $f always contains the running total of all previous multiplications, so all that's necessary to do in each iteration is multiply $f by the current value in $j, save that value back into $f, and then decrement $j, which is performed by this statement:

```
$f *= $j--;
```

The *= assignment operator is ideal in this situation because it performs both the multiplication and the assignment of the result back to $f using a single operator. Also, the post-decrement operator applied to $j makes for more efficient coding, too.

The Example in Detail

In detail, what occurs in the preceding example is that j is a loop counter that is initialized to the value 10 (because there are 10 numbers to multiply) and f is the factorial, which is initialized to 1 because the loop will start with the expression $f *= $j--;, which the first time around the loop will be the equivalent of $f = 1 * 10;.

The post-decrement operator after the j ensures that each time around the loop, the multiplier is decremented by 1 (but only after the value in j is used in the expression). The second time around the loop, f will have a value of 10, and j will be 9, so the expression will be equivalent to $f = 10 * 9;.

Then, on the next iteration, f will have a value of 90 as it enters the loop, and j will be 8, so these two values will be multiplied together and placed back into f. The expressions evaluated in the loop are therefore as follows:

```
$f =        1 * 10; // Results in 10
$f =       10 *  9; // Results in 90
$f =       90 *  8; // Results in 720
$f =      720 *  7; // Results in 5040
$f =     5040 *  6; // Results in 30240
$f =    30240 *  5; // Results in 151200
$f =   151200 *  4; // Results in 604800
$f =   604800 *  3; // Results in 1814400
$f =  1814400 *  2; // Results in 3628800
$f =  3628800 *  1; // Results in 3628800
```

When the expression at the end of the loop (in the while() part) evaluates to FALSE, this means that j is no longer greater than 0. Therefore, the loop is not re-entered, and program flow continues at the first instruction following the loop.

When this example is loaded into a browser (as shown in Figure 12-2), the result shown in the final line is displayed, by the echo instruction that follows the loop.

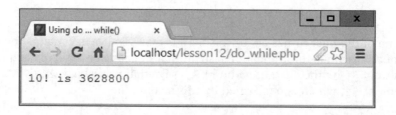

FIGURE 12-2 Using do ... while() to calculate the factorial of a number

Note As with many other PHP constructs, if there is only one statement inside the loop, you can omit the curly braces if you like. Therefore, the loop could also be written as follows:

```
do $f *= $j--;
while ($j > 0);
```

Using `for()` Loops

Although the preceding two types of loop structure may seem sufficient for most requirements, they can actually be improved on, especially because you must first initialize variables outside of these loops before they are even entered, and then you generally have to increment or decrement at least one variable inside the loop, too.

For these reasons, a third type of loop structure is supported, the `for()` loop—and it is one of the most compact and most-used forms of loop structure for these reasons:

- It allows you to initialize all the variables you need, within the creation of the loop.
- It allows you to specify the test condition within the creation of the loop.
- It allows you to specify variables to change after each loop iteration within the creation of the loop.

Let's look at how you can do this by rewriting the previous example, as follows:

```
for ($j = 10, $f = 1 ; $j > 0 ; --$j)
{
  $f *= $j;
}

echo "10! is $f";
```

Doesn't that look much simpler than the do … `while()` version? As before, there's still a single statement inside the loop, but it no longer uses the post-decrement operator, because `$j` is decremented within the setup section of the loop. Also, no variables are preassigned outside of the loop because that is also handled within the loop setup.

The Example in Detail

Here's what's going on: a `for()` loop's setup section (the part within parentheses) is divided into three parts, separated with semicolons. Each part performs the following tasks, in order:

1. Initialize any variables used within the loop.

2. Perform a test to see whether the loop should be entered.

3. Change any variables required after each loop iteration.

The first and third sections may include more than one statement, as long as you separate them using commas. Therefore, in the first section of the preceding example, $j is initialized to a value of 10, and $f to a value of 1, like this:

```
$j = 10, $f = 1
```

Next comes the loop test:

```
$j > 0
```

And finally $j is pre-decremented (or in this situation it could also be post-decremented):

```
--$j
```

The three sets of arguments inside the parentheses look like this:

```
$j = 10, $f = 1 ; $j > 0 ; --$j
```

And that's really all there is to it. When the loop is first entered, the variables are initialized—this will not happen in any other iterations. Then the test in part two of the loop setup is made, and if the expression evaluates to TRUE, the loop is entered.

Next, the statements in the loop are executed (in this case there's only one), and then the third section of the loop setup is executed, which in this case decrements $j. Then, the second time and all subsequent times around the loop, section one of the setup is skipped and program flow goes straight to the test in section two.

If this is TRUE, the loop is again entered, the statements in it are executed, and then the statements in the third part of the setup section are executed and the loop goes around again. However, if the test doesn't evaluate to TRUE, program flow goes to the code following the loop, which in this case is the echo statement, to print the calculated factorial value.

Because there is only a single statement within the loop of the preceding example, the braces may be omitted from the code, as follows (or you can make the code even more compact by placing the statement directly after the loop section):

```
for ($j = 10, $f = 1; $j > 0 ; --$j)
    $f *= $j;
```

Because for () loops are so powerful, their usage has become widespread, and you will find that you rarely need to use a while () or do ... while () loop because for () loops can compactly and neatly accomplish almost every type of looping structure you could want in PHP.

Have you spotted a simple optimization that could be made to this (and the preceding do ... while ()) example? Well, there's actually a wasteful iteration of the loop as these examples stand. The expression $10 \times 9 \times 8 \times 7 \times 6 \times 5 \times 4 \times 3 \times 2 \times 1$ is being calculated, but the final × 1 is unnecessary because multiplying by 1 doesn't change the result. Therefore, instead of making the loop conditions test for whether $j is greater than 0, you can change the expression to test for $j > 1, and you'll get the same result, in a shorter amount of time.

Breaking Out of a Loop

Amazingly I still haven't yet finished introducing you to everything that PHP loops can do for you, because there's still the matter of a couple of keywords you can employ to further enhance their use.

The first of these is the break keyword, which I already showed being used with the switch() statement in Lesson 11 to stop fall-through of program flow between cases. However, the break keyword is not exclusive to switch() statements, because it can also be used inside loops too.

But why would you want to use a break within a loop? Surely you have all the tests for conditions you could want already? Well, not quite, as it turns out. Sometimes you may want to terminate a loop early, as with the following example, which searches an array for a particular value:

```php
$HayStack = array(1, 23, 16.3, 88.23, 11, 24.46, 30, 99);
$Needle   = 11;

echo "Searching for $Needle: ";

for ($j = 0 ; $j < sizeof($HayStack) ; ++$j)
{
  if ($HayStack[$j] == $Needle) break;
}

if ($j < sizeof($HayStack)) echo "Found at index $j";
else                        echo 'Not found';
```

If the value being searched for is found, it would be a waste of time to continue searching the array (unless multiple occurrences are being looked for), and so terminating the loop early makes sense. This is done with a break statement, as shown in Figure 12-3 (in which an additional search for the value 17.3 is also made).

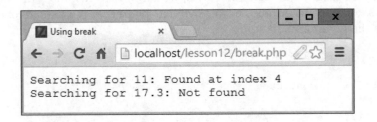

FIGURE 12-3   Using break to exit from a loop if a condition is met

As with other PHP structures, because this example has only a single statement in the loop, the braces can be omitted for simplicity, like this:

```
for ($j = 0 ; $j < sizeof($HayStack) ; ++$j)
  if ($HayStack[$j] == $Needle) break;
```

Breaking Out of Multiple Loops

When you use the break keyword within a loop that is itself inside one or more other loops, only the current loop will be broken out from, because the break keyword applies only to the scope of the current object in which it exists.

However, if you wish to break out of further levels of loop nesting, you can do so by supplying an extra argument with the break keyword, indicating the number of nested enclosing structures to break out of in total, like this:

```
if ($condition == $met) break 2;
```

The continue Statement

The break statement diverts flow to the statement immediately following the loop in which it exists, but sometimes this is too drastic a measure, because you may only want to skip the current iteration of a loop, and not all remaining iterations.

When this is the case, you can use the continue statement, which forces program flow to skip over any remaining statements in a loop and to start again at the next iteration of the loop. One reason for wanting to do this might be (for example) to avoid encountering a division-by-zero error, which could generate invalid results.

For example, consider the case of some code that must calculate the reciprocal of all numbers between –5 and 5 (the reciprocal of a number is found by dividing 1 by that number).

When calculating a reciprocal, though, if the number happens to be zero, an attempt would be made to divide 1 by 0, which in PHP results in the value infinity, which is not a useful number in this context. Therefore, we need to check for it and remove the possibility, like this:

```
for ($j = -5 ; $j < 6 ; ++$j)
{
  if ($j == 0) continue;

  echo "1/$j is " . 1 / $j . '<br>';
}
```

Figure 12-4 shows this code being run in a browser. As you can see, when the value 0 is reached for $j, nothing is displayed, because the continue keyword has forced the loop to skip to its next iteration.

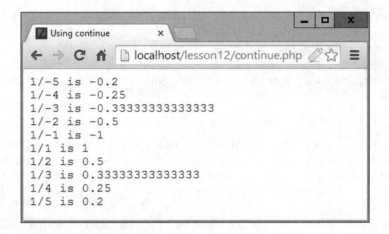

FIGURE 12-4   Avoiding division by 0 with a `continue`

Continuing Within Multiple Loops

If you follow the `continue` keyword with a number, the level of nesting indicated by that number becomes the place in the code that will be skipped from, and the PHP code pointer will be moved from there onto the next iteration of that loop, not the current loop and iteration.

For example, take the case of calculating the prime numbers between 1 and 100. One way to do this is to create an outer loop that counts from 1 to 100, and an inner loop to test each of these values to see whether it is prime, as follows (saved as *continue2.php* in the accompanying archive):

```
for ($i = 1 ; $i <= 100 ; ++$i)
{
  for ($j = 2 ; $j <= sqrt($i) ; ++$j)
    if (!($i % $j)) continue 2;
  echo "$i ";
}
```

Here, the outer loop iterates the variable $i from a value of 1 up to 100:

```
for ($i = 1 ; $i <= 100 ; ++$i)
```

Then the inner loop iterates the variable $j from the value of 2 up to the square root of $i. The square root is chosen because it is the pivot point for all pairs of factors, as indicated by the fact that the square root of a number's pivot factor is the same number. For example, 8 × 8 is 64. Therefore, only values up to (and including) the square root of a number require testing—a great optimization, and programmers love optimizations! Here's what this looks like:

```
for ($j = 2 ; $j <= sqrt($i) ; ++$j)
```

Then the test for primality is made, in which the modulus of $i and $j is calculated. Remember that the modulus is the value remaining after a division, so the ! operator makes the expression say, "if there is not any remainder, then do this...."

Therefore, if there's no remainder, the number cannot be prime (because $i is exactly divisible by $j with no remainder), and the statement continue 2; is issued, like this:

```
if (!($i % $j)) continue 2;
```

Here, the value 2 following the keyword says, "Go back two levels of nesting and then continue." So what happens is that the code drops back to the $i for() loop, from where the current iteration is skipped (so as not to execute echo "$i ";), moving the PHP statement pointer onto the next value of $i, and then loop iteration continues.

Therefore, in this context, the continue 2; statement has acted like a break statement for the $j loop, returning execution to the containing structure, and then it has the effect of acting as a normal continue statement at that point, forcing the outer loop to move onto its next iteration.

Meanwhile, if the value in $i is found to be prime (by process of elimination, in that the continue 2; statement has never been accessed), its value is output to the browser:

```
echo "$i ";
```

The output of this code displays as follows:

```
1 2 3 5 7 11 13 17 19 23 29 31 37 41 43 47 53 59 61 67 71 73 79 83 89 97
```

Summary

Now that you know how to use the wide variety of looping structures provided by PHP, you'll begin to develop your own programming style, because you can write most types of code that rely on loops in a number of different ways, and before long you'll begin to settle on the structures that fit your way of thinking the best.

For example, most programmers tend to generally use for() loops, but then they may need to occasionally use the break keyword for special instances. On the other hand, those who prefer while() and do ... while() loops rarely need to use break. It's a matter of personal style.

Anyway, regardless of which type of loop structure you find yourself migrating toward, in the next lesson you'll discover even more powerful things you can do with PHP, including writing functions and using global and local variables.

Self-Test Questions

Test how much you have learned in this lesson with these questions. If you don't know an answer, go back and reread the relevant section until your knowledge is complete. You can find the answers in the appendix.

1. Which type of PHP loop is not entered unless an expression evaluates to TRUE, and then continues looping until the expression is FALSE?

2. Are curly braces required around loop statements?

3. With which type of loop is at least one iteration guaranteed to occur?

4. With which type of loop can you initialize variables, test for conditions, and modify variables after each iteration, all in a single statement?

5. Which character separates the three sections of a for() loop?

6. How can you include additional variable initializations and post-iteration assignments in a for() loop?

7. With which keyword can you cease execution of a loop, and move program flow to the following statement after the loop?

8. How can you break out of the current loop as well as another loop that contains it?

9. With which keyword can you skip the current iteration of a loop, and move onto the next iteration?

10. While in a loop, how can you drop out of the loop and skip an iteration in the enclosing loop structure?

PART II

Advanced PHP

Writing Functions

To view the accompanying video for this lesson, please visit mhprofessional.com/nixonphp/.

In addition to using conditional constructs and statements such as `if()` and `switch()` as well as loops such as `while()` and `for()`, there's another way you can control program flow—by using functions. *Functions* are sections of code you call from any other part of code (or even the function itself, which is known as *recursion*), which then perform one or more actions and then return.

When functions return, they may also return a value back to the calling code, or they can simply return without doing so, in which case the returned value will be undefined. Interestingly, since PHP 5.3, functions can also be anonymous (not given a name) and can even be passed as values or stored in arrays.

Using Functions

PHP comes with many in-built functions. For example, to obtain the square root of the number 49, you can call the `sqrt()` function, like this, which will return the value 7:

```
echo sqrt(49);
```

The optional value you pass to a function is called an *argument,* and you can have any number of these arguments, or even none. In the case of `sqrt()`, a single value is required. The square root of that number is then calculated, and the value derived is returned. That's how the `echo` command in the preceding example can display the square root value, because that value is returned directly to the calling code, which is the `echo` statement.

You create functions using the keyword `function`, followed by the name to give to the function, and then a pair of parentheses, within which you list the arguments being passed to the function, separated with commas. The code of the function must be enclosed within curly braces.

Following is what the code to emulate the built-in sqrt() function might look like, based on the fact that the square root of a number can be calculated by raising that number to the power of 0.5, with the pow() function serving to calculate the power:

```
function SquareRoot($n)
{
   return pow($n, 0.5);
}
```

In this example, the function created is SquareRoot(), and it accepts one argument (the value passed in the variable $n).

The function code comprises a single statement that simply calls the built-in pow() function, which accepts two values: a number and a value by which power the number should be raised. Therefore, the two values passed to pow() are $n and 0.5.

The return Statement

The function then calculates the square root and returns it, at which point the return statement causes that value to be returned. It is then a simple matter of calling the function in the following manner to display a square root in the browser:

```
echo SquareRoot(49);
```

Alternatively, the value returned can be used in an expression, assigned to a variable, or used in numerous other ways.

 Of course, this code slightly cheats because it calls another built-in function called pow() (in which case we might as well simply call the built-in sqrt() function in the first place), but it serves to illustrate how to write a simple function that takes one value and returns another after processing it.

Passing Arguments

In the preceding example, you saw how to pass a single argument to a function, but you can pass as many as you need (or none), as shown with the following function, which shows how you might re-create the built-in PHP str_repeat() function:

```
function StrRepeat($s, $r)
{
   return implode($s, array_fill(0, $r + 1, ''));
}
```

This function uses the sneaky trick of creating a new array using the array_fill() function, which has the number of elements in the value $r, plus 1. So, if $r has the value 3, the new array is given four elements by pre-incrementing the value in $r. Each element is given the value '' (the empty string).

With the array now created, the `implode()` function is called in the outside expression. As you will recall from Lesson 9, `implode()` concatenates all the elements in an array into a string, placing the separator string in the value passed to `implode()` between each element value.

Therefore, if `$r` has the value 3, a four-element array is created (with each element being empty). Then the `implode()` function concatenates these four elements together, placing the string in the variable `$s` between each occurrence. Therefore, because the array elements are empty, this entire statement will simply create three copies of the string in `$s` concatenated together, and that is the string that is returned from the function using the `return` keyword. Neat, huh?

Accessing Arguments

Arguments received by a function are given the names you supply between the parentheses. These do not need to be (and probably will mostly not be) the same as the variables or values passed to the function.

Variables are assigned to the values received by a function in the order in which they are listed, and there can be as many or as few arguments as you like. Generally the number of arguments supplied to a function should be the same as the number the function expects to receive, but not always.

If a function receives fewer arguments than it is expecting, the remaining values will be undefined, and PHP may well issue one or more warnings, as shown in the following example (see Figure 13-1) in which the third argument has not been passed:

```
Example(1, 2);

function Example($a, $b, $c)
{
  echo "[$a - $b - $c]";
}
```

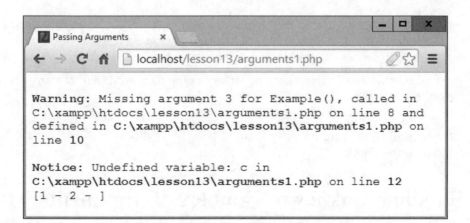

FIGURE 13-1   No third argument has been passed to the function.

One way to improve on this is to provide default values for arguments that will be assigned if no value is passed, like this (highlighted in bold):

```
function Example($a, $b, $c = 0)
{ ... }
```

Now PHP will not generate an error, and if no third argument is passed, a value (in this instance) of 0 will be assigned to $c (or you could choose any other default value, even including NULL).

Let's see how to make good use of this feature by considering the built-in PHP function implode(), which joins the elements of an array together into a string, separating them (optionally) with a string separator value. By default, though, implode() concatenates without any separator (the same as an empty string separator), running all the array elements together.

However, if that's not the behavior you require, you can write a new version of implode() to work in the same way as the JavaScript join() function, such that when no separator is specified, a comma will be assumed as the separator, like this:

```
function NewImplode($arg1, $arg2 = ',')
{
  return implode($arg1, $arg2);
}
```

Here, if only one value is passed, it will be an array to be imploded, and will arrive in $arg1, whereas $arg2 will not receive a value (and will therefore be assigned the default string value of ','). But if two values are passed to NewImplode(), then no default value is assigned to $arg2.

In either case, once inside the function, the two values (either both received, or one received and one assigned as a default) are then passed onto implode(), which conveniently allows arguments passed to it to be in any order (for historical reasons), so it processes them correctly regardless of their order.

This means that NewImplode() will also accept *its* arguments in any order; therefore, all the following are legal statements:

```
echo NewImplode('|', array('cow', 'horse', 'duck')          ) . '<br>';
echo NewImplode(    array('cow', 'horse', 'duck'), ' and ') . '<br>';
echo NewImplode(    array('cow', 'horse', 'duck')           ) . '<br>';
```

These will result in the following strings being displayed (without any error messages):

cow|horse|duck
cow and horse and duck
cow,horse,duck

Handling Unknown Numbers of Arguments

Rather than passing and accepting a known number of arguments, you can also access an unknown number of arguments by calling the func_num_args() function. This returns the number of arguments that have been passed to a function. Using this value and the func_get_arg() function, which retrieves a single argument, you can access all the arguments passed to a function as if it were an array using an index (from 0 to the number of arguments minus 1).

To illustrate this, let's emulate the array() function, which itself supports any number of arguments passed to it, and then places them in an array to be returned, like this:

```
function NewArray()
{
  $n = func_num_args();
  $a = array();

  for($j = 0 ; $j < $n ; ++$j)
    array_push($a, func_get_arg($j));

  return $a;
}
```

This function first looks up the number of arguments that have been passed to it, and it saves that value in $n. Then it creates a new array called $a. After that, it iterates through all the arguments passed to the function, using $j as an index into the list. Each time around the loop, the argument indicated is pushed onto the $a array. When the loop has completed the array, $a is returned.

It is now possible to call this new function in place of array(), like this, for example:

```
$Flowers = NewArray('Daisy', 'Lilly', 'Crocus');
```

Here, the array $Flowers is created and populated with three elements. To verify that this is the case, the following loop displays all these elements:

```
foreach($Flowers as $flower) echo "$flower<br>";
```

 The archive of example files at the companion website includes *arguments1*
.php, arguments2.php, and *arguments3.php*, which illustrate all the preceding discussions of argument passing and handling.

Passing by Reference

In earlier versions of PHP you used to be able to pass arguments to functions by reference, by prefacing them with the & symbol. This would tell the parser to supply a reference to the variable, *not* the value, which would grant the function full access to the variable being passed, rather than a copy of its value. But as of PHP 5.4.0, passing by reference was removed.

However, you may choose for a PHP function to *receive* the reference of a variable by prefacing its name with & in the function declaration, like this example, which will swap the values of the two variables passed to the function:

```
function swap(&$v1, &$v2)
{
  $t  = $v1;   // Create temporary copy of $v1
  $v1 = $v2;   // Move value from $v2 to $v1
  $v2 = $t;    // Assign $v2 previous value of $v1
}
```

 Even though the procedure is called *passing by reference,* in PHP it is now probably better thought of as *receiving by reference.*

Global and Local Variable Scope

Up to this point I have left out a very important keyword, which you will certainly have seen if you have viewed the source of any PHP code—and that's the `global` keyword. I left out its inclusion until now because I didn't want to get you bogged down by the difference between *local* and *global* variables. But you are ready for it now!

So far I have treated all the variables created in the lessons as having local scope (except when we are passing a value to a function, which chooses to receive it by reference). This means that once they are defined, you can access their values and modify them from the current part of the program, which is either of the following:

- If it is created outside of a function, the scope covers all code that resides outside of function calls, as well as those in included files.
- If it is created within a function, the scope covers that function only.

Using Local Variables

So far in this book, I have used only local variables in functions. Let me illustrate this to you with some code:

```
$MyVar = 1;
echo 'Outside: $MyVar == ' . "$MyVar<br>";

Example();

function Example()
{
  echo 'Inside: $MyVar == ' . "$MyVar<br>";
}
```

In this example, the variable $MyVar is created in the main part of the program (outside of any functions) and is assigned the value 1. Then the variable's value is displayed, and if you run the code you will see the value 1 is output.

But then the function Example() is called, which also displays the value in $MyVar, and when this code is run nothing is output. The reason for this is that $MyVar has only global scope when it is defined outside of a function, and therefore it can be read from and written to only outside of any functions (and also in any included code that is also outside of any functions). In order to give the Example() function access to the global variable, we must define it as being global using the following statement:

```
global $MyVar;
```

Therefore, the following updated version of the previous example will now display the value of 1 both outside and inside the function:

```
$MyVar = 1;
echo 'Outside: $MyVar == ' . "$MyVar<br>";

Example();

function Example()
{
  global $MyVar;
  echo 'Inside: $MyVar == ' . "$MyVar<br>";
}
```

 Note Even though you can do so, there is no point using the global keyword outside of a function because it will not make that variable available to any functions. Only by using the global keyword from *inside* a function will access be granted to the variable.

You can make more than one variable have global scope within a function by separating their names with commas, like this:

```
global $MyVar, $ThisVar, $ThatVar;
```

You may not, however, try to assign a value to a variable from a global statement, as in the following example, which is invalid syntax and will not work because you may only provide variable names (not expressions) after the global keyword:

```
global $MyVar = 2; // This is not a valid statement
```

The correct alternative is to use two statements, like this:

```
global $MyVar;
$MyVar = 2;
```

The following code illustrates more clearly the difference between local and global scope:

```php
$MyVar1 = 1;
$MyVar2 = 2;

echo 'Outside of any functions<br><br>';
echo '$MyVar1 == ' . "$MyVar1<br>";
echo '$MyVar2 == ' . "$MyVar2<br><br>";

Example();

function Example()
{
  global $MyVar2;

  echo 'Inside a function<br><br>';
  echo '$MyVar1 == ' . "$MyVar1<br>";
  echo '$MyVar2 == ' . $MyVar2;
}
```

Here, $MyVar1 is given a value of 1 and $MyVar2 a value of 2. Both these assignments occur outside of any functions, and the echo statements verify these assignments have been successfully made.

Then Example() is called and the code in this function only gives $MyVar2 global scope, so when the value of $MyVar1 is displayed nothing is output because (as far as the function is concerned) that variable doesn't exist. However, because it has global scope, the value in $MyVar2 is displayed.

Figure 13-2 shows the result of running this code (available as *local.php* in the companion archive) in a browser.

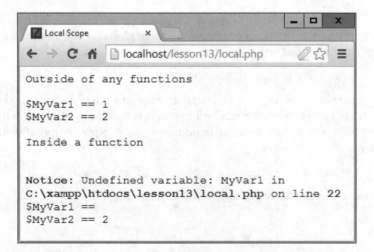

FIGURE 13-2   Only $MyVar2 is global, so accessing $MyVar1 causes an error.

Notice how there is an error message in Figure 13-2 because $MyVar1 was created outside of the Example() function, and because there is no global keyword making it accessible to the function, an error is thrown. There are a couple of possible fixes for this. One is to make $MyVar1 global, like this:

```
global $MyVar1;
```

Alternatively, you can simply give $MyVar1 a value before accessing it, to create a local variable of that name, perhaps like this:

```
$MyVar1 = 23;
```

What this means is that all variable names are free for reuse inside all functions so that, for example, you could reuse the variable $count to keep count of something many times over in different functions, without any use conflicting with any other use.

This is possible because when a function returns, it also forgets all the local variables that have been used in it. However, any changes the function makes to any variables it has given global scope to remain in place when the function returns.

The use of the global keyword in PHP is not the same as in some other programming languages, because what the keyword really means in PHP is "Give access to that variable, which was created outside of this function." It does not make a variable fully global to all code in a program. Therefore, even though the global keyword may be applied to a variable within one function, that same variable will *not* have global scope in any other functions *unless* they too use the global keyword to gain access to it.

The $GLOBALS[] Superglobal Array

Normally in PHP you can manage almost every programming task using local variables, with occasional use of giving a function global access to the odd variable. It also makes for clear and more bug-free code to avoid extensive use of global variables.

However, there are occasions when you find no simpler way to manage a particular task, and for these times PHP provides you with a special "superglobal" $GLOBALS[] array. This is a predefined array that has full global scope both outside and inside functions.

To access a global variable, you place its name in the $GLOBALS[] array, like this:

```
echo $GLOBALS['MyVar'];
```

Therefore, even though no global keyword has been used, as long as $MyVar was created outside of any functions, you can access it in the $GLOBALS[] array. Think of using $GLOBALS[] as a quick way to access a global variable, without actually specifying it as global to a function by using the global keyword.

 You can also create a global variable within a function by first creating it using the global keyword and then assigning it a value. This value will then be accessible from all parts of a program, outside and within any functions, and also via the $GLOBALS[] array.

Let's look at a slightly modified version of the `Example()` function in the previous section, which will now display all values, with the difference highlighted in bold:

```
function Example()
{
  global $MyVar2;

  echo 'Inside a function<br><br>';
  echo '$MyVar1 == ' . $GLOBALS["MyVar1"] . '<br>';
  echo '$MyVar2 == ' . $MyVar2;
}
```

Now, the value in `$MyVar1` is correctly output (as shown in Figure 13-3) because it has been looked up using the `$GLOBALS[]` array. The file *globals.php* in the companion archive contains this updated code.

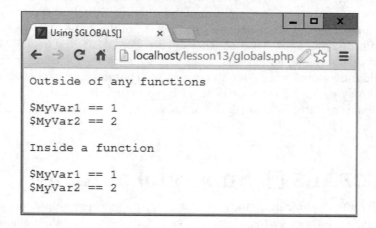

FIGURE 13-3   Using `$GLOBALS[]`, it is now possible to access `$MyVar1`.

You can also write a value back to a global variable using `$GLOBALS[]`, like this:

```
$GLOBALS["MyVar1"] = 3;
```

The main benefit of using the `$GLOBALS[]` array is that it is immediately obvious to you (or any other programmer who updates your code) that a global variable is being accessed, whereas when you use the `global` keyword, it is not always apparent that a variable has global scope.

Note   Remember that when accessing a global variable via the `$GLOBALS[]` array, you must omit the preceding `$` and place the remainder of the variable name inside quotes.

Global Naming Convention

I write a lot of PHP code, and I used to find that for each variable I used, I would still have to keep referring back to see whether it had a `global` keyword applied at any point in a function (making it global). If no `global` keyword was used, it would then be local. So, to save having to keep rechecking, I came up with the following simple convention.

Whenever a variable is created that requires global scope, I use all uppercase letters, and when a local variable is created, I use lowercase, or a combination of uppercase and lowercase (sometimes called *CamelCase*), like this:

```
$HIGHSCORE  = 0;    // Creates a global variable
$HighScore += 100;  // Increments a local variable
```

Therefore, for any variables I use that have any lowercase letters, I can be sure that they are being used in local context. I also tend to make array index and temporary variables all lowercase (not even CamelCase), to emphasize their transience in my code. Also, the more important a variable, the longer a name I generally give it, and the less important, the shorter a name it gets.

For example, `$MASTER_INVENTORY` could be the name of a global array containing the inventory of an online shopping site, `$Basket`, might be the name of a local shopping basket on that site, and `$i` might be the name of an index variable used to iterate through either of these.

Of course, you can use any other conventions you like (such as prefacing global variables with `G_`, floating points with `F_`, integers with `I_`, strings with `S_`, and so on), or no convention at all (but be prepared for longer debugging sessions).

Summary

Congratulations. With the handling of functions under your belt, you can now call yourself a PHP programmer. However, there are still a few more steps to take before you can call yourself a master of the language—starting with the next lesson on PHP objects, which will teach you how to write using object-oriented programming (OOP).

Self-Test Questions

Test how much you have learned in this lesson with these questions. If you don't know an answer, go back and reread the relevant section until your knowledge is complete. You can find the answers in the appendix.

1. What is a function, and what does it do?

2. Are curly braces required around the statements in a function?

3. How do you call a function?

4. How does a function receive the values upon which to work?

5. How can you assign default values to arguments that are passed to a function?

6. With which two functions can you handle variable numbers of arguments to a function?

7. How does a function return to the calling code?

8. In PHP, what is the difference between local and global scope?

9. With which keyword can you access a global variable from a PHP function?

10. With which array can you access global variables from a function?

14

Manipulating Objects

To view the accompanying video for this lesson, please visit mhprofessional.com/nixonphp/.

PHP is so much more than simply a scripting language because it also offers the power and flexibility of object-oriented programming (OOP). This is a style of programming in which the data used by a program, and the code to manipulate it, are all provided together in bundles called *objects*.

For example, a standard (or procedural) programming language will treat data and code as two separate entities, although some steps toward using objects are made in terms of providing access to functions. Indeed, enabling the use of local variables in functions also takes a further step toward modularity. But that's about as far as a non-OOP language generally goes.

On the other hand, a language that embraces OOP encourages you to place data where it is not directly accessible by the rest of the program. Instead, the data is accessed by calling specially written functions (commonly called *methods)* that are either bundled in with the data or inherited from class objects.

An object-oriented program will usually contain different types of objects, with each type corresponding to a particular kind of complex data to be managed, or a real-world object or concept such as a car, football team, or dental practice. For example, in the case of providing social networking capability to a website, there may be a number of objects to program, such as one for signing up new users, another for users to manage their accounts, another to enable messaging between accounts, and so on.

OOP Terminology

You need to get used to a number of terms when you first start to program using OOP. To start with, the combination of code and the data it manipulates is called a *class.* Each new object created that is based on a class is called an *instance* of that class (also known as an *occurrence).*

Within a class, the data associated with it are called its *properties,* while the functions it uses to access that data are called its *methods* (other programming languages may call them *member functions).* Whenever you see the term "method" used in relation to programming, it's simply another word for "function," but it implies that OOP programming is being discussed.

The objective of OOP is to write methods in such a way that only they can access their associated properties. This is known as *encapsulation,* and the idea is to prevent tainting of data by preventing any functions other than the methods of a class from manipulating its properties. The methods you build into a class are known as the *interface.* Classes may contain a special method used to initialize an instance of the class, and this type of method is called a *constructor.*

The reason OOP can be much safer than procedural programming is that, due to encapsulation, only the methods in a certain class can access its properties. Therefore, there is only one place to go when you need to debug your code—the methods of a class. You will not need to look anywhere else in your code to solve a bug relating to how the properties of a class are manipulated.

Other benefits are that once you have created and debugged a class, you may find you later need another one that is similar. Whenever that happens, you can save yourself a tremendous amount of development time by simply defining a new class based on the existing one. This is called *inheritance,* with the original class then becoming a *superclass* (also known as a *base* or *parent* class), while the new one is a *subclass* (also known as a *derived* class). This new subclass can then add its own properties and methods, as required.

Declaring a Class

The first step in object-oriented programming is declaring a class, which defines a new type of object but doesn't actually create an instance of the object. Classes group together a combination of data and the program code required to manipulate the data into a single object. To declare a class you use the `class` keyword, like this:

```
class UserClass
{
  public $firstname, $lastname;
```

```
    function GetName()
    {
        return $this->firstname . ' ' . $this->lastname;
    }
}
```

This creates the new class UserClass and gives it two items of data it can hold: $firstname and $lastname. It also sets up a method (another name for a function) called GetName() that can be applied to the class and returns a string with $firstname and $lastname concatenated together, separated with a space character.

The $this keyword refers to the current object (instance), and the -> operator refers to a property of that object. It can also refer to a method of an object as well.

 Notice how the example refers to $this->firstname and $this->lastname, and not $this->$firstname and $this->$lastname, because when you're accessing a property of a class using the -> operator, the property names should *not* include a $ symbol.

Creating an Object

You can now create a new object (known as an *instance)* based on this class, as follows (in which the new object $User is created):

```
$User = new UserClass;
```

This creates the new object $User, which has all the properties and methods defined in the class. The object doesn't (yet) have any data in it, though.

Accessing Properties and Objects

Once an instance of a class has been created using the new keyword, you can supply or modify the object data like this:

```
$User->firstname = 'Julie';
$User->lastname  = 'Jones';
```

And you can view these values by calling the GetName() method, like this:

```
echo "The user's first and last names are: " . $User->GetName();
```

In this instance, the result will look like Figure 14-1.

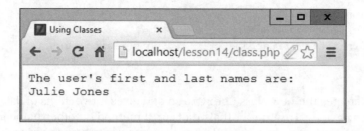

FIGURE 14-1 Assigning data to an object and reading it back with a method of the object

Using a Constructor

To be able to create a new object and populate it with data all at the same time, you can create a constructor method in one of two ways. The first is to repeat the class name as a class method, like this (with the new constructor method shown in bold):

```
class UserClass
{
  public $firstname, $lastname;

  function UserClass($firstname, $lastname)
  {
    $this->firstname = $firstname;
    $this->lastname  = $lastname;
  }

  function GetName()
  {
    return $this->firstname . ' ' . $this->lastname;
  }
}
```

Now you can prepopulate the object (in the same manner as prepopulating a new array) when you create an instance of the class (rather than creating the object and adding the data values afterwards), like this:

```
$User = new UserClass('Julie', 'Jones');
```

Note But now you must beware—if you create a new object from this revised class without supplying values for $firstname and $lastname (for example: $User = new UserClass()), you will get a PHP warning or error.

These days there's a better way that is recommended instead of using the preceding constructor, which is to use a method called __construct() as your constructor (two underscores followed by the word construct), like this:

```
function __construct($firstname, $lastname)
{
  $this->firstname = $firstname;
  $this->lastname  = $lastname;
}
```

It is always recommended to use a constructor method to ensure encapsulation. Without one, data properties must be separately assigned, and it may be tempting to do so by directly manipulating the property values of an object (for example, by the statement $User->lastname = 'Jones';). However, you can avoid this if you require the initial values to be assigned to an object's properties when the object is first created. To maintain full encapsulation, you should also write methods for the object's class to update the properties in the future, rather than directly updating them. In other words, it's best to only use an object's methods to read, change, or update the object's properties, and to avoid directly accessing or manipulating an object's properties.

Destructors

You can also provide a destructor method to be called when the code has no more references to an object, or when a script reaches the end. To create a destructor method, use code such as this (where the method name is two underscores followed by the word destruct):

```
function __destruct()
{
  // Place your destructor code here
}
```

Object Cloning

After you create an object, it will be passed by reference when passed as a parameter. This means that when assigning a new object based on an existing one, you don't actually copy the old object to the new one—you simply create a reference to the existing object. Therefore, the following code does *not* create a copy of $OldObject:

```
$NewObject = $OldObject; // Creates a reference to $OldObject
```

All that has happened here is that both $NewObject and $OldObject now refer to the same object. This is important to remember because it can result in unexpected bugs for beginners to OOP.

If you actually *do* want to create a new (and totally independent object) from an existing one, you must use the clone operator, like this:

```
$NewObject = clone $OldObject; // Creates a copy of $OldObject
```

This creates a brand-new instance of the object with its own methods and properties that is completely unconnected to the original object. It creates a new instance of the class used by the original object, then it copies all the properties from the old object to the new one.

Static Methods and Properties

Sometimes you want to be able to supply a method that is called on a class and not on an instance of the class (an object). This type of method is suitable where you wish to perform an action that relates to the class and not to any particular instance of that class.

For example, you might need a method to ask users for their first and last names so that you can create a new object. This method will apply to the class but not to the objects, so you would write it like this (placing it inside the class definition):

```
static function EnterName()
{
  // Display a form with input fields etc
}
```

Static methods are called differently from regular ones, in that you don't use the -> operator. Instead, you use a double colon operator (known as the *scope resolution* operator), like this (assuming that EnterName() is a static method of the class UserClass):

```
UserClass::EnterName();
```

Alternatively, from within another method of the class, you can refer to the static method like this:

```
self::EnterName();
```

Likewise, you can create static properties that relate only to the class and not to any specific instances. For example, you may wish to track the number of users you have, and the place to store that figure would be in a static property, like this:

```
static $UserCount;
```

From within a method of a class, you could then refer to this property with the self keyword and the scope resolution operator, like this:

```
self::$UserCount = 47362;
```

From outside the class, you could access it like this (assuming the class it is attached to is `UserClass`):

```
echo UserClass::$UserCount;
```

Predefined Properties

In the same way as providing default values to regular functions, when declaring properties in a class you may supply default values that will be used if none are supplied, like this:

```
function __construct($firstname = 'anonymous', $lastname = 'user')
```

If values are supplied to the constructor, these default values will be ignored and the supplied ones will be applied. This is the recommended way to ensure that errors are not displayed when arguments are not supplied to methods that expect them.

OOP Constants

PHP supports the creation of constants in classes but you must use a different syntax from the standard `define()` function, as required for regular constants. Instead, you use the `const` keyword, like this:

```
class UserClass
{
  const VERSION = 1.21;

  function DispVer()
  {
    echo self::VERSION;
  }
}
```

For a method within a class, the constant's value is returned by applying the `self` keyword, followed by the scope resolution operator (`::`) and the constant's name. You can also access it directly, like this:

```
echo UserClass::VERSION;
```

Like regular constants, they cannot be changed once they are defined. Also like regular constants, the `'$'` character is not used.

Property and Method Scope

So far, all the properties and methods in this lecture have been `public` so that they have been fully accessible, even to the point of directly assigning values to object properties. However, this is not considered good OOP practice because it breaks the encapsulation.

Therefore, PHP provides a means for you to restrict access to properties and methods by controlling what is known as their *visibility,* using three keywords:

- **public**   Public visibility is the default when declaring a variable using the public (or deprecated var) keyword, or when one is implicitly declared on first use. Don't confuse the var keyword in PHP, which is retained only to support legacy code, with var in JavaScript, which actually creates a local variable. In fact, because var is deprecated, you should always use the public keyword instead. PHP methods are assumed to be public by default.
- **protected**   A property or method with protected visibility can be referenced only by the object's class methods, and those of any subclasses.
- **private**   Members with private visibility can be referenced only by methods within the same class—and not by subclasses.

Here's how to decide which you need to use:

- Use public when outside code should be able to access this member, and extending classes should also inherit it.
- Use protected when outside code should not be able to access this member, but extending classes should inherit it.
- Use private when outside code should not be able to access this member, and extending classes also should not inherit it.

The following example illustrates these keywords in use:

```
class User
{
  var       $firstname;   // As public but deprecated
  public    $lastname;    // A public property
  protected $age;         // A protected property

  private function Admin() // A private method
  {
    // Code for administration goes here
  }
}
```

In most cases, for proper encapsulation, you should set your properties to protected or private. Methods that should only be used internally in the class should also be set to protected or private. Use public visibility only when absolutely required. That way, you'll keep your objects as self-contained as possible.

Applying Inheritance

When you've written a good general-purpose class that you'd like to use elsewhere, you can use the extends keyword when building a new class to incorporate all the features of the existing one. For example, assume you have the following class:

```
class UserClass
{
  public $firstname, $lastname;

  function UserClass($firstname, $lastname)
  {
    $this->firstname = $firstname;
    $this->lastname  = $lastname;
  }

  function GetName()
  {
    return $this->firstname . ' ' . $this->lastname;
  }
}
```

Now, let's say you want to create a new class that will deal with a first name and last name and that also handles usernames and passwords. To do so, all you need to add is the following, for example:

```
class Subscriber extends UserClass
{
  public $username, $password;

  function ShowDetails()
  {
    echo "Firstname: " . $this->firstname . '<br>';
    echo "Lastname : " . $this->lastname  . '<br>';
    echo "Username : " . $this->username  . '<br>';
    echo "Password : " . $this->password  . '<br>';
  }
}
```

The new class, Subscriber, now embodies all the properties and methods of both classes, as can be verified by issuing the following statements, which results in Figure 14-2:

```
$User           = new Subscriber('Julie', 'Smith');
$User->username = 'jsmith01';
$User->password = 'letmein';
echo $User->ShowDetails();
```

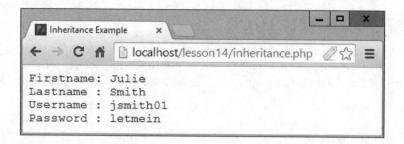

FIGURE 14-2   Extending a class with additional properties and methods

Using the **parent** Keyword

If you write a method in a subclass with the same name as a method in its parent class, its statements will override those of the parent class. Sometimes this is not the behavior you want, because you need to access the parent's method. To do this, you can use the **parent** keyword, as demonstrated by the following example:

```
$object = new Child;
$object->output1();
$object->output2();


class Father
{
  function output1()
  {
    echo "This is the parent object (class Father) responding<br>";
  }
}

class Child extends Father
{
  function output1()
  {
    echo "This is the child object (class Child) responding<br>";
  }
  function output2()
  {
    parent::output1();
  }
}
```

This code creates a base class called Father and then a subclass called Child that inherits its properties and methods, then overrides the method output1(). Therefore, when line 2 calls the method output1(), the new method is executed. The only way to execute the overridden output1() method in the Father class is to use parent, as shown in function output2() of class Child. The code results in Figure 14-3.

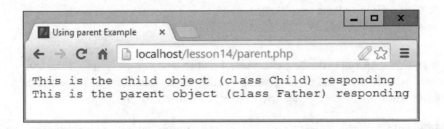

FIGURE 14-3   Calling a parent class method from a child class

If you wish to ensure that your code calls a method from the current class, you can use the self keyword, like this:

```
self::method();
```

Writing Subclass Constructors

When you extend a class and declare your own constructor, PHP will not automatically call the constructor method of the parent class. Therefore, to be certain that all initialization code is executed, subclasses should almost always call the parent constructors, like this:

```php
$object = new ChocChip();
echo 'Choc Chip Cookies have these properties...<br>';
echo 'Chewy     : ' . $object->chewy . '<br>';
echo 'Chocolate : ' . $object->chocolate;

class Cookie
{
  public $chewy;            // Cookies are chewy

  function __construct()
  {
    $this->chewy = 'TRUE';
  }
}

class ChocChip extends Cookie
{
  public $chocolate;        // Choc Chip cookies have chocolate
```

```
function __construct()
{
  parent::__construct(); // Call parent constructor first
  $this->chocolate = 'TRUE';
}
}
```

In this example, the `Cookie` class has created the property `$chewy`, which is reused in the `ChocChip` subclass that inherits it. Additionally, the `ChocChip` class creates another property, `$chocolate`, as shown in Figure 14-4.

 Note how the `ChocChip` subclass constructor calls its parent class constructor using the `parent` keyword and the scope resolution operator (`::`).

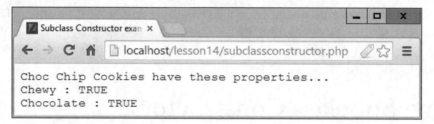

FIGURE 14-4 Using subclass constructors

Using the `final` Keyword

Sometimes you may wish to prevent a method from being overridden by a subclass, and you can do this using the `final` keyword, like this:

```
final public function Author()
{
  echo 'Written by Fred Bloggs';
}
```

When you use code such as this, the function will be inherited by all subclasses and cannot be overridden by a method of the same name. You cannot, however, use the `final` keyword on properties. Instead, you should probably think about using a constant. The `final` keyword can also be used on a class to prevent it from being extended.

Summary

You are now becoming a power PHP programmer, capable of bending the will of the language itself to your whims. Before you can move onto using PHP in meaningful ways in your web pages, though, a few things still remain outstanding in your training.

For example, in the following lesson you'll further flesh out your knowledge by looking at how to handle errors gracefully in your code, and also how to use regular expressions for powerful pattern matching.

Self-Test Questions

Test how much you have learned in this lesson with these questions. If you don't know an answer, go back and reread the relevant section until your knowledge is complete. You can find the answers in the appendix.

1. In object-oriented programming (OOP), what is the combination of code and the data it manipulates called?

2. How do you declare a class in PHP?

3. How can you create an object from a class?

4. With which operator can you modify properties of an object?

5. What is the recommended way to create a constructor method for a class?

6. Why is it a good idea to include a `__destruct()` method in your classes?

7. How can you copy an object?

8. How can you access a method in the parent of a class?

9. How can you create a new class that inherits the properties and methods of an existing one?

10. What are the three types of visibility you can apply to properties and methods?

Handling Errors and Expressions

To view the accompanying video for this lesson, please visit mhprofessional.com/nixonphp/.

There's no getting away from it. Even the most careful programmers build unexpected errors (or bugs) into their code, and so will you—it's perfectly normal. And even after you think you've fully debugged your code, the likelihood remains that there may still be obscure bugs lurking somewhere.

The last thing you want on a published website is for users to encounter errors, or sometimes even worse, just find your code doesn't work for them—making them leave to never return. But PHP comes with ways you can minimize the problem by attaching your own function to the standard error-trapping routines.

In this lesson I'll show you how you can manipulate PHP's built-in error trapping for dealing with bugs, and also how you can use regular expressions to perform powerful and complex pattern matching in simple statements, thus cutting back on lots of lines of code with potential for bugs to lurk in.

Error Trapping

Although you can't catch fatal errors (such as typing echho instead of echo) in PHP, it is possible to trap runtime errors in your code by adding the following statement and function to the start of any PHP program:

```
set_error_handler("ErrorHandler");

function ErrorHandler($no, $str, $file, $line)
{
```

```
echo
  "<div style='border:2px dotted;padding:5px 10px;background:tan'>" .
  "Line $line: <span style='color:red'>$str</span> " .
  "in <span style='color:blue'>$file</span></div>";
}
```

Then, whenever a runtime error occurs, such as from the following typographical error, a message similar to that shown in Figure 15-1 will be displayed:

```
$fred = 1;
echo $fredd;
```

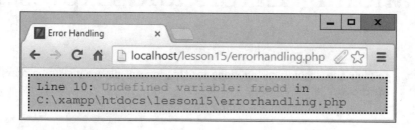

FIGURE 15-1 Trapping PHP errors

 If you plan on working with HTML in your variables, you may also want to process the value of $str in the preceding code through the htmlentities() function, in order to see the HTML tags in a variable rather than how the HTML displays.

The four values passed to the function you provide (in this case, received in the variables $no, $str, $file, and $line) are the error number, the error message, the file containing the error, and the line number within the file. If you prefer, to reduce the size of code, you can also use an anonymous (unnamed) function instead, like this:

```
set_error_handler(function($no, $str, $file, $line)
{
  echo
    "<div style='border:2px dotted;padding:5px 10px;background:tan'>" .
    "Line $line: <span style='color:red'>$str</span> " .
    "in <span style='color:blue'>$file</span></div>";
});
```

Here, the error-handling function is not given a name, but is simply supplied directly as an argument to the set_error_handler() function. Now you only need to copy the single, combined statement and function into pages that you'll be using it on. Alternatively, you could place the code in its own file, which you can then include where required using one of the include or require statements.

This makes it far quicker to catch and correct obscure errors you may introduce into your code and is achieved simply by pointing PHP's standard error-trapping code to a new function that replaces it. If you want to revert to the previous error handler at some point in your code, just add the following statement:

```
restore_error_handler();
```

You can copy and paste this code from the file *errorhandling.php* in the archive of examples on the companion website. Just remember to remove the error-trapping code when you move your files to a production website (once all bugs have been corrected).

Regular Expressions

Regular expressions were invented as a means of matching an enormous variety of different types of patterns with just a single expression. Using them, you can replace several lines of code with a simple expression, and can even use regular expressions search and replace operations.

To properly learn everything there is to know about regular expressions could take a whole book (and, indeed, many books have been written on the subject), so I'm just going to introduce you to the basics in this lesson. If you need to know more, I recommend you check out wikipedia.org/wiki/Regular_expression as a good starting point:

In PHP, you will use regular expressions mostly in two functions: `preg_match()` and `preg_replace()`. The `preg_match()` function tells you whether its argument matches the regular expression, whereas `preg_replace()` takes a second parameter: the string to replace the text that matches.

Using `preg_match()`

Let's say you want to find out whether one string occurs within another. For example, if you wish to know if the string whether occurs in Hamlet's famous soliloquy, you might use code such as the following:

```
$s = "To be, or not to be, that is the question: "   .
     "Whether 'tis Nobler in the mind to suffer"      .
     "The Slings and Arrows of outrageous Fortune, "  .
     "Or to take Arms against a Sea of troubles, "    .
     "And by opposing end them.";

$r = '/whether/';
$n = preg_match($r, $s, $match);
echo "$s<br><br><b>$r</b> matches: $match[0]";
```

In this example, the variable $r is a string that is given the value /whether/. This is how you denote a regular expression using the / character as a delimiter (in much the same way that quotation marks delimit strings).

First, you place a / character, then the text to match, followed by a closing / character. In this example, however, a match is not made because (by default) regular expressions are case-sensitive, and only the word Whether (with an upper case W) exists in the string.

If you wish to make a case-insensitive search, you can tell PHP by placing the letter i (a pattern modifier) after the closing / character, like this (in this case, a match will be made):

```
$r = '/whether/i';
```

You don't have to first place a regular expression in a variable if you don't want to, so two lines can be replaced with the following single statement:

```
$n = preg_match('/whether/i', $s, $match);
```

The result of executing these statements results in $match[0] containing the match (if there was one). The variable $match[] is an array, so it is able to store more than a single value, even though this particular statement only looks for a single match.

When it completes running, preg_match() returns a value of 1 if there was a match, 0 if none was found, or FALSE if an error occurred. Figure 15-2 shows the result of loading the previous program into a browser.

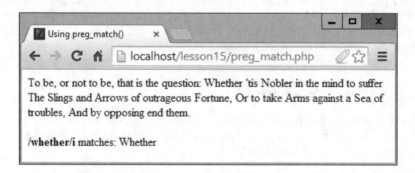

FIGURE 15-2   Testing for a match with **preg_match()**

 If all you are doing is testing whether one string appears in another, you may prefer to use strpos() or strstr() instead because they will be much quicker than using regular expressions. For more details on preg_match(), see the page php.net/manual/en/function.preg-match.php.

Using `preg_match_all()`

The preceding code is great for when you need to see whether there's at least a single instance of a search word in a target string. However, when you want to find out how many matches there are, you need to use the `preg_match_all()` function, like this:

```
$s = "To be, or not to be, that is the question: "  .
    "Whether 'tis Nobler in the mind to suffer"      .
    "The Slings and Arrows of outrageous Fortune, " .
    "Or to take Arms against a Sea of troubles, "    .
    "And by opposing end them.";

$r = '/to/i';
$n = preg_match_all($r, $s, $match);
echo "$s<br><br><b>$r</b> matches " . sizeof($match[0]) . ' times: ';
echo join(', ', $match[0]);
```

In this example, the word `to` is being searched for in a case-insensitive manner. The matches are returned into the array `$match[0]`, so the `sizeof()` function is used to display how many matches there were. Then the `join()` function (an alias of `implode()`) displays all occurrences, separated with commas. The array `$match[]` now contains a sub-array in `$match[0]` containing all the matches found, resulting in Figure 15-3.

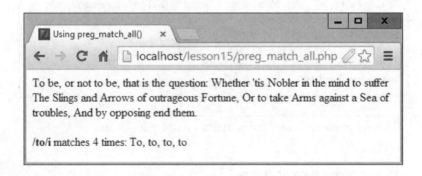

FIGURE 15-3 Four occurrences of the word **to** have been located.

The contents of `$match[1]` and other elements will contain text that matched the first captured parenthesized subpattern (if any). If all you require is the number of matches found (returned in this instance into `$n`), you can omit the `$match` argument because it is optional.

When pattern matching, you may place subpatterns within parentheses, and when they are matched they will appear in these elements of $match[], like this:

```
$s = "To be, or not to be, that is the question: "    .
     "Whether 'tis Nobler in the mind to suffer"      .
     "The Slings and Arrows of outrageous Fortune, " .
     "Or to take Arms against a Sea of troubles, "    .
     "And by opposing end them.";


$r = '/out(rage)ous/i';
$n = preg_match_all($r, $s, $match);
echo "$s<br><br><b>$r</b> matches " . sizeof($match[0]) . ' times: ';
echo join(', ', $match[0]);
echo '<br>Sub-pattern found: ' . $match[1][0];
```

Here, the word `rage` is placed in parentheses within the search pattern in $r. When this code is run, the `rage` subpattern is found, and it's placed in the first element of a sub-array of $match[1], as shown in Figure 15-4.

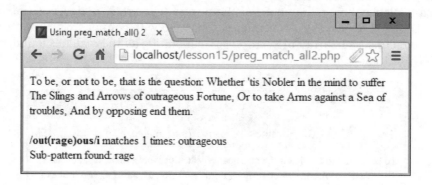

FIGURE 15-4 The main pattern and subpattern have been found.

Using `preg_replace()`

You can also replace matched text using the `preg_replace()` function. The source string is not modified by this because `preg_replace()` returns a new string with all the changes made.

For example, to replace the string `'tis` in the soliloquy with the word `it's` (although Shakespeare would surely object), you could use a regular expression and the `preg_replace()` function like this:

```
preg_replace("/'tis/", "it's", $r);
```

Figure 15-5 shows the result of executing this statement (using the file *preg_replace.php* in the accompanying archive). In it, you can see that the word after Whether is now it's. For the screen grab, the replaced word has been underlined to make it stand out better.

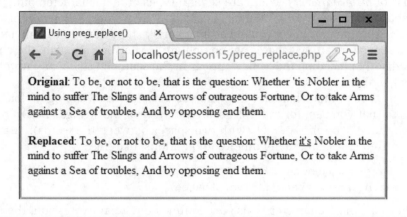

FIGURE 15-5   Searching and replacing content with `preg_replace()`

As with `preg_match()`, you can specify a case-insensitive replace with `preg_replace()` by placing an i character at the end of the regular expression, as in the following example :

```
preg_replace("/'tis/i", "it's", $r);
```

Unlike `preg_match()`, though, the `preg_replace()` function will automatically replace all matches it discovers. It's also more powerful, in that the subject of the replace operation can be an array, in which case the replacement will occur on all matches in the array.

To limit the number of replacements, you can supply an optional fourth argument, specifying the maximum number to allow. By default, this value is -1, which means there is no limit.

You may also provide an optional fifth argument to the function (which means you'll also have to give a value for the limit argument) into which the number of replacements made will be saved, like this:

```
preg_replace("/'tis/i", "it's", $r, -1, $count);
```

Upon return, $count will contain the number of replacements made.

Fuzzy Matching

Regular expressions are a lot more powerful than simply searching for and replacing words and phrases, because they also support complex fuzzy logic features through the use of *metacharacters*. There are several types of metacharacter, but let's look at just one for now (the * character) to see how they work. When you place * in a regular expression, it is not treated as an asterisk character, but as a metacharacter with a special meaning—that is, when you are performing a match, the character immediately preceding the * may appear in the searched string any number of times (or not at all).

This type of metacharacter is particularly useful for sweeping up lots of blank space so that you can, for example, search for any of the strings `'back pack'`, `'backpack'`, `'back  pack'` (with two spaces between the words), `'Back Pack'` (with mixed case), and many other combinations, like this:

```
$s = "Have you seen my BackPack anywhere?";
preg_match('/back *pack/i', $s, $match);
```

Because the i character is also used after the regular expression, the matching is case-insensitive; therefore, the word BackPack is found by the regular expression, and the echo command displays the result in the browser. You can try this for yourself using the file *fuzzy.php* in the archive file available at the companion website, as shown in Figure 15-6.

FIGURE 15-6 Matching variations of search patterns

 Note If you want to use any of the characters that are metacharacters as regular characters in your regular expressions, you must escape them by preceding the characters with a \ character. For example, * will turn the * from a metacharacter into a simple asterisk.

Matching Any Character

You can get even fuzzier than that, though, with the period (the dot or full stop) character, which can stand in for any character at all (except a newline). For example, to find all

HTML tags (which start with < and end with >), you could use the following regular expression (in any `preg_match()`, `preg_match_all()` or `preg_replace()` calls):

```
$expression = "/<.*>/";
```

The left and right angle brackets on either side serve as the start and end points for each match. Within them, this expression will match any character due to the dot metacharacter, whereas the `*` after the period says there can be zero, one, or any number of these characters. Therefore, any size of HTML tag, from the meaningless <> upwards, will be matched.

Other metacharacters include the + symbol, which works like `*`, except that it will match one or more characters, so you could avoid matching <> by ensuring there is always at least one character between the angle brackets, like this:

```
$expression = "/<.+>/";
```

 Unfortunately, because the `*` and + characters will match all the way up to the last > on a line, as well as catching entire elements such as `<h1>Heading</h1>`, they will also catch any nested HTML such as `<h1><i>Heading</i></h1>`.

Not Matching a Character

A solution to the multitag matching problem is to use the ^ character, whose meaning is "anything but," but it must be placed within square brackets, like this:

```
$expression = "[^>]+";
```

This regular expression is like `.+` except there is one character it refuses to match, which is the > symbol. Therefore, when presented with a string such as `<h1><i>Heading</i></h1>`, the expression will now stop at the first > encountered, so the initial `<h1>` tag will be properly matched. Table 15-1 summarizes the basic metacharacters and their actions.

Some of the characters in Table 15-1 have already been explained, and some should be self-explanatory. Others, however, you may find confusing, so I would recommend only using those you understand until you have learned more about regular expressions, perhaps from the Wikipedia article listed a little earlier, or from the comprehensive, multipage tutorial at *tinyurl.com/phpregex*.

Table 15-2 lists a selection of escape metacharacters and numeric ranges you can also include.

To help you better understand how these various metacharacters can work together, in Table 15-3 I have detailed a selection of regular expression examples as well as the matches they will make.

Remember that you can place the character i after the closing / of a regular expression to make it case-insensitive and can also place the character m after the final / to put the expression into multiline mode, so that the ^ and $ characters will match at the start and end of any newlines in the string, rather than the default of the string's start and end.

TABLE 15-1 The Basic Metacharacters

Metacharacters	Action
/	Begins and ends a regular expression.
.	Match any character other than newline.
*	Match the previous element zero or more times.
+	Match the previous element one or more times.
?	Match the previous element zero or one time.
[chars]	Match any single character contained within the brackets.
[^chars]	Matches any single character not contained within the brackets.
(regexp)	Treats regexp as a group for counting, or following *, +, or ?.
left|right	Match either left or right.
l-r	(In square brackets) Match a range of characters between l and r.
^	(Not in square brackets) Match at the search string's start.
$	(Not in square brackets) Match at the search string's end.

TABLE 15-2 Escape and Numeric Range Metacharacters

Other	Action
\b	Matches a word boundary
\B	Matches where there isn't a word boundary
\d	Matches a decimal digit
\D	Matches a nondecimal digit
\n	Matches a newline character
\s	Matches a whitespace character
\S	Matches a nonwhitespace character
\t	Matches a tab character
\w	Matches a word character (one of a-z, A-Z, 0-9, or _)
\W	Matches a nonword character (anything but a-z, A-Z, 0-9, or _)
\x	Means treat x as normal character (where x is a metacharacter)
{n}	Matches exactly n times
{n,}	Matches n times or more
{min,max}	Matches at least min and at most max times

TABLE 15-3   Some Example Regular Expressions and Their Matches

Example	Matches
`\.`	The first . in `Hello there. Nice to see you.`
`h`	The first h in `My hovercraft is full of eels`
`lemon`	The word `lemon` in `I like oranges and lemons`
`orange|lemon`	Either `orange` or `lemon` in `I like oranges and lemons`
`bel[ei][ei]ve`	Either `believe` or `beleive` (also `beleeve` or `beliive`)
`bel[ei]{2}ve`	Either `believe` or `beleive` (also `beleeve` or `beliive`)
`bel((ei)|(ie))ve`	Either `believe` or `beleive` (but not `beleeve` or `beliive`)
`2\.0*`	`2.`, `2.0`, `2.00`, and so on
`[j-m]`	Any of the characters j, k, l, or m
`house$`	Only the final `house` in `This house is my house`
`^can`	Only the first `can` in `can you open this can?`
`\d{1,2}`	Any one- or two-digit number from 0 to 9 and 00 to 99
`[\w]+`	Any word of at least one character
`[\w]{3}`	The first three consecutive word characters

Summary

This lesson has covered some fairly advanced topics, including error handling and sophisticated pattern matching, and it tops off the last items of basic knowledge you need about the PHP language. Therefore, starting with the following lesson, I will concentrate on how to use PHP to interact dynamically with users.

Self-Test Questions

Test how much you have learned in this lesson with these questions. If you don't know an answer, go back and reread the relevant section until your knowledge is complete. You can find the answers in the appendix.

1. How can you add your own error handler to PHP, and which four values will it be passed?

2. How can you disable (or turn off) your own error handler to restore PHP's default error handling?

3. With which function can you search for occurrences of a search string in another string?

4. How must you format a search string?

5. How can you set a regular expression to match regardless of case?

6. With which function can you match all occurrences of a search string?

7. How many arguments must be passed to the `preg_match()` and `preg_match_all()` functions, and what are they?

8. How can you replace any matches with a replacement string as well as find out how many replacements were made?

9. What regular expression might you use to search for any occurrences of either `car` or `automobile`?

10. With what statement could you case-insensitively find all six-letter words (not merely sequences of six letters) in a string (hint: think about word boundaries)?

16

Building Web Forms

▶ To view the accompanying video for this lesson, please visit mhprofessional.com/ nixonphp/.

Even modern websites with hyper-interactivity and self-updating pages, using behind-the-scenes communication with web servers via Ajax (detailed in Lesson 20), still rely on trusty old HTML forms for requesting input from users. HTML forms are simple, easily implemented, and have passed the test of time. What's more, they can be simply constructed in HTML or output from a scripting language such as PHP.

There is a downside, though: even on a securely encrypted connection there's no guarantee that the data being sent from the user isn't going to be potentially malicious. And especially on unencrypted links it's possible for hackers to construct copies of web forms either in HTML or created from software to send badly formed data to a web server, hoping to somehow gain entry to it or otherwise compromise or harm the server.

Therefore, this lesson focuses on how you can create effective forms that are easily processed via PHP. It also points out potential security hazards and pitfalls, and shows you how you can avoid them.

Creating a Form

Whether created in a simple HTML page or assembled via output from a program such as PHP, all web forms must have the following:

- Opening and closing <form> and </form> tags
- A submission method of either Post or Get
- One or more input fields (although you can omit them, but you won't be able to send any data if you do)
- A destination URL of a program or script to receive the form data

The following example illustrates how to build a very simple form to ask someone for their username and password, using straightforward HTML:

```
<!DOCTYPE html>
<html>
  <head>
    <title>A Simple Form</title>
  </head>
  <body style='font-family:monospace;white-space:pre'>
    <form method='post' action='simpleform.php'>
    Enter Username: <input type='text'     name='username'>
    Enter Password: <input type='password' name='password'>
    <input type='submit'></form>
  </body>
</html>
```

 Note I have used some CSS in the `<body>` element to keep the output tidy, by using a monospaced font, and ensuring that all whitespace and linefeeds are displayed.

This HTML starts off by specifying the standard HTML5 `!DOCTYPE` and then outputs a `<form>` element, two text-based `<input>` elements, and a submit `<input>` element. The type of data expected for the Username field is `text`, and for the Password field it is `password`, which has the effect of displaying only * characters when data is entered into this field, thus keeping it secure from any prying eyes. When loaded in a browser, the result of displaying this unsubmitted form looks like Figure 16-1.

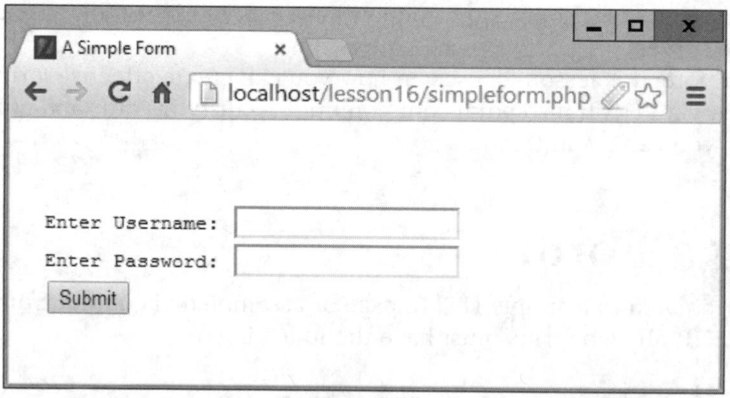

FIGURE 16-1 A simple form created with PHP

The Difference Between Post and Get Requests

In this example, the data is being sent using a Post request, which sends the information using headers (which are transmitted separately to HTML) so that they are not visible to the user. It could equally have used a Get method instead, but this would require the receiving program to retrieve the data slightly differently.

The reason is that Get request data is attached to the end of the URL receiving the form data, in the form of a query string. This is a tail containing various information that you often see following regular URLs. For example, when you search Google for the term PHP, the results page may display a URL similar to the following in the address field (where I have highlighted the query string in bold):

```
http://www.google.com/search?q=PHP&ie=utf-8&oe=utf-8
```

In fact, the URL will likely be longer than that, because I'm showing only the first three items of data in the query string, as follows:

- **q** has the value PHP.
- **ie** has the value utf-8.
- **oe** has the value utf-8.

The query string starts with the characters following a ? character (which is the character that separates a query string from a URL), and is then followed by one or more pairs of field names and values (data on the Internet is often handled in key/ value pairs). Each pair is separated by a & character, and the field names and values themselves are separated with an = character.

> **Note** Some programmers refer to Post and Get as POST and GET, but just like the term AJAX started fully capitalized, but now generally only has the first letter capitalized (Ajax), I prefer not to fully capitalize terms when avoidable, especially because these particular names are based only on the words *post* and *get,* and are not acronyms. It's up to you, however, how you choose to write these terms.

Security Issues with Get Requests

Because Post requests are sent using headers, they are not revealed to the user. But with the way that Get requests are appended to the URL being posted to, it is easy for the user (or any anyone else with access to that computer) to see the query data by referring to the address field.

Therefore, if the data contains sensitive information such as a password, even though it has been displayed using * characters in the input field, it is out in plain view in the address field. More than that, if a page that was arrived at from a Get request is bookmarked, then all that query data will be stored in the bookmark URL, which can be easily located by even the most casual of snoopers.

There's an additional security risk with Get requests in that most web servers save the full URLs of all pages called up in their log files, and many web pages also use third-party analytics services that may also store this data. This means there's a chance that these logs could get into the wrong hands, and any sensitive data might be compromised.

 I always recommend that you avoid using Get requests for posting form data, unless you have a compelling reason for doing so, and the data being transmitted is not of a sensitive nature.

Accessing Form Data from PHP

It is possible for a PHP program to extract Get data from the query string directly, but it takes some fiddly code to separate out all the fields and values. However, whichever method is used to send form data to a PHP program, there's an easy way of accessing it, via either the $_GET[] or $_POST[] superglobal array, which is prepopulated with data by PHP.

For example, the following code can be added into the previous example to place the data posted into a pair of variables:

```
$username = $_POST['username'];
$password = $_POST['password'];
```

Or you can also retrieve data sent with a Get request like this:

```
$username = $_GET['username'];
$password = $_GET['password'];
```

In fact, it's possible to make your PHP programs accept either type of input with code such as this:

```
$username = '';
$password = '';

if (isset($_POST['username'])) $username = $_POST['username'];
if (isset( $_GET['username'])) $username =  $_GET['username'];
if (isset($_POST['password'])) $password = $_POST['password'];
if (isset( $_GET['password'])) $password =  $_GET['password'];
```

Here, the two variables are first assigned the empty string, to ensure they have a value when PHP later comes to read them (variables should be assigned values at the earliest possible opportunity after creating them to avoid the potential for a warning being given or an error being thrown).

Then the two arrays $_POST[] and $_GET[] are tested for the keys username and password, with any matches then stored in $username and $password, overwriting the empty string values. This approach ensures that at all times PHP is dealing with sensible and processable values, and will not display any error or warning messages.

About `register_globals`

In the early days of PHP there was a `register_globals` setting that was enabled by default, and it caused all form data sent to a PHP program to automatically be saved into variables of the same names as the fields.

In the preceding example, therefore, there would have been no need to access the `$_POST[]` and `$_GET[]` arrays, because `$username` and `$password` would be automatically assigned values from these arrays (if present). At first this seemed like a great idea (and plenty of programmers thought it was a wonderful timesaver), until enterprising hackers discovered that they could use this feature to hijack uninitialized variables using simple form injection.

For example, assume a programmer has created a variable called `$adminaccess`, which is to be used to prevent unauthorized access to certain code, like this:

```
if ($adminaccess == 1)
{
  // Access to sensitive functions
}
```

Only if the variable has a value of 1 will that section of code be entered. And in the early days of PHP, if `$adminaccess` didn't have a value, this `if()` statement would simply be passed over (it would be ignored).

Then, elsewhere in the code, there would be a statement for setting this variable, which might look like this:

```
if ($username == 'Admin' && $password == 'secret')
  $adminaccess = 1;
```

Normally all this would mean that only once `$username` and `$password` had been correctly verified by this statement would `$adminaccess` be set to 1. And if they were not verified, then `$adminaccess` would have no value (having not been set) and so it would prevent unauthorized access—or would it?

Well, nowadays a warning would be issued by this code because an unassigned variable would be encountered. But in earlier versions of PHP, because `$adminaccess` has never been initialized to a non-1 value, a malicious hacker would only need to create an edited version of the form on their own computer, in which the field name adminaccess is given a default value of 1. If this form were then posted, the variable `$adminaccess` would be automatically created by PHP and assigned the value 1— and, bingo, they would be in!

Of course, a hacker would have to know the precise names of specific variables in your code. But in popular programs where the source code was generally available, it was easy to find omissions like this and create hacks to take advantage of them.

This is why `register_globals` was set to off by default in version 4.2 of PHP, was deprecated in version 5.3, and was finally removed altogether in version 5.4.

You should always assign a value to any variable you use before you read or access it. You never know, the server your code runs on may have an old version of PHP and your code could therefore be vulnerable to this hack. More importantly these days, though, predefining all your variables is good practice because it helps you (and other people) better maintain your code, because you can see at a glance all the variables being used—especially if you document them at each assignment too.

Redisplaying a Form

Having both the form HTML and the code to process submitted data in the same PHP file makes it easy for your code to process the data received and resubmit the form (or parts of it) if any data is missing or invalid. It can also prepopulate any valid data to save users from having to type it in again.

The following revision of the earlier example shows how to do this by allowing you to keep posting the form back to the PHP program, which then prepopulates the fields with the data previously posted to it:

```php
<!DOCTYPE html>
<html>
  <head>
    <title>A Simple Form (2)</title>
  </head>
  <body style='font-family:monospace;white-space:pre'>
<?php
  $username = '';
  $password = '';

  if (isset($_POST['username'])) $username = $_POST['username'];
  if (isset( $_GET['username'])) $username =  $_GET['username'];
  if (isset($_POST['password'])) $password = $_POST['password'];
  if (isset( $_GET['password'])) $password =  $_GET['password'];

  echo <<< _EOT
<form method='post' action='simpleform2.php'>
Enter Username: <input type='text'     name='username'
  value='$username'>
Enter Password: <input type='password' name='password'
  value='$password'>
  <input type='submit'></form>
_EOT;
?>
  </body>
</html>
```

The PHP section of the example first assigns any posted values sent (whether via a Get or Post request) to the variables $username and $password. Then it outputs the HTML to create a form, specifies a method of post for sending the data, and sets a destination of *simpleform2.php*. If this example file is saved using that filename, it will post to itself.

The main differences between this combined HTML/PHP example and the previous HTML-only example are highlighted in bold. They are the addition of values passed to the value attributes of the <input> elements, in the form of the two variables that have had their values extracted from the $_GET[] and $_POST[] arrays.

This keeps the form populated with user data ready for reposting. Figure 16-2 shows what this page looks like when displayed in a browser, after the form is filled in and submitted.

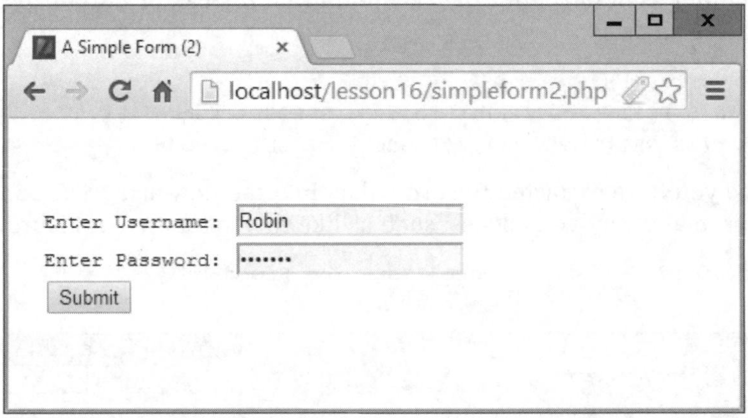

FIGURE 16-2   The posted form data is redisplayed.

You can also use the value attribute of an <input> element to offer default values to your users. For example, if you're creating a loan repayment calculator, most mortgages tend to be offered over 25 years, so you might choose to make that a default value, to save users from typing it in. However, being in a user-editable field, it can easily be changed if users require.

The **checkbox** and **select multiple** Input Types

Other types of <input> tags you will need to be able to process in PHP are checkbox and select with multiple enabled. It is fully legal HTML to create multiple checkboxes or select lists using the same name, and these types of input arrive at a

PHP server in an array, with the different values in each element. For example, you might ask a user for their favorite foods out of a selection, like this:

```
Hamburger <input type='checkbox' name='foods[]' value='burger' >
   Pizza <input type='checkbox' name='foods[]' value='pizza'  >
  Burrito <input type='checkbox' name='foods[]' value='burrito'>
```

 The values supplied to the name properties end with [] (square brackets). This indicates to the receiving program that the data being posted is an array, and that it should be processed as such. Without the [] characters, only the most recent value would be posted, and it would be just a single string.

You can extract this array data from either the $_GET[] or $_POST[] array in the same manner as before, with the exception that instead of initializing a variable, this time it's an array:

```
$foods = array();
if (isset($_POST['foods'])) $foods = $_POST['foods'];
if (isset( $_GET['foods'])) $foods =  $_GET['foods'];
```

Once you have extracted the array data into the new array $foods[], you can process it in any way you choose, such as like this (as shown in Figure 16-3):

```
foreach($foods as $food) echo "You like $food<br>";
```

```
Form Array Data

localhost/lesson16/formarraydata.php

You like burger
You like pizza
You like burrito


Hamburger
    Pizza
  Burrito
  Submit
```

FIGURE 16-3   Processing form array data

Alternatively, instead of simply displaying these values, you can do whatever else you need to do with them, such as processing items individually, like this:

```
$firstfood = $food[0];
```

Similarly to multiple checkboxes, when a type of `select` is used with the option `multiple` enabled, an array will also be posted to PHP, as with this HTML (note the use of `veggies[]` with square brackets):

```
Vegetables <select name="veggies[]" size="5" multiple="multiple">
  <option value="Peas">Peas</option>
  <option value="Beans">Beans</option>
  <option value="Carrots">Carrots</option>
  <option value="Cabbage">Cabbage</option>
  <option value="Broccoli">Broccoli</option>
</select>
```

And, after extracting the array data (remember that the name you provide in the form must end with `[]`, otherwise only one item will be stored), you can iterate through the resulting array in a similar manner to the previous example, like this (as shown in Figure 16-4):

```
foreach($veggies as $veg) echo "You like $veg<br>";
```

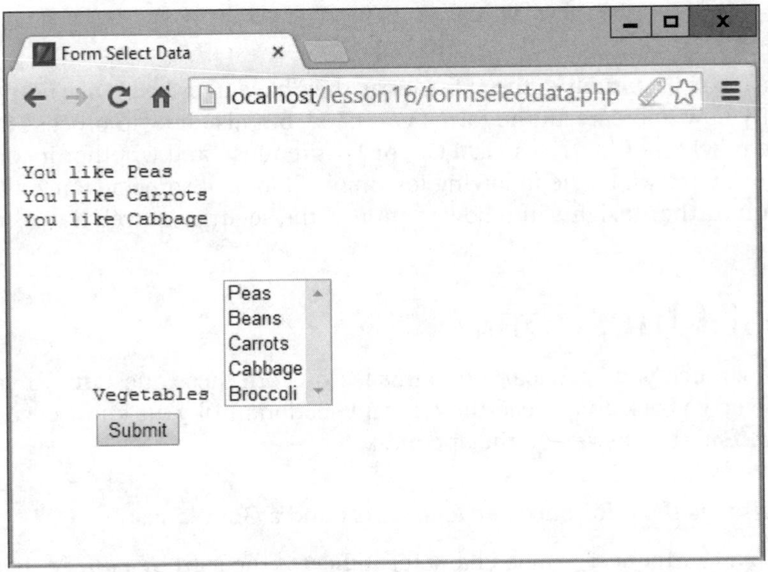
Form Select Data
localhost/lesson16/formselectdata.php
You like Peas
You like Carrots
You like Cabbage
Peas
Beans
Carrots
Cabbage
Vegetables
Broccoli
Submit

FIGURE 16-4 Processing data from a form using **`select multiple`**

Note Radio button values do not get passed in an array (and can be treated as regular form input) because only one can be selected in any group. Also, for brevity, remember that instead of using the attribute `multiple='multiple'`, you can simply add the attribute `multiple` to a `<select>` element without assigning it a value (as long as you're not using XHTML), like this: `<select name='options[]' multiple>`.

Using Hidden Fields

A great way of helping a user navigate through more than one page of input (perhaps as part of an online shopping website) is to track the user by placing one or more hidden fields in a form. This lets you keep track of items already in their basket and/or any other data they may have entered, and you don't want to confuse the user by continually displaying them.

To do this, simply prepopulate a field with a `value` of your choice and give it a `type` of `hidden`, like this:

```
<input type='hidden' name='purchases' value='11324,6463,921'>
```

In this instance, the `value` attribute has three numbers in it, which could represent inventory ID numbers of goods ordered so far by the user. When the form that this input is part of is later posted back to the server with any additional item(s) to be purchased, the info about the existing items will also be posted to keep track of the order, without (yet) having to save any data to disk or a database.

Summary

Forms are as important to the Internet as they have ever been, but now you know not only how to create all the forms you need, but also how to process the data posted via them, whether it arrives via a Get or Post request, and whether it comes in single items or in arrays. In the following lesson, we'll look at some advanced uses for forms and gain further insights into how to protect the security of web transactions.

Self-Test Questions

Test how much you have learned in this lesson with these questions. If you don't know an answer, go back and reread the relevant section until your knowledge is complete. You can find the answers in the appendix.

1. What is the difference between a Post and a Get request?
2. In a Get request, which character indicates the start of a query string, which character separates keys and values, and which character separates pairs of keys and values?
3. How can you access form data sent to PHP via a Post request?
4. How can you access form data sent to PHP via a Get request?
5. How can you ensure that your PHP program doesn't throw an error if no submitted data can be retrieved?

6. How can you let users resubmit a form with a problem in one of its inputs, without requiring them to reenter all the data?

7. How can you submit a collection of checkbox inputs to PHP?

8. How can you submit a collection of options from a `<select>` element that uses the `multiple` attribute?

9. How can you access array data submitted from a web page using PHP?

10. How can you store data your program needs in a form, without showing it to the user?

Maintaining Security

To view the accompanying video for this lesson, please visit mhprofessional.com/
nixonphp/.

There is one overriding consideration to take into account when you work on
anything more than a simple product or personal web page. As soon as you begin
to work with data, accept input from users, process it, and return information based
on that input, opportunities for compromise can occur.

It doesn't matter what the website is; if it has a vulnerability, it will be discovered
and exploited. And this won't necessarily be by human beings. More and more
recently when I process my log files, I see bots of all kinds rummaging through my
websites. They used to be very rare, but now can be upwards of 25 percent of traffic
in some instances. And you can be sure that although some are beneficial, such as
search engine spiders, a few of these have malign intent—you can often tell them
because they make unusual requests, often for pages that don't exist.

So get used to the fact of life that not only will your websites be subject to hacking
attempts by being explored for vulnerabilities, this will happen continuously on a
daily basis—forever. And one of your biggest jobs as a developer is to ensure that the
bad guys never find a way in.

Sanitizing Input

Looking back at the form-processing examples in the previous lesson, in the code that
extracts form data from the $_GET[] and $_POST[] arrays, it is always a good idea
to insert some extra security to prevent malicious hacking attempts. For example,
suppose you have created a bulletin board program in PHP and use it to accept input
from your users, which you then display on the board.

Although this may seem quite a simple thing to do—just accept the input and then echo it to the browser—what if the user has entered some HTML of their own, which totally messes up the display? Or, worse still, what if they entered some JavaScript that hijacks the page and redirects the user to a different website, for example?

Obviously, you can't allow that, so your best safety measure is to run all user input through the htmlentities() function. This takes the string that is passed to it and replaces all characters that could be interpreted by HTML with simple entities. For example, the < and > characters (which could be used to enter HTML tags) are replaced with < and >. This renders them harmless, but still allows < and > to be displayed in the browser.

In the same way, all & characters are replaced with & and all double quotes are replaced with ", along with any other characters that have HTML character entity equivalents.

The end result is that a string such as <h1>"Hello"</h1> will be changed to <h1>"Hello"</h1>. This will display in the browser as typed in by the user, and not as an actual <h1> heading.

Therefore, I recommend that as soon as you have some user data ready for processing, you immediately sanitize it, as with these two lines:

```
$username = htmlentities($username);
$password = htmlentities($password);
```

However, because the default setting of this function is to convert only double quotes, it is advisable to also supply a second argument to the function with the value ENT_QUOTES, to deal with this case. Therefore, the following is the recommended final version of these statements, which should ideally be added to the examples in Lesson 16:

```
$username = htmlentities($username, ENT_QUOTES);
$password = htmlentities($password, ENT_QUOTES);
```

Should you ever need to convert sanitized input back, you can always call the inverse function html_entity_decode().

There is also a less sweeping function called htmlspecialchars() with which you can assert greater control over which characters are to be converted. See the following URL for more details (it has quite a number of options): php.net/manual/en/function.htmlspecialchars.php.

It will also probably require supplying the ENT_QUOTES argument to ensure that single quotes are also converted.

Note Sometimes you may wish to first process raw user data in one way or another, and only later sanitize it. But this can be dangerous if something in the process causes it to skip the sanitization; therefore, you must fully test any code where you do so, each time you modify it. This is the reason I always recommend sanitizing input as soon as it arrives, even if the data is going to be stored in a file or database (because you know it is sanitized, your code can always account for this). This way, you never again have to worry about it being tainted.

Uploading Files to a Server

Uploading files to PHP is almost as simple as sending plain data. The trick is to use a special type of encoding that works with binary data (as opposed to textual form data, for example) called `multipart/form-data`; your browser will then know what to do with it, and so will PHP. It is, however, a procedure ripe for exploitation if you don't take the correct security measures.

The following example supports the uploading of an image to PHP:

```
<!DOCTYPE html>
<html>
  <head>
    <title>File Upload</title>
  </head>
  <body>
    <form method='post' action='fileupload.php'
       enctype='multipart/form-data'>
      Choose File: <input type='file' name='filename' size='27'>
      <input type='submit' value='Upload'>
    </form>
<?php
    if ($_FILES)
    {
      $name = $_FILES['filename']['name'];
      move_uploaded_file($_FILES['filename']['tmp_name'], $name);
      echo "Uploaded image '$name'<br><br><img src='$name'>";
    }
?>
  </body>
</html>
```

There are two parts to this example. The first contains all the HTML for setting up a web page, along with a form for selecting and uploading an image. The second part of the example is the PHP that processes the uploaded image, and you can see the result of running the code in a web browser in Figure 17-1.

The way the example works is that a form-encoding type of `multipart/form-data` is specified, along with an `<input>` type of `file`, so that a Browse button (or a Choose File button, depending on the browser) is displayed alongside, with which a file can be located on the local file system. When the form is submitted, the form data is posted to the script *fileupload.php*.

In the PHP section, an array called `$_FILES[]` is tested in the first line. If it has no value, then no file was posted to the program; otherwise, `$_FILES['filename']['name']` contains the name that was used when the file was selected by the user.

At this point, though, the file is held in a temporary storage area, so next it is moved to a permanent location, using the filename just obtained:

```
move_uploaded_file($_FILES['filename']['tmp_name'], $name);
```

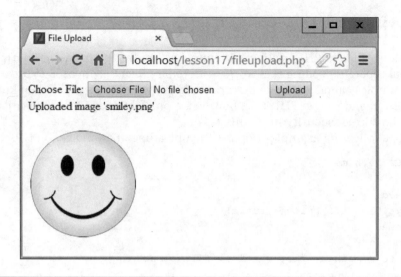

FIGURE 17-1   Uploading a file to a web server

The value `tmp_name` is a temporary name that uploaded files are first given by PHP, and the `move_uploaded_file()` function copies this file to the current folder (or a subfolder or other location), as specified in the final parameter, which in this case is simply the filename in `$name`.

To move the file to */usr/home/robin* (for example) on a Linux computer, you might use the following statement instead (assuming that directory exists, and PHP has permission to write to it):

```
move_uploaded_file($_FILES['filename']['tmp_name'],
    "/usr/home/robin/$name");
```

However, in this example, I have simply copied the file into the current folder so that it can be quickly displayed by the final line of code:

```
echo "Uploaded image '$name'<br><br><img src='$name'>";
```

 Ensure that the correct write permissions for the destination folder have been enabled when using this function, or you may find that the file cannot be copied.

The `$_FILES[]` Array

The `$_FILES[]` superglobal array can contain five different items after a file upload, as follows:

- `$_FILES['file']['name']`   The name of the uploaded file
- `$_FILES['file']['type']`   The content type (such as `image/png`)

- **`$_FILES['file']['size']`**   The file size in bytes
- **`$_FILES['file']['tmp_name']`**   The name of the temporary file
- **`$_FILES['file']['error']`**   Any error code resulting from the upload

Using these values, you will know what the file was called when selected by the user, the type the file is (image, video, and so on), how big it is, its temporary name on the server, and any error that may have occurred.

Some of the file types (also known as MIME types) you may encounter include the following:

- **Applications**   application/pdf, application/zip
- **Audio**   audio/mpeg, audio/x-wav
- **Images**   image/gif, image/jpeg, image/png, image/tiff
- **Text**   text/html, text/plain, text/xml
- **Video**   video/mpeg, video/mp4, video/quicktime

The `$_FILES[]` array is cleared when PHP exits, so if you do not copy an uploaded file to a permanent location, it will be lost on exit.

File Security

There is potential for a hacker to seriously mess up your server using file uploading, unless you are careful. They could do this by entering a special filename for the uploaded file, such as *C:/Windows/System32/calc.exe* (for just one example), which on a Windows computer could replace your calculator with a malicious program (if the write permissions are not set securely)!

Therefore, the example is unsafe as I have written it, because it needs any characters other than alphanumeric characters (and the period) stripped out before being used, which can be done by replacing the line of code

```
$name = $_FILES['filename']['name'];
```

with the following:

```
$name = strtolower(preg_replace('/[^\w.-]/', '',
  $_FILES['filename']['name']));
```

This uses the `preg_replace()` function (as described in Lesson 15), along with a regular expression that allows through only word characters, and the `.` and `-` characters, and then uses a replacement value of the null (empty) string to remove any unwanted characters, thus rendering the filename safe to use. The `/` character, quotation marks, and any operating system control characters will be unable to get through this conversion.

Finally, enclosing the name conversion code is a call to `strtolower()`, which sets the resulting filename to all lowercase so that it will work on all file systems—whether case-sensitive or not.

There's a lot more to dealing with files than this, so I cover file handling in much greater depth in Lesson 18.

Other Potential Insecurities

In the following lesson, we'll look at file handling and discuss maintaining security when doing so. But even before you get to that lesson, you should be thinking about how to help your websites and your users be more secure. For example, if you intend to support logging in with usernames and passwords, will you evaluate the passwords and either inform a user if a chosen password is weak, or perhaps insist on certain minimum lengths and/or required types of characters (such as combinations of uppercase, lowercase, digits, and punctuation)?

You see, even without finding a vulnerability in your website, an intruder may find a way in to the accounts with short and/or simple passwords, by using simple brute-force, repeated login attempts. Speaking of which, any account that receives more than a set number of failed login attempts should probably be flagged for the system admin to investigate. And it may also pay to use a CAPTCHA service (many free services are available, such as *captcha.net*, which is shown in Figure 17-2) to try and ensure that only humans can create accounts on your websites. If you don't, you may find your sites overwhelmed with bot-created logins.

FIGURE 17-2 Restricting access to websites with a CAPTCHA

Also, PHP is often used in conjunction with database programs such as MySQL. Although I don't cover these programs in this course, if you choose to learn how to use MySQL (or another database) in conjunction with PHP, be sure to keep security in mind from the very first examples you try. Many of the cases you hear about in the news where passwords and other details have been hacked on major websites have resulted from some form of database injection (similar to the form injection discussed here).

There are ways to further sanitize user input for databases, such as PHP functions you can call to strip out potentially malicious characters, but let me advise you right now that the one absolutely failsafe method to use with MySQL is *prepared statements*. So make sure that any book or course you purchase on MySQL (or any other database) comprehensively works with prepared statements, rather than sending user input directly to the database.

I would also advise you to be aware of the term *salting*, in which (very roughly) you add your own strings of characters to user passwords before encoding or hashing them (and then remove them upon retrieval), so that even if your database is hacked, if the salt string you have applied is not found by the intruder, that database will be useless to them. So make sure any database book or course you buy fully discusses salting.

Summary

You will now be able to effectively sanitize user input to make it safe to work with, and know how to upload any type of file to PHP without creating a security risk. In the following lesson, we'll move onto processing such submitted data by setting and reading cookies and using file handling.

Self-Test Questions

Test how much you have learned in this lesson with these questions. If you don't know an answer, go back and reread the relevant section until your knowledge is complete. You can find the answers in the appendix.

1. With which function can you sanitize user input, converting HTML special characters into safe entities?

2. What encoding type should an HTML form use in order to be able to upload files to a web server?

3. What input type should an `<input>` element use in order to allow a file to be selected for uploading via a form?

4. When a form has uploaded a file to a web server, which PHP superglobal array will contain all the details about the file?

5. What are the five pieces of information you can retrieve from PHP after a file upload, and how?

6. Assuming the uploaded file is an image, what are the three main types that it could be?

7. How can you ensure that an uploaded file will not compromise your web server?

8. Once you have received a file and sanitized its filename, what must you do to place it on your system?

9. What can you do to lessen the possibility that "bots" are accessing your websites instead of humans?

10. When processing filenames, what function is it a good idea to call if your program may have to run on different platforms?

LESSON 18

Accessing Cookies and Files

> To view the accompanying video for this lesson, please visit mhprofessional.com/nixonphp/.

Your journey to become a master PHP programmer is almost complete, but there are just a few odd bits and pieces I still have to tell you about in these final lessons—sort of the icing on the cake of PHP.

In this lesson these items include how to save cookies on your users' computers to personalize their browsing experience on your web pages, how to get useful information from the browser's environment, and how to work with files and the file system.

Using Cookies

Cookies are those little snippets of data that get saved on your computer and that everyone makes such a fuss about because some companies use them to track your surfing and buying habits. However, cookies are extremely useful and, in fact, invaluable for making your users' visits to your web pages as smooth and enjoyable as possible.

You see, cookies are the means used by sites such as Facebook and Twitter to keep you logged in so that you can keep going back without having to continually reenter your username and login details. And I'll now show you how easy it is for you to set and read cookies using PHP, so that you can provide the same functionality.

Cookies are sent to (and retrieved from) a web browser in header messages that get sent before the body of a page is sent to the browser. Therefore, you must always ensure that your cookie setting takes place before any part of a web page is sent. Otherwise, if even one character of a web page body has already been sent to a browser by your PHP script, then setting a cookie will fail.

Setting a Cookie

To create a cookie, you simply assign it a value that contains the various details it needs to store on the user's computer. These include the cookie name, its contents, its expiry date, the domain to which it applies, the path to the server issuing it, and whether or not it is secure, as follows:

- **name**   The name of the cookie as used by your PHP code to access the cookie on subsequent browser requests.
- **value**   The value of the cookie (the cookie's contents). It can hold up to 4KB of alphanumeric text (but is not suitable for the storing of sensitive data).
- **expire**   The Unix timestamp of the expiration date. Most easily set in an expression using `time()` plus a number of seconds. (This setting is optional; the default is that the cookie expires when the browser closes.)
- **path**   The path of the cookie on the server. If this is a /, the cookie is available over the entire domain. If it is a directory, the cookie is available only within that directory and its subdirectories. (This setting is optional; the default is the current directory that the cookie is being set in.)
- **domain**   The Internet domain of the cookie. If this is *myserver.com*, the cookie is available to all of that web domain and its subdomains, such as *www.myserver.com* and *sport.myserver.com*. If it's a subdomain, such as *sport.myserver.com*, the cookie is available only to that subdomain and its sub-subdomains such as *tennis.sport .myserver.com*, but not to any other main subdomains such as *news.myserver.com*. (This setting is optional; the default is all domains and subdomains of the current server.)
- **secure**   If this is set to TRUE, the cookie must be sent over an https:// secure connection or it is not sent at all. (This setting is optional—the default is FALSE.)
- **httponly**   If this is set to TRUE, the cookie will be made accessible only through the HTTP protocol; therefore, cookies set in PHP will not be retrievable from scripting languages such as JavaScript. Additionally, this setting may not be supported in all browsers, so I recommend you probably shouldn't rely on it unless you have a very good reason. (This setting is optional; the default is FALSE.)

The name, value, and expire arguments should now be quite clear, but let me expand on the optional path argument. Don't supply an argument (or just pass ' ') if you want cookies to apply in the current directory or deeper. Alternatively, you can give a value of / for the cookie to apply across all directories on the server, or you can supply the location of another subdirectory, such as /login/, and cookies will apply only in that directory or deeper.

The same goes for the optional domain argument. Don't supply an argument (or just pass ' ') for the cookie to apply to the entire domain of the website. Otherwise, specify a subdomain such as *subdomain.mysite.com* to restrict access to the cookie to that domain only.

Finally, if you have a secure web server running and wish to restrict cookie exchanges to using only a secure HTTPS connection, then set the optional secure argument to TRUE. Otherwise, don't pass an argument.

Therefore, to simply set a cookie's value and expiry, and have it apply only in the current folder (or deeper) of the current website, you might issue a simple statement such as this:

```
setcookie('username', 'FJones', time() + 60 * 60 * 24 * 7);
```

The cookie set by this assignment will have the name username and the value FJones. It will stay on the user's computer (unless manually removed) for a week, as calculated by multiplying 60 (seconds) by 60 (minutes) by 24 (hours) by 7 (days). Alternatively, a precalculated numeric value (in this case, 604800) can be supplied (but time() must still be added to it).

Reading a Cookie

Reading back a cookie's value is simply a matter of accessing the $_COOKIE[] superglobal array, like this:

```
$username = isset($_COOKIE['username']) ? $_COOKIE['username'] : FALSE;
```

The variable $username will now either have the value FALSE if the cookie was not found, or it will contain the cookie's value. You could also use the value NULL, the empty string (''), or other similar values to indicate that no value was retrieved into the variable.

However, as previously cautioned, remember that you cannot read back a cookie's value immediately after setting it, because you can only read cookies from a web browser after they are sent to PHP as part of the header exchange prior to sending a web page to the browser. Therefore, you can only check that the value was correctly assigned on the subsequent page load.

Deleting a Cookie

To delete a cookie, you simply need to use the setcookie() function in the same way you did to set the cookie in the first place, but with an expiry time set in the past, like this:

```
setcookie('username', '', time() - 3600);
```

This function simply saves a cookie of the name username with no value (actually an empty string), and sets its expiry to time() - 3600 seconds (one hour in the past), the result of which is that the cookie expires. You could even use a value of just time() - 1, but it makes sense to go further back than that to account for any timing delays caused by slow or interrupted data transfer.

Once you've set a cookie for a user, upon their next return to your website, just check for the existence of that cookie, and if it has a value, you can use it to look up their details and personalize your content for them. You can also store other values in cookies, too (although you should avoid storing a password, and instead save a unique token your server has created for identifying the user). The generous 4KB size limit per domain means you can probably store all the cookies you could want for most purposes.

Combining These Three Functions

Following is an example that combines all three of these functions (cookie creation, reading, and deletion) in a single web document, as shown in Figure 18-1:

```html
<!DOCTYPE html>
<html>
  <head>
    <title>Using Cookies</title>
  </head>
  <body>
    <h3>Press Reload to allow the cookie to be set and erased</h3>
<?php
  $username = isset($_COOKIE['username']) ? $_COOKIE['username'] : FALSE;

  echo "The username is: $username";

  if (!$username)
  {
    $username = 'admin';
    setcookie('username', $username, time() + 604800);
  }
  else setcookie('username', $username, time() - 3600);
?>
  </body>
</html>
```

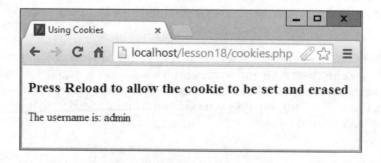

FIGURE 18-1 Creating, reading, and deleting a cookie

The beginning part of this example simply outputs some HTML, before entering a section of PHP code where the first thing that happens is the variable $username is assigned the value in the cookie with the name of username. If there is no such cookie, $username is given the value FALSE.

If an attempt was made to simply read the cookie directly, there is potential for an error to be thrown if the cookie doesn't have a value. Therefore, instead a call to the isset() function is first made, and only if it returns TRUE (indicating that there is a retrievable value) is the value then read by extracting it from the $_COOKIE[] array:

```
$username = isset($_COOKIE['username']) ? $_COOKIE['username'] : FALSE;
```

Next, the value in $username is output. This will either be a string, the value FALSE (which will cause the variable's value to be displayed), or nothing:

```
echo "The username is: $username";
```

After this, $username is then tested using an if() statement. If it doesn't have a value, it is assigned the string admin:

```
$username = 'admin';
```

Then a cookie is set with the name of username and given the value in $username. The cookie is set to expire in one week:

```
setcookie('username', $username, time() + 60 * 60 * 24 * 7);
```

The matching else part of the if() statement is selected only if $username does have a value, in which case it erases the cookie username:

```
else setcookie('username', $username, time() - 3600);
```

The result of this is to toggle the variable $username between having the value FALSE and the value admin each time the page is reloaded. Although not particularly useful in a production website, this is a good example of the three main things you can do with cookies. Try the program for yourself by loading *cookies.php* from the companion archive into a browser and clicking the Reload button a few times.

Browser Identification

Even in the current times of greater browser compatibility, there still remain differences between all the major browsers, and sometimes you'll find you need to determine the user's browser in order to tailor your PHP output to provide the best possible experience. For example, it can be helpful to know if a user is browsing on a mobile device such as a phone or tablet.

To do this, you can process the user agent string that the browser passes to PHP. Every web page request supplies a user agent string passed to it by well-behaved browsers, and you can usually rely on this string to determine information about the user's computer and web browser. However, some browsers allow the user to modify the user agent string, and some web spiders and other "bots" use misleading user agents, or even don't provide any user agent string.

Nevertheless, on the whole it is a very handy item of data to make use of, and takes a form such as the following formidable-looking user agent string. (Note that each string can be different from any other due to the way the browser is configured, its brand and version, the add-ons in it, the operating system used, and so on.)

```
Mozilla/5.0 (Windows NT 6.3; WOW64; Trident/7.0; MALNJS; rv:11.0) like
Gecko
```

This string states that the browser is Internet Explorer 11 (because of the layout engine `Trident/7.0` and version string `rv:11.0`). The browser is broadly compatible with version 5 of Mozilla-based browsers such as Firefox (both the terms `Mozilla/5.0` and `like Gecko` supply this information). The operating system is Windows 8.1 (because of the string `Windows NT 6.3`), and the browser is a Windows-On-Windows program (a 32-bit application running on a 64-bit operating system), as indicated by the string `WOW64`. The string `MALNJS` is a manufacturer code, which indicates that the current device is a Lenovo PC.

Many of these you can normally ignore, but the most useful piece of information is the browser type, because sometimes you need to tailor code to specific browsers (most frequently with Internet Explorer, due to a history of incorporating nonstandard features).

The `GetBrowser()` Function

To extract this information from the user agent string, you can use a function such as the following (the result of which is shown in Figure 18-2):

```
function GetBrowser()
{
  $UA = $_SERVER['HTTP_USER_AGENT'];

  if      (strstr($UA, 'MSIE'))     return 'IE';
  elseif (strstr($UA, 'Trident')) return 'IE';
  elseif (strstr($UA, 'Opera'))   return 'Opera';
  elseif (strstr($UA, 'OPR'))     return 'Opera';
  elseif (strstr($UA, 'Chrome'))  return 'Chrome';
  elseif (strstr($UA, 'iPod'))    return 'iPod';
  elseif (strstr($UA, 'iPhone'))  return 'iPhone';
  elseif (strstr($UA, 'iPad'))    return 'iPad';
  elseif (strstr($UA, 'Android')) return 'Android';
  elseif (strstr($UA, 'Safari'))  return 'Safari';
  elseif (strstr($UA, 'Firefox')) return 'Firefox';
  elseif (strstr($UA, 'Gecko'))   return 'Firefox';
  else                            return 'Unknown';
}
```

In this code, the user agent string is retrieved from the `$_SERVER[]` superglobal array and then tested for all major browsers such as Internet Explorer, Opera,

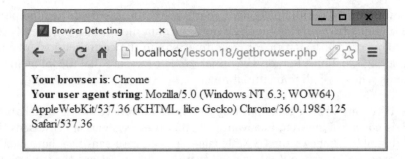

FIGURE 18-2   Reporting the browser type and user agent string

Google Chrome, Apple Safari, Mozilla Firefox, Google Android, and various Apple iOS devices. The function uses the `strstr()` function to interrogate the user agent string, and the result is saved in the variable $UA. It returns the browser found (or the string Unknown if no browser is recognized).

There is more than one test for some browsers due to differing user agent strings for older versions, so all browsers of the last few years should return the correct string. You can test the code for yourself using the file *getbrowser.php* in the archive downloadable from the companion website at *20lessons.com*.

 Another PHP function, called `get_browser()`, will return information about the features the current browser is capable of handling, including frames, JavaScript, cookies, and more. See the URL php.net/manual/en/function.get-browser.php for more details.

File Handling

One of the best ways to store and retrieve large amounts of data in PHP is using the MySQL database. However, just teaching MySQL involves enough material that it would take up a separate book—in fact, several books have been written on the subject.

Because this is a course on PHP, not PHP/MySQL, I won't digress into how you use it here. Anyway, as a beginner there's no need to quite yet, because you can perform an amazing amount of data storage and retrieval using simple flat files and the built-in PHP file-handling commands.

They are fast and even support file locking (explained in the following lesson) to allow multiple accesses to the same file at the same time (taking turns, though, of course). In fact, to gain maximum speed where complex database functions are not required, I sometimes use flat files for basic data storage, because it removes all the overhead that running MySQL requires, enabling many more users to interact with the data at a time.

However, once you need to start searching through data or need to perform more complicated data operations such as merging data files and so on, the MySQL overhead starts to become less significant in comparison to the complications of convoluted file-handling functions. But for a beginner to PHP, I'm sure that the following file-handling functions will serve all your initial needs.

> If you are writing code that may be used on a variety of PHP installations, there is no way of knowing in advance whether these systems are case-sensitive. For example, Windows and OS X filenames are not case-sensitive, but Linux and Unix ones are. Therefore, I recommend that you always assume the system your program is running on is case-sensitive, and therefore stick to a convention such as only allowing all lowercase filenames.

Testing for a File Existing

One of the first things you may need to do is test whether a file already exists before writing to it. Often this will be because you are going to keep updating the file, but it hasn't yet been created. To determine whether a file exists, simply call the `file_exists()` function with the filename of the file to examine, like this:

```
if (file_exists('myfile.info')) echo 'File exists';
```

The `file_exists()` function returns TRUE if a file already exists; otherwise, it returns FALSE. If you don't specify a path along with the filename, the file is looked for in the current folder (the one the PHP code has been called up from). To access a different location, preface the filename with a suitable path.

If your code will be distributed, and therefore might be running on any of a number of platforms, you will not be able to specify an absolute path, so I recommend using relative paths, like this (not just for testing for a file's existence, but for all file operations):

```
if (file_exists('../myfiles/myfile.info')) echo 'File exists';
```

If you are writing code for a particular server, though, you can use absolute paths, but I still caution you that you could well find you have to port your code at some future time. Therefore, I recommend you keep these paths in global variables specified at the head of your code, like this:

```
$GLOBALS['mypath'] = '/usr/home/peter/';
```

Then, whenever you access files, you can attach the path, like this:

```
if (file_exists($GLOBALS['mypath'] . 'myfile.info'))
  echo 'File exists';
```

Now, should you ever have to modify your code, all you need to do is change this and any other global path variables you have defined, and your code should be set to run on a new server and/or from a new location.

Of course, another method you might employ to save such a global value is to create a constant, like this: `define('MYPATH', '/usr/home/peter/');`. (This was discussed in Lesson 4.) You can then refer to the constant's value using simply the word `MYPATH` (without a $ symbol). For the sake of brevity, though, the following examples use only local filenames, so if you intend to modify any of the code to your own purposes, it's up to you to add in any paths.

Creating or Opening a File

To open files for reading or writing, you use the `fopen()` function and pass the filename (and optional path), along with a second argument that tells PHP in what mode to open the file. So, to open one for writing, you would use a statement such as this:

```
$filehandle = fopen('myfile.info', 'w');
```

This opens the file *myfile.info* for writing because of the w argument. A handle with which the file can be accessed while it is opened is returned by `fopen()`, and here it is saved in the variable `$filehandle`.

You can supply several different values to `fopen()` for specifying the way to open a file:

- **r**   Opens a file for reading only, and places the file pointer at the start of the file. If the file doesn't exist, FALSE is returned.
- **r+**   Opens a file for reading and writing, and places the file pointer at the start of the file. If the file doesn't exist, FALSE is returned.
- **w**   Opens a file for writing only, and places the file pointer at the start of the file. If the file exists, the file's length is truncated to 0. If it doesn't exist, the file is created. On error, FALSE is returned.
- **w+**   Opens a file for writing and reading, and places the file pointer at the start of the file. If the file exists, the file's length is truncated to 0. If it doesn't exist, the file is created. On error, FALSE is returned.
- **a**   Opens the file for writing only, and places the file pointer at the end of the file. If it doesn't exist, the file is created. On error, FALSE is returned.
- **a+**   Opens the file for reading and writing, and places the file pointer at the end of the file. If it doesn't exist, the file is created. On error, FALSE is returned.
- **b**   On systems such as Windows that differentiate between text and binary files, when writing binary data you will need to include a b alongside whichever preceding specifier you also apply (for example, `fopen('file', 'wb');` or `fopen('file', 'rb+');`).

Writing to a File

To write to a file that is open, you use the `fwrite()` function, to which you pass the file handle that was returned by calling `fopen()`, and the data to be written, like this:

```
fwrite($filehandle, 'Hello, this is a test');
```

You can write a small string (as in the preceding statement), or a very large one, up to the single file length capacity of the current file system. The data written is saved in the file starting at the current file pointer location. In addition to strings, you can also write binary data (such as an image file).

If the file has only just been opened using an argument of r+, w, or w+, the writing will begin at the start of the file. But if it was opened using a or a+, the writing will take place at the file's end (the data will be appended).

If fwrite() cannot write to the file, it will return a value of FALSE (otherwise, on success, it returns the number of bytes written), so it's always a good idea to access fwrite() in a manner such as the following:

```
$flag = fwrite($filehandle, 'Hello, this is a test');
if (!$flag == FALSE) die('Fatal error: could not write to file.');
```

The die() function outputs the string passed to it and then exits from PHP, so it's equivalent to the following two statements, but is simpler and more compact:

```
echo 'Fatal error: could not write to file.';
exit;
```

You would probably use more user-friendly error handling than this, by the way, but you get the picture.

Closing a File

To close a file when you have finished accessing it, you issue a call to fclose(), passing it the file handle, like this:

```
fclose($filehandle);
```

This will flush any as yet unwritten data to the file and then close it. After that point, $filehandle will be invalid, unless that variable is used again when opening another file.

Reading from a File

A file that has been opened in one of the modes that supports reading can be read from in different ways. First, you can read in a single character using fgetc(), like this:

```
$char = fgetc($filehandle);
```

This will advance the file pointer by 1 and store the character retrieved in $char. But this is an unwieldy way to read from a file, so there's also the fgets() function, which will read in a line from the file up to the next newline character (\n) that it encounters, or the end of file, whichever comes first, like this:

```
$line = fgets($filehandle);
```

If a newline is encountered, it will be returned as part of the line. You can also specify a maximum number of characters to read in a second argument, like this (ensuring, in this case, that no more than 249 characters will be read in):

```
$line = fgets($filehandle, 250);
```

As you can see, you must supply a value plus 1, so if you want to read up to 250 characters, you should provide an argument value of 251. If fgets() encounters an error or if there is no more data to read, it will return FALSE, so it's also a good idea to check the returned value before using it, like this:

```
$line = fgets($filehandle, 250);
if ($line == FALSE) die('Fatal error: could not read from file.');
```

Or you can use the following shorthand equivalent:

```
$line = fgets($filehandle, 250) or die('Fatal error: could not read from
file.');
```

The preceding functions are handy for reading text files, but if you are reading from a binary file, you will probably want to use the fread() function, which reads in an exact number of bytes, unless the end of file is reached, like this:

```
$data = fread($filehandle, 512);
```

This statement will read in 512 bytes from the file (or less if the end of file is reached first). Should you want to read in an entire file at once, you can issue a statement such as this:

```
$data = fread($filehandle, filesize($filename));
```

By using filesize() to return the length of the file (remembering to also enter a path, if necessary), you can quickly pull in the entire file in one go. As with the other similar functions, if an error is encountered, fread() will return FALSE.

Summary

You now know how to tailor code to individual browsers whenever it (unfortunately) is necessary. You can also save and read cookies from a user's device and know how to create, read from, write to, and test for the existence of files. In the following lesson, we'll look at some more advanced file-handling techniques as well as ways of maintaining sessions to help keep your users logged in or their shopping carts active across multiple pages on a site.

Self-Test Questions

Test how much you have learned in this lesson with these questions. If you don't know an answer, go back and reread the relevant section until your knowledge is complete. You can find the answers in the appendix.

1. How can you set a cookie with the name `cookie` and value `choc-chip`, with an expiry date of 30 day's time?

2. How can you read the value (if there is one) of a cookie named `cookie`?

3. How can you delete a cookie (give an example)?

4. What is a good way to determine the make of browser and the platform it is running on?

5. How can you test for the preexistence of a file on your web server?

6. How can you open a file for writing to, and how do you retain access to that file for later write operations?

7. With what command can you write the string `'This is a sentence'` to a file opened in write mode?

8. How can you open a file for reading?

9. With a file opened in read mode, which command can you use to read in a string of up to a maximum of 100 characters, or the next newline or file end (whichever comes first)?

10. With a file opened in read mode, how can you read in exactly 1,000 bytes (or up to the file end, if sooner)?

Advanced File Handling

To view the accompanying video for this lesson, please visit mhprofessional.com/
nixonphp/.

In this lesson, we'll clear up the remaining aspects of file handling by introducing
functions with even greater power to make the manipulation of on-server data even
easier (even across servers in different locations). We'll also look at reading from or
writing to just parts of files using random access techniques, where you seek to the
part of the file you need and just read or write at that location, as well as how to lock
files when accessing them to prevent concurrent users corrupting data.

Combining File Functions

Let's start by looking at an example that brings many of the file functions from the
previous lesson together in the form of a very simple shopping list app (or it could
serve as a reminder or to-do list app) that allows you to add and delete entries from
the list, keeping track of the current contents in a text file, as shown in Figure 19-1:

```php
<?php
  $message = '';

  if (isset($_POST['list']))
  {
    $mylist = htmlentities($_POST['list']);
    $handle = @fopen('shopping.txt', 'w')
      or $message = 'Could not open file for writing';
    @fwrite($handle, $mylist) != FALSE
      or $message = 'Could not save file';
    @fclose($handle);
```

```php
    }
    elseif (file_exists('shopping.txt'))
    {
      $handle = @fopen('shopping.txt', 'r')
        or $message = 'Could not open file for reading';
      $length = filesize('shopping.txt');
      $mylist = @fread($handle, $length)
        or $message = 'Could not read file';
      @fclose($handle);
    }
    else $mylist = "Bread\nCheese\nMilk\nEggs\nButter\nChips\n";

    $self = $_SERVER['PHP_SELF'];

    echo <<<_EOT
<!DOCTYPE html>
<html>
  <head>
    <title>File Handling 1</title>
    <style>
      textarea {
        width :150px;
        height:150px;
        resize:none;
      }
    </style>
  </head>
  <body>
    <h3>Your Shopping List</h3>
    <form method='post' action='$self'>
      <textarea name='list'>$mylist</textarea><br>
      <input type='submit' value='Save list'>
      <a href='$self'>Reload</a>
    </form><br>
    $message
  </body>
</html>
_EOT;
?>
```

There are two separate parts to this program. In the first, all the file-handling operations take place. In the second part, rather than dropping out of PHP back to HTML, PHP is used to output all the HTML for the web page, so that PHP variables can be placed right into the HTML at the relevant places. This is managed using a heredoc structure, located within the <<<_EOT and _EOT; tags.

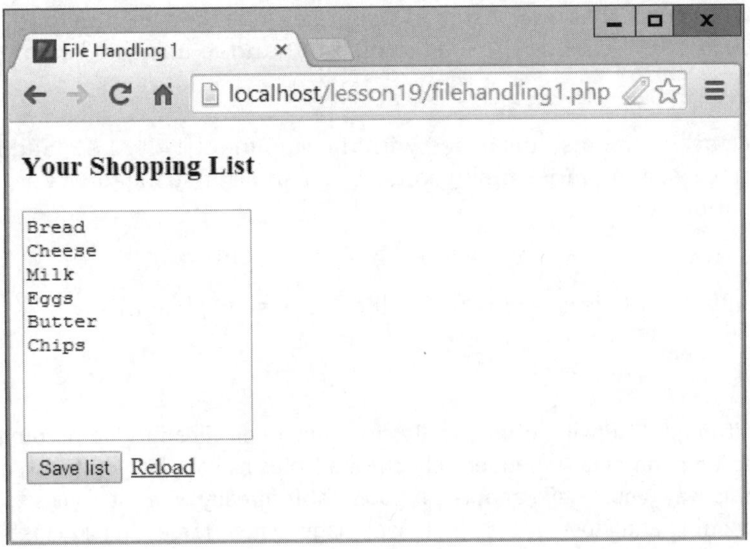

FIGURE 19-1   Maintaining a shopping list on the server

Saving Any Form Data

Looking at the first section, you can see that it is divided into three subsections. The first of which uses the isset() function to test whether any form data has been posted using the name (or key) list:

```
if (isset($_POST['list']))
```

If it has, the user has updated the information and it therefore needs processing, beginning with sanitizing the input to make it safe for use with the htmlentities() function:

```
$mylist = htmlentities($_POST['list']);
```

With the sanitized form data now safely in the variable $mylist, a handle called $handle is then created to access a file in the current folder named *shopping.txt*, using write mode:

```
$handle = @fopen('shopping.txt', 'w') != FALSE
```

If an error occurs during this process, a result of -1 will be returned, which is tested with the trailing != FALSE statement. If so, the following or statement sets the variable $message (initialized to '' at the start of the program, so that by default no error will be displayed) to a string explaining the problem:

```
or $message = 'Could not open file for writing';
```

Next, the data that was posted to the program is then written to the disk with a call to `fwrite()`, passing the file handle in `$handle` and the data in `$mylist`:

```
@fwrite($handle, $mylist) != FALSE
```

Once again, the result is tested with the statement `!= FALSE`, and if there was an error, the `or` statement is employed to assign an error string to `$message` should the file operation fail:

```
or $message = 'Could not save file';
```

Finally, the file is closed with a call to `fclose()`, like this:

```
@fclose($handle);
```

 Although PHP will automatically close any open files for you on program exit, it's still a good idea to deliberately close all files as soon as you finish accessing them. This way, you'll have adopted a good habit already when it comes to multiple file opening and closing in a single web page, where forgetting to close a file could cause very nasty mangling of data.

I'm sure you'll have noticed something strange in this code, in that `@fopen()`, `@fwrite()`, and `@fclose()` all have an `@` symbol prefacing them. The reason for this is that you can suppress PHP error messages by placing that symbol in front of the functions you call.

Although this is usually not a good idea on its own (because you'll be oblivious to important information you may need to know), if you have written your own error-handling (as we have here), it does makes sense to disable the system messages in favor of your own more user-friendly ones. It also means users aren't confronted with two different types of messages for each error.

Reading from the Data File

In the next section (which is entered only if no data was posted), an `elseif()` statement calls the `file_exists()` function to determine whether the file *shopping. txt* exists:

```
elseif (file_exists('shopping.txt'))
```

If it does, a handle to the file in read mode is created in `$handle`, and if an error is encountered, an `or` statement ensures a message will be placed in `$message`:

```
$handle = @fopen('shopping.txt', 'r')
  or $message = 'Could not open file for reading';
```

Then, we assign the length of the file to `$length` by looking it up with the `filesize()` function:

```
$length = filesize('shopping.txt');
```

Using the variables just assigned, we read in the contents of the file, with an or statement setting $message to a relevant value if there is any problem with the operation, and then the file is closed:

```
$mylist = @fread($handle, $length)
  or $message = 'Could not read file';
@fclose($handle);
```

Prepopulating the Shopping List

In the third section (which is only reached if no data was posted, and the file *shopping .txt* was not found), the variable $mylist is populated with six items, each followed by a \n escape character to place a new line after it when displayed in the HTML <textarea> element later on:

```
else $mylist = "Bread\nCheese\nMilk\nEggs\nButter\nChips\n";
```

There is one further instruction before the HTML is output, which simply sets the variable $self to refer to the current web document. This will enable the page to link to itself no matter where on a server it is located or what name it is given:

```
$self = $_SERVER['PHP_SELF'];
```

 In a larger program it might be a good idea to create a constant to hold a value such as this (which cannot change throughout the life of the script). See Lesson 4 for more details on constants.

The HTML Section

The HTML begins at the start of a heredoc section, like this:

```
echo <<<_EOT
```

It uses a little CSS to style the <textarea> element and then displays it within a <form> element, alongside an <input> element to submit edited data for saving to disk.

The variable $self is used to refer to the document itself in two places: once where the form action is set, and again where a link is made to enable the page to be reloaded without submitting the current contents of the form.

The variable $mylist is placed inside the <textarea> element to display the shopping list data, and, finally, $message is placed just before the <body> closes. If no errors have been encountered, it will contain the empty string; otherwise, the error string assigned to it will be displayed. The heredoc is then closed and the page is complete:

```
_EOT;
```

When you load this document into a web browser, you can update the shopping list and click the Save List button to save it to the server's hard disk. You can verify that this has correctly occurred by clicking the Reload link at any time, which forces the program to start from scratch without posting the current data. You need to use the link, because if you use a browser's Reload button, it will prompt you to resubmit the form data, which you don't want to happen.

Anyway, when you click the Reload link, if there is any data saved on the web server, it will be read in and displayed. Therefore, if you have updated the list and saved it, you will see your changes have been recorded—that is, if all is working as it should (and you have set appropriate file permissions).

Even Simpler File Accessing

For very quickly grabbing the contents of a file, you can use the `file_get_contents()` function. Simply call it with the filename to read, and the entire contents of that file will be returned. For example, the second section of PHP code can be replaced with the following, much more concise equivalent:

```
elseif (file_exists('shopping.txt'))
{
  $mylist = @file_get_contents('shopping.txt') != FALSE
    or $message = 'Could not retrieve file';
}
```

As you can see, this function opens, reads, and closes the requested file for you, so it's very powerful, and generally the better option when you want to read in an entire file.

And you can also replace the first `if` statement with the following shorter replacement, which uses the partner `file_put_contents()` function, as shown in Figure 19-2:

```
if (isset($_POST['list']))
{
  $mylist = htmlentities($_POST['list']);
  @file_put_contents('shopping.txt', $mylist) != FALSE
    or $message = 'Could not save file';
}
```

In fact, the function is so powerful that you can even supply a URL to it, and the document (or even binary data) at that URL will be returned. Now this *is* handy because in the old days of the Net, programmers used to have to play with opening web sockets and other arcane features in order to access documents from across the Web, but now it's as easy as the following short example (as shown in Figure 19-3):

```
<?php
  $url  = 'http://upload.wikimedia.org/wikipedia/commons/thumb/' .
          '8/85/Smiley.svg/600px-Smiley.svg.png';
```

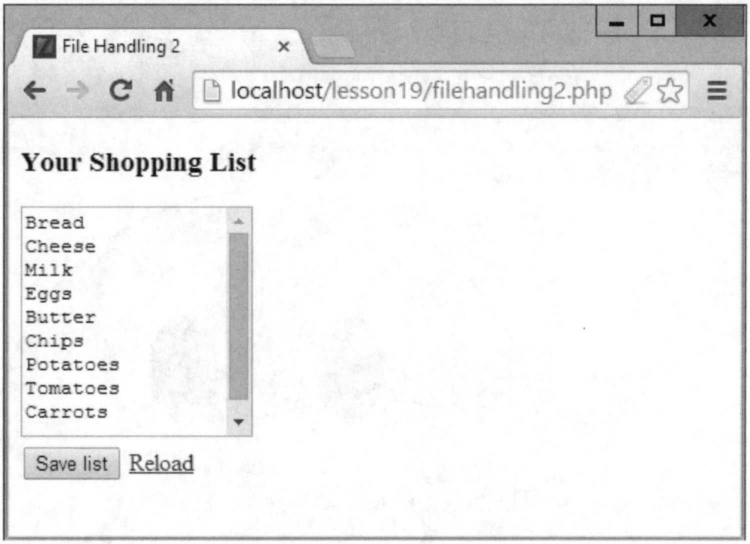

FIGURE 19-2   The shorter and simpler code works just as well.

```php
    $name = 'smiley.png';

    if (!file_exists($name))
    {
      $image = file_get_contents($url);
      file_put_contents($name, $image);
    }

    echo <<<_EOT
<!DOCTYPE html>
<html>
  <head>
    <title>Cross-Web File Handling</title>
  </head>
  <body>
    <h3>Here's a smiley from Wikimedia</h3>
    The image was fetched from <i>$url</i> and saved locally<br>
    (Examine the page source to confirm)
    <img src='$name'>
  </body>
</html>
_EOT;
?>
```

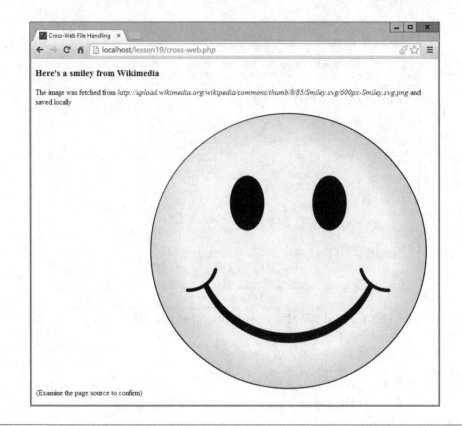

FIGURE 19-3 Copying an image from a remote server to serve up locally

This code fetches an image from the Wikimedia servers and stores it in `$smiley`, before saving a copy to the local disk using `file_put_contents()`, and then displaying it later on in the HTML section. It's also very web friendly in that the cross-web access is made only once, because after the image has been fetched for the first request, the `file_exists()` function call in future requests will report that the local copy exists, and so no further attempt will be made to get that file.

 Using `file_put_contents()`, you can also write to other servers to which you have access, but this is too complex a procedure for this lesson. However, if you are interested in doing this, you can check out the following URL for details: php. net/manual/en/function.file-put-contents.php. Also, you should always ensure that you have sufficient rights to access third-party servers in these ways.

File Copying

To copy a file, you don't need to open one, read it in, and then write out another; instead, there's a PHP function to do it for you, called simply copy(). Just supply the source and destination filenames (including paths as necessary), like this:

```
copy('original.file', 'copied.file') != FALSE
  or die("Could not copy file");
```

The != FALSE statement tests the returned value, whereas the or keyword saves you from having to use an if() statement for evaluating the test, and thus is simpler than (for example) the following:

```
$flag = copy('original.file', 'copied.file');
if ($flag == FALSE) die("Could not copy file");
```

File Deleting

To delete a file, you use the unlink() function, like this:

```
if (unlink('original.file') == FALSE)
  die("Could not delete file");
```

This statement also shows another way of catching and dealing with an error. In this case, the returned value is directly tested. It's not quite as elegant as using or after the function, but it's another method you can choose to use.

 Beware that if you are calling unlink() based on user input, you must make sure to first sanitize the input sufficiently that you won't be deleting something on your server that you shouldn't be.

File Moving

If you no longer need it, you can always delete the original file after making a copy, but it's probably quicker and simpler to simply move the original file using the rename() function, like this:

```
rename('original.file', 'copied.file') != FALSE
  or die("Cannot rename.");
```

Like with the other functions, if the file cannot be renamed, FALSE is returned.

Random Access

Using the file pointer that every open file has, you can move about within files. This gives you what is called *random access* to the file, in which you can move the file pointer wherever you like, to read in and (if the file was opened in the right way) write out data.

To move a file's pointer, you use the fseek() function, to which you pass the file handle, an offset value, and (optionally) an argument that specifies where the seek should be from. For example, to seek all the way back to the start of a file, you would issue this call:

```
fseek($filehandle, 0);
```

This is directly equivalent to using the rewind() function, like this:

```
rewind($filehandle)
```

You can supply three optional values as a third argument to fseek(), as follows:

- **SEEK_SET** Seeks from the file's start
- **SEEK_CUR** Seeks from the current file pointer
- **SEEK_END** Seeks from the file's end

Of these, SEEK_SET is the default, so the following are equivalent to each other:

```
fseek($filehandle, 0);
fseek($filehandle, 0, SEEK_SET);
```

To move the file pointer to the end of a file, you would use this statement:

```
fseek($filehandle, 0, SEEK_END);
```

When using the default or SEEK_SET, you must use positive seek values to seek forward into the file. Likewise, when using SEEK_END, you must use negative values to seek backward from the end (because positive values always advance the file pointer further away from the file's start, but with SEEK_END the pointer is already at the file's end).

When you use SEEK_CUR, you can supply either negative values to seek backward from or positive values to seek forward from the current file pointer location. And to determine where the file pointer is in a file, you can call the ftell() function, like this:

```
$filepointer = ftell($filehandle);
```

Note If you have opened the file in append (a or a+) mode, any data you write to the file will *always* be appended, regardless of the file position, and the result of calling fseek() will therefore be undefined.

Writing to a Random Access File

To write to a file, you use the `fwrite()` function, which takes a file handle, the data to write, and (optionally) the length of data to write, like this:

```
fwrite($filehandle, $string);
```

If a length argument is given, writing will stop after the number of bytes specified have been written, or the end of string is reached, whichever comes first. Therefore, the following will write a maximum of 64 bytes:

```
fwrite($filehandle, $string, 64);
```

The writing always takes place at the current file pointer position, which then gets updated after the write (to the next location following the data that was just written).

If `fwrite()` fails, it returns FALSE; otherwise, it returns the number of bytes that were written. The second argument doesn't necessarily have to be a string, because you can also supply binary data.

Managing Directories

To create a new directory (assuming PHP has the correct permissions in the file system to do so), you call the `mkdir()` function, like this:

```
mkdir('newfolder');
```

This will create a new directory called *newfolder* in the current directory. Include a path with the filename if you need a directory created elsewhere. Upon error, this function returns FALSE.

On a Unix/Linux system, the default file mode for the directory will be 0777, which means full access for all users. This is not very secure, so you can restrict the mode with a second argument, like this (which allows full access by the file's owner, but limits write access by other users):

```
mkdir('newfolder', 0755);
```

To remove (delete) a directory (which must be empty), use the `rmdir()` function, like this (along with any path, as necessary):

```
rmdir('newfolder');
```

The complete list of PHP file-handling functions (of which there are dozens) can be found at php.net/manual/en/ref.filesystem.php.

 Note   Again, always be careful if you are creating and/or deleting folders based on user input.

File Locking

PHP has a built-in locking mechanism you can call on so that multiple users can access the same file at the same time, but via a queuing system so that each user gets access to the file in turn. One reason you might do this would be, for example, to update a guestbook with comments from your users (or perhaps to allow concurrent access to the shopping list example data file for additional family members).

Without locking, if two users were to submit an entry at precisely the same time, it's quite likely that only one comment would get posted. But worse than that, if two PHP scripts had the file open at the same time, it could even become corrupted and result in data loss.

Therefore, file locking is an absolutely must-have feature on multiuser websites, and to implement it you use the `flock()` function, in conjunction with the other file system function, like this:

```php
$handle = @fopen("guestbook.txt", 'a+') != FALSE
  or die("Cannot open file");

if (@flock($handle, LOCK_EX))              // Request lock
{
  $flag = @fwrite($handle, $comment);      // Write to file
  @flock($handle, LOCK_UN);                // Release lock
  if (!$flag) die("Cannot write to file"); // Must be after unlocking
}

@fclose($handle);
```

In this example, the file *guestbook.txt* is opened for appending to, which places the file pointer at the file's end ready for writing. If the opening didn't fail, the `flock()` function is called. It is passed the file handle of the newly opened file, along with a value of LOCK_EX, which locks the file exclusively.

This places a request to PHP saying, "Please give me exclusive access to this file," and then `flock()` waits patiently in any queue of similar requests until its turn comes up, and only then will it release access to the file.

Upon returning from `flock()`, the PHP code knows it now has exclusive access to the file, and so it writes out the contents of `$comment` to the file (or quits with an error message if that fails).

Once the file has been written to, the code calls `flock()` once more, but this time with a value of LOCK_UN, which tells PHP that it has finished with its exclusive access to the file and that PHP can now assign it to the next script (if any) waiting in the queue.

The initial `flock()` call is placed within an `if()` statement, because some file systems (such as FAT—particularly Windows 98) do not support file locking, and so it's a good idea to see whether or not you actually achieved a secure lock before trying to write to a file. In this case, if the attempted locking fails, program flow will fall through to the `fclose()` statement and nothing will be written to the file. This is better than possibly having corrupted files.

If you plan to use code such as this, you should probably consider placing a matching set of `else` statements after the `if()` to try another means of safely saving the file (or at least offering an error message to the user).

A Practical Example

Here's a very simple example of a working guestbook that you could incorporate on a website with a few tweaks:

```php
<?php
  $message   = '';
  $self      = $_SERVER['PHP_SELF'];
  $guestbook = '';

  if (isset($_POST['comment']))
  {
    $comment = '<li>' . htmlentities($_POST['comment']) . "</li>\n";
    $handle  = @fopen("guestbook.txt", 'a+')
      or $message = 'Cannot open file';

    if ($handle)
    {
      if (@flock($handle, LOCK_EX))
      {
        $flag = @fwrite($handle, $comment);
        @flock($handle, LOCK_UN);
        if ($flag == FALSE) $message = 'Cannot write to file';
      }

      @fclose($handle);
    }
  }

  $handle = @fopen("guestbook.txt", 'r') != FALSE
    or $message = 'Cannot open file';

  if ($handle)
  {
    $flag = TRUE;

    if (@flock($handle, LOCK_EX))
    {
      $length    = @filesize('guestbook.txt');
      $guestbook = @fread($handle, $length) or $flag = FALSE;
      @flock($handle, LOCK_UN);
```

```
      if ($flag == FALSE) $message = 'Cannot read file';
    }

    @fclose($handle);
  }

  echo <<<_EOT
<!DOCTYPE html>
<html>
  <head>
    <title>Guestbook</title>
    <style>
      textarea {
        width :300px;
        height:100px;
        resize:none;
      }
    </style>
  </head>
  <body>
    <h3>Guestbook</h3>
    <ol>$guestbook</ol>
    <form method='post' action='$self'>
      <textarea name='comment'></textarea><br>
      <input type='submit' value='Add Comment'>
    </form><br>
    $message
  </body>
</html>
_EOT;
?>
```

This code is similar to the previous couple of examples, and looks like Figure 19-4 when in use. It is split into the two parts—file handling and HTML output—and starts by assigning three variables:

```
$message   = '';
$self      = $_SERVER['PHP_SELF'];
$guestbook = '';
```

The $message variable will be used to display any errors, $self ensures the program will always post to itself, and $guestbook will contain any previously posted comments.

Next, a test is made to see whether a comment has been posted. If one has, it will be in $_POST['comment'], from where it is extracted, sanitized with the htmlentities() function, and placed within <li> and </li> tags for later display.

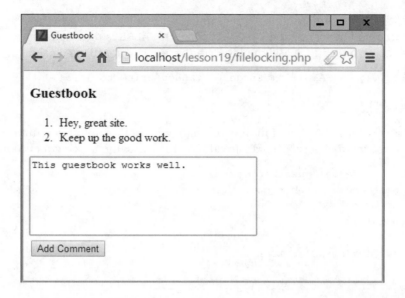

FIGURE 19-4 A simple guestbook with file locking

A \n escape character is also appended to enable the data file to be loaded into a text editor for manual viewing and editing:

```
if (isset($_POST['comment']))
{
  $comment = '<li>' . htmlentities($_POST['comment']) . "</li>\n";
```

Next, the file *guestbook.txt* is opened in append mode, and a handle to it is saved in $handle. If the file could not be opened, $message is assigned an error message string:

```
$handle = @fopen("guestbook.txt", 'a+') != FALSE
  or $message = 'Cannot open file';
```

Next, $handle is tested; if it has a value, the code to append to the file is entered and an exclusive file lock is obtained on it:

```
if ($handle)
{
  if (@flock($handle, LOCK_EX))
```

As soon as the program obtains the lock, it writes the contents of $comment to the file using fwrite(), assigning the value returned to $flag, and then the file lock is immediately released:

```
$flag = @fwrite($handle, $comment);
@flock($handle, LOCK_UN);
```

With the lock released, the program can then determine whether the file append was successful by testing the variable $flag. If FALSE is returned, there was a problem, and so an error string is assigned to $message: and the file is closed:

```
    if ($flag == FALSE) $message = 'Cannot write to file'
}
@fclose($handle);
```

Lastly, in the PHP section, regardless of whether or not any comment was just appended, the file *guestbook.txt* is read in using the same locking technique:

```
$handle = @fopen("guestbook.txt", 'r') != FALSE
  or $message = 'Cannot open file';

if ($handle)
{
  if (@flock($handle, LOCK_EX))
  {
    $length    = @filesize('guestbook.txt');
    $guestbook = @fread($handle, $length) or $flag = FALSE;
    @flock($handle, LOCK_UN);
    if (!$flag) $message = 'Cannot read file';
  }

  @fclose($handle);
}
```

Finally, any comments in the guest book are displayed within <ol> and </ol> tags, and then a form is displayed for adding new comments, underneath which $message displays any errors that are encountered.

For maximum response time (and minimum disruption to other waiting scripts), you should only lock a file exclusively immediately before you intend to access it. You should then release the lock as soon as possible after that. Any unnecessary delays between locking a file and releasing it will mount up on a busy system, and make it quite sluggish.

As it stands, until the first comment is posted, this example will display an error due to no guestbook file currently existing. To avoid this, you could create an empty *guestbook.txt* file in the current folder, or simply post a first welcome message yourself.

Note Because reading a file doesn't change it, you might think you wouldn't need file locking for file reading because there's no danger of corrupting a file. But on busy web servers it's possible that a read request could occur halfway through an update by another user, and so only a partial file might get read back. Therefore, you also need to lock files subject to updates by other users when reading from them. Also, never forget to close a file lock when you have finished with it, or you'll very quickly grind a server to a halt as all the requests back up.

Summary

This completes your introduction to all aspects of PHP file handling, and you're now able to manipulate files in multiple ways, across servers or locally, and with the necessary locking if required for concurrent users.

In the final lesson, we'll use these skills for maintaining a user's presence throughout the pages of a website with authentication and session handling, and even conduct background Ajax communications with the web server, to allow partial updates to web pages without requiring them to be reposted or reloaded.

Self-Test Questions

Test how much you have learned in this lesson with these questions. If you don't know an answer, go back and reread the relevant section until your knowledge is complete. You can find the answers in the appendix.

1. How can you prevent PHP from displaying its own messages when you call a function?

2. How can you determine the length of a file?

3. When writing text to a file, how can you insert newline characters?

4. With which single function can you open, read, and then close an entire file?

5. With which single function can you open, save, and then close an entire file?

6. How can you read in a web document or object from a URL?

7. With which command can you create a copy of a file?

8. With which command can you delete a file?

9. With which command can you move the pointer into an open file?

10. How can you prevent file accesses by one user conflicting with those by another, potentially causing file corruption?

Authentication, Sessions, and Ajax

 To view the accompanying video for this lesson, please visit mhprofessional.com/nixonphp/.

In this final lesson, we'll look at ways to keep track of the state of a user's interaction with a website (perhaps the contents of a shopping cart, or just their username and password) and maintain it across all pages on that site, by first authenticating users and then managing their access to your server with sessions.

Then we'll finish off by conducting background Ajax communications between a browser and web server. Ensuring that your server and your user's data remain secure is always a priority, and is also fully encompassed throughout this lesson.

Authentication

Using HTTP authentication, you can prevent access to certain areas of a website to unauthorized users. To do this, you maintain a list of valid usernames and passwords that are accepted by the server, and then add some code to your PHP that requests identification before granting access.

Let's start using an example where only one person, the administrator, is granted access, like this (see Figure 20-1):

```php
<?php
$username = 'admin';
$password = 'password';

if (!isset($_SERVER['PHP_AUTH_USER']) ||
    !isset($_SERVER['PHP_AUTH_PW']))
```

```php
{
  header('WWW-Authenticate: Basic realm="Restricted Section"');
  header('HTTP/1.0 401 Unauthorized');
  die ("Please enter your username and password");
}
else
{
  if ($_SERVER['PHP_AUTH_USER'] != $username ||
      $_SERVER['PHP_AUTH_PW']    != $password)
    die("Invalid username/password combination");
}
?>
<!DOCTYPE html>
<html>
  <head>
    <title>HTTP Authentication</title>
  </head>
  <body>
    <h2>Welcome. You are now logged in</h2>
  </body>
</html>
```

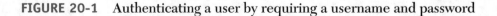

FIGURE 20-1 Authenticating a user by requiring a username and password

Here, the variables $username and $password are given values, and then the global array $_SERVER [] is tested to see whether both PHP_AUTH_USER and PHP_AUTH_PW have been entered by the user.

```
if (!isset($_SERVER['PHP_AUTH_USER']) ||
    !isset($_SERVER['PHP_AUTH_PW']))
```

If they haven't, the following statements are executed. These send headers to the browser that will cause the browser to request a username and password (the die() function being an easy way to display some text to the user and quit from PHP at the same time):

```
header('WWW-Authenticate: Basic realm="Restricted Section"');
header('HTTP/1.0 401 Unauthorized');
die ("Please enter your username and password");
```

Otherwise, if a username and password have been submitted, the ones received are checked against those stored in $username and $password. If they are not the same, the program exits with a suitable error message.

```
if ($_SERVER['PHP_AUTH_USER'] != $username ||
   $_SERVER['PHP_AUTH_PW']   != $password)
  die("Invalid username/password combination");
```

However, if they do match, program flow drops through to the HTML below to take over (or you could have more PHP code after the if() ... else and it would fall through to that).

Once a user has been authenticated, they can revisit the same page and, as long as they have not restarted their browser, they should be able to access the page without reauthenticating. A successful authentication is shown in Figure 20-2.

FIGURE 20-2   The user has been successfully authenticated.

 Using the file-handling functions, you could easily extend this code to support additional username/password pairs, which you could check against those input over HTTP authentication. I leave that as an exercise for you to practice your new PHP skills on.

Using Sessions

Sessions allow you to maintain a set of variables across multiple page loads for a user. Sessions are stored by default in special cookies in the user's browser, but if cookies are disabled, they will be saved in the query string, attached to the URL of subsequent web pages.

Because cookies are the most likely means of maintaining a session, you must start your session before any part of a web page has yet been output to the web browser, like this:

```
session_start() != FALSE
  or die('Could not start session');
```

Then you can store and retrieve session values using the superglobal $_SESSION[] array, like this:

```
$_SESSION['username'] = $username;
$_SESSION['password'] = $password;
```

 It is very rare for `session_start()` to return FALSE, and will probably only happen when you specify that cookies should be used for all session communication, but the user has disabled cookies in the browser. In such cases, you may have no alternative other than to ask the user to reenable cookies for the current website (or you could switch to allowing less secure Get requests for sessions). If, after this, you still encounter a return value of FALSE, you may need to ask the user to reload their browser, reboot their computer, or use a different browser.

Retrieving Session Variables

Once you have set these session variables, they will maintain their values throughout the user's current session on your site, and you can access these values from other web pages as long as you call `session_start()` before doing so (and before any part of the web page has been output), like this:

```
session_start() != FALSE
  or die('Could not start session');

$username = $_SESSION['username'];
$password = $_SESSION['password'];
```

You can also store other pieces of information in a session, such as any other user details (like their email address), products they have in a shopping cart, and so on.

Combining Authentication with Sessions

Once authenticated for a given folder on a server, a user has access to all the files in that folder (and subfolders), but you don't necessarily know anything else about that person. However, using sessions you can store all the data you need about a user so that, in conjunction with authentication, you not only have a secure web server that only users with the correct credentials can access, you can also track them throughout the website, keeping details such as preferences and items in shopping carts fully up to date.

So let's add session handling to the authentication example so that after successful authentication, a session is started in which (for this example) the username and password are saved. To do this, all that needs to be added to the previous example (before any HTML is output) is the following:

```
session_start();
$_SESSION['username'] = $username;
$_SESSION['password'] = $password;
```

Then let's test the session by adding a link to the HTML section, like this:

```
<a href='sessions.php'>Check out this page</a>
```

Now, as Figure 20-3 shows, when you log in, there is a link you can click.

FIGURE 20-3   A link has been added to the authentication page.

Picking Up Session Details

Following is what the *sessions.php* program just referred to might look like. It's a simple program that displays some HTML, and within it the username and password of the user, as retrieved from the current session, are displayed:

```
<?php
  $username = '';
  $password = '';
```

```
  session_start() != FALSE
    or die('Could not start session');

  if (isset($_SESSION['username'])) $username = $_SESSION['username'];
  if (isset($_SESSION['password'])) $password = $_SESSION['password'];

  echo <<<_EOT
<!DOCTYPE html>
<html>
  <head>
    <title>Using Sessions</title>
  </head>
  <body>
    <h2>You are currently logged in as '$username'</h2>
    (And your password is: '$password')
  </body>
</html>
_EOT;
?>
```

First, $username and $password are initialized to empty strings, and then there's a call to session_start() to begin a session:

```
$username = '';
$password = '';

session_start() != FALSE
  or die('Could not start session');
```

Then, if the $_SESSION[] array contains username or password keys, their associated values are extracted into $username and $password:

```
if (isset($_SESSION['username'])) $username = $_SESSION['username'];
if (isset($_SESSION['password'])) $password = $_SESSION['password'];
```

The remainder of the program simply consists of outputting some HTML using a heredoc construct, in which the values in $username and $password are included. As shown in Figure 20-4, it's extremely easy to provide sessional support to your web users and customize your websites to their needs.

You can now reload the page as often as you like and, without you pasting any data from a form, or otherwise sending the username or password details, they are still available to the document because they have been saved in the session that is being managed by PHP. Through the use of cookies (or sometimes the query string), PHP knows the same user is accessing the page and can therefore provide the correct session variables when requested.

FIGURE 20-4   The session variables are easily accessed.

Closing a Session

To close a session, you need to reset the $_SESSION[] array so that it is empty and then remove any cookies. The following function will do all that's needed for you:

```
function CloseSession()
{
  $_SESSION = array();
  if (session_id() != "" || isset($_COOKIE[session_name()]))
    setcookie(session_name(), '', time() - 3600, '/');
  session_destroy();
}
```

The first line empties the $_SESSION[] array; then the second line uses the session_name() function to find the name of the current session (if there is one), which is then removed from the user's computer by saving a new cookie of the same name, but with an expiry date and time of one hour in the past. Finally, the session_destroy() function is called to clean everything up.

Between all these things, you can be sure that a session is completely closed. However, you must ensure you call the function prior to outputting any part of the HTML page.

Session Security

There is a hack whereby a malicious user will log in to a website so that a session gets started, and they make sure they have cookies disabled so that the session ID gets displayed in the address bar where they can see it. Then they may pass this URL on via spam or social networking sites in the hope that someone will click it.

If someone does click it, they could find themselves inheriting the malicious person's session, and might even enter sensitive details about themselves that also get stored in the session. And if the hacker then comes back and also enters that URL (with the same session ID), they might be able to retrieve those details.

To prevent this possibility, when you first create a session for a user, I recommend you also save a copy of that user's IP address and their User Agent string, saving them as session variables. Having done that, on each new page load, you can check the user's IP and User Agent against those in the session. If they match, then all's well and good. If not, then something funny's going on, and you can close the session immediately.

Here's how to add those items of data to a session:

```
$_SESSION['ip'] = $_SERVER['REMOTE_ADDR'];
$_SESSION['ua'] = $_SERVER['HTTP_USER_AGENT'];
```

Now, each time you load in session variables, you can perform a quick security check at the same time, like this:

```
session_start();

if (($_SESSION['ip'] != $_SERVER['REMOTE_ADDR']) ||
    ($_SESSION['ua'] != $_SERVER['HTTP_USER_AGENT'])
{
  CloseSession();
  // Code here to open a new session
}
```

In this code, a session is started (before outputting any part of the web page to the browser), and then the first thing after that is a test to see whether the saved User Agent string and IP numbers match those for the current browser. If not, the `CloseSession()` function (in the previous section) is called, and then you need to place code of your own to open a brand-new session for this user—perhaps with a message saying, "Sorry, you were logged out; please sign in again," or something similar.

 A simpler alternative is to require your users to always allow cookies from your site (not an unreasonable request on a shopping or similar site) and force sessions to only use cookies by issuing the statement: `ini_set('session.use_only_cookies', 1);`. Now you won't need to keep checking for session hacking, and life will be a lot easier for everyone.

Using Ajax

Ajax is the power behind what came to be known as Web 2.0. It transformed the Internet, because it replaced static pages that had to be posted using forms to make changes, with much simpler behind-the-scenes communication with a web server—you merely had to type on a web page for that data to get sent to the server. Likewise, Ajax-enabled sites offer assistance whenever you need it (for example, by instantly telling you whether a username you desire is available, before you submit your signup details).

The term *Ajax* actually stands for Asynchronous JavaScript and XML. However, nowadays it almost never uses XML, because Ajax can communicate so much more than just that particular markup language. For example, it can transfer images and videos as well as other files.

Initially, writing Ajax code was considered a black art that only the most advanced programmers knew how to implement, but that's not actually the case. Ajax is relatively straightforward. However, it does require you to use JavaScript—but even if you are not familiar with the language, you should still be able to make use of the following examples in your own web pages.

Creating an Ajax Object

The first thing you need to do in order to communicate with a web server via Ajax is to create a new JavaScript object, as performed by the following `CreateAjaxObject()` function:

```
function CreateAjaxObject(callback)
{
  try
  {
    var ajax = new XMLHttpRequest()
  }
  catch(e1)
  {
    try
    {
      ajax = new ActiveXObject("Msxml2.XMLHTTP")
    }
    catch(e2)
    {
      try
      {
        ajax = new ActiveXObject("Microsoft.XMLHTTP")
      }
      catch(e3)
      {
        ajax = false
      }
    }
  }

  if (ajax) ajax.onreadystatechange = function()
  {
    if (this.readyState    == 4    &&
        this.status        == 200 &&
```

```
            this.responseText != null)
        callback.call(this.responseText)
    }
  else return false

  return ajax
}
```

Let's break this down, because it's quite long (although easy to understand). To start with, the `CreateAjaxObject()` function accepts the argument `callback`, which I'll explain shortly. Then, a sequence of `try` and `catch()` keywords attempt to use three different methods to create a new Ajax object in `ajax`.

The reason for this is that various older versions of Microsoft's Internet Explorer browser use different methods for this, while all other browsers use yet another method. The upshot of the code is that if the browser supports Ajax (which all major modern browsers do), then a new object called `ajax` is created.

In the second part of the function is a pair of nested `if()` statements. The outer one is entered only if the `ajax` object was created; otherwise, `false` is returned to signal failure. On success, an anonymous (unnamed) function is attached to the onreadystatechange event of the `ajax` object:

```
ajax.onreadystatechange = function()
```

This event is triggered whenever anything new happens in the Ajax exchange with the server. So, by attaching to it, the code can listen in and be ready to receive any data sent to the browser by the server:

```
if (this.readyState    == 4    &&
    this.status        == 200 &&
    this.responseText != null)
  callback.call(this.responseText)
```

Here, the attached function checks the readyState property of the `this` object (which represents the `ajax` object), and if it has a value of 4, the server has sent some data. If that's the case, if `this.status` has a value of 200, the data sent by the server was meaningful and not an error. Finally, if `this.responseText` doesn't have a value of null, the data was not just an empty string, so the `callback.call()` method is called:

```
callback.call(this.responseText)
```

I mentioned `callback` at the start of this explanation. It is the name of a function passed to the `CreateAjaxObject()` function, so that `CreateAjaxObject()` can call `callback()` when new Ajax data is received. The `callback()` function takes the value received in `this.responseText`, which is the data returned by the web server. I'll explain what goes into the `callback()` function a little later.

The `PostAjaxRequest()` Function

You will never have to call `CreateAjaxObject()` yourself, because there are two more functions to complete the Ajax process (which will do the calling of `CreateAjaxObject()` for you): one for communicating with the server by Post requests, and the other for using Get requests.

The `PostAjaxRequest()` function takes three arguments: the name of your callback function to receive data from the server, a URL with which to communicate with the server, and a string containing arguments to post to the server. It looks like this:

```
function PostAjaxRequest(callback, url, args)
{
  var contenttype = 'application/x-www-form-urlencoded'
  var ajax        = new CreateAjaxObject(callback)
  if (!ajax) return false

  ajax.open('POST', url, true)
  ajax.setRequestHeader('Content-type',   contenttype)
  ajax.setRequestHeader('Content-length', args.length)
  ajax.setRequestHeader('Connection',     'close')
  ajax.send(args)
  return true
}
```

This function first sets `contenttype` to a string value that enables encoded form data to be transmitted:

```
var contenttype = 'application/x-www-form-urlencoded'
```

Then, either the new `ajax` object is created or `false` is returned to indicate an error was encountered:

```
var ajax = new CreateAjaxObject(callback)
if (!ajax) return false
```

Now that an `ajax` object has been created, the following lines open the Ajax request with a call to the `open()` method of the `ajax` object as well as send headers to the server via a Post request, including the `contenttype` string, the length of the `args` argument, and a header to close the connection when done (instead of keeping the connection alive):

```
ajax.open('POST', url, true)
ajax.setRequestHeader('Content-type',   contenttype)
ajax.setRequestHeader('Content-length', args.length)
ajax.setRequestHeader('Connection',     'close')
```

The data is then sent, the connection is closed, and a value of true is returned to indicate success:

```
ajax.send(args)
return true
```

The `GetAjaxRequest()` Function

The PostAjaxRequest() function comes with a sister function that performs exactly the same process, but it sends the data using a Get request. You need to have both functions in your toolkit because some servers you may interact with require Post requests, and some will need Get requests for their Ajax calls.

Here's what the partner GetAjaxRequest() function looks like:

```
function GetAjaxRequest(callback, url, args)
{
  var nocache = '&nocache=' + Math.random() * 1000000
  var ajax = new CreateAjaxObject(callback)
  if (!ajax) return false

  ajax.open('GET', url + '?' + args + nocache, true)
  ajax.send(null)
  return true
}
```

One of the main differences between this and the PostAjaxRequest() function is that a variable called nocache is created from a random number so that a unique value can be added to the query string sent by each Get request, which will prevent any caching the server might perform, by ensuring that every request sent is unique:

```
var nocache = '&nocache=' + Math.random() * 1000000
```

The next couple of lines are the same as the PostAjaxRequest() function. They create a new ajax object, or return false if that fails:

```
var ajax = new CreateAjaxObject(callback)
if (!ajax) return false
```

Finally, the Get request is made with a call to the open() method of the ajax object, the request is sent, and then true is returned to indicate success:

```
ajax.open('GET', url + '?' + args + nocache, true)
ajax.send(null)
return true
```

The `callback()` Function

Now we are ready to create our `callback()` function that will receive the data sent back to PHP via Ajax, as follows:

```
function callback()
{
  document.getElementById('mydiv').innerHTML = this
}
```

This code supplies the value passed to the function in `this` to the `innerHTML` property of a `<div>` with the `id` of `mydiv`. All that remains to do is create the `<div>`, like this:

```
<div id='mydiv'></div>
```

And now we are ready to call either the `PostAjaxRequest()` or the `GetAjaxRequest()` function, like this:

```
PostAjaxRequest(callback, 'ajax.php',
  'url=http://wikipedia.org/wiki/AJAX')
```

Or, like this:

```
GetAjaxRequest(callback, 'ajax.php',
  'url=http://wikipedia.org/wiki/AJAX')
```

In either instance, a program in the same folder as the calling code, called *ajax.php*, is chosen for the communication, and the URL is sent to the program as the value of the key `url`.

The ajax.php Program

The last part of the Ajax puzzle is to write the *ajax.php* program that will reside on the web server and communicate with the web browser, and that's this short snippet of PHP:

```
echo isset($_POST['url']) ?
  file_get_contents($_POST['url']) :
  file_get_contents($_GET['url']);
```

 Note This code assumes that either a Post or a Get request has been made to it, with the value of the key `url` being the URL of a web document to fetch. If this is not the case, it will fail and generate an error.

What it does is test whether the key `url` has been sent to it, either in a Post request (as `$_POST['url']`) or in a Get request (as `$_GET['url']`). In either case, the PHP `file_get_contents()` function is called on the value passed to it (in this case, a Wikipedia page). This fetches the web page referred to, which is then returned to the calling Ajax function using the PHP echo keyword.

Figure 20-5 shows the result of running the Ajax example at the end of this lesson (saved as *ajax.htm* in the accompanying archive), which then communicates with *ajax.php* (also in the archive) on the web server, to insert the contents of a Wikipedia page into a `<div>` element.

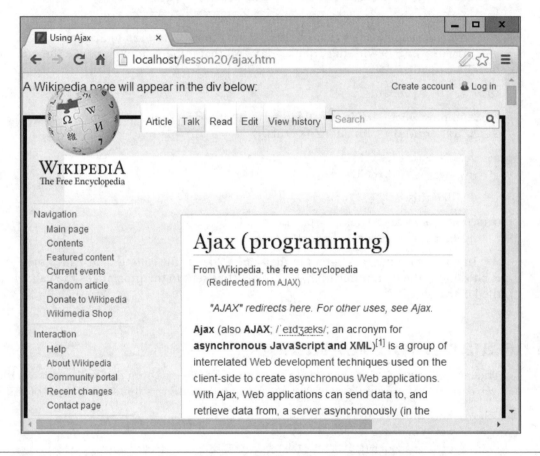

FIGURE 20-5   The Wikipedia page on Ajax has been pulled in via Ajax.

Note   Loading an entire web page and all its sub-elements from a third-party web server and then inserting it into a `<div>` element is not a great way to embed such pages—for that there are `<iframe>` elements. However, this example illustrates how to fetch any data from the web server and then use it (in this case, by displaying it in a `<div>`)—and grabbing a Wikipedia page is as easy as anything else.

For your convenience, I have saved the three Ajax functions in the file *ajaxfunctions.js* in the accompanying archive so that you can include them in the `<head>` of any web page you create that will employ Ajax communication, like this:

```
<html>
  <head>
    <script src='ajaxfunctions.js'></script>
    <!-- etc... -->
```

Using this method to pull in the JavaScript functions from an external file, here's the short and simple code with which Figure 20-5 was created:

```
<!DOCTYPE html>
<html>
  <head>
    <title>Using Ajax</title>
    <script src='ajaxfunctions.js'></script>
    <script>
      PostAjaxRequest(function() {
        document.getElementById('mydiv').innerHTML = this
      }, 'ajax.php', 'url=http://wikipedia.org/wiki/AJAX')
    </script>
  </head>
  <body>
    <p>A Wikipedia page will appear in the div below:</p><br>
    <div id='mydiv' style='border:5px solid'>Loading...</div>
  </body>
</html>
```

As you can see, all you need at the bare minimum is a single call to `PostAjaxRequest()` (or `GetAjaxRequest()`) containing an anonymous (unnamed) function, where you do something with the value in `this`, which is the result returned by the Ajax call. In this instance, the returned value is inserted into the `innerHTML` property of the `<div>` element with the ID of `mydiv`. This is all simply and easily achieved with a single function call—even if you've never used JavaScript before!

Summary

And that, as they say, is that! You've reached the end of the lessons, and I hope you found them as easy to follow as I promised at the start. You now have all the skills you need to be a proficient PHP programmer (and have even picked up a little JavaScript, if you didn't already know it), and are well on your way to creating popular and dynamic websites.

As ever, all comments and suggestions are very welcome via the website at *20lessons.com*. Also, if you feel so motivated, I will be especially grateful if you have a moment to leave a quick review for this book at your preferred online book retailer. Thanks again, and good luck with your web development!

Self-Test Questions

Test how much you have learned in this lesson with these questions. If you don't know an answer, go back and reread the relevant section until your knowledge is complete. You can find the answers in the appendix.

1. How can you initiate HTTP authentication?

2. How can you verify a user's authentication credentials?

3. How can you initiate a PHP session?

4. How can you save values into a session?

5. How can you read a value from a session?

6. How do you close a PHP session?

7. Without enforcing the use of cookies, how can you prevent sessions from being hijacked maliciously?

8. How can you force a session to only use cookies, and to never show session IDs in the address bar in the query string?

9. How can you conduct Ajax background communications with a web server?

10. What is a simple PHP statement to receive an Ajax Post request with a key named `ajax`, whose value is the name of a file in the local folder, and then return the contents of the file to the calling web page?

Answers to the Self-Test Questions

This appendix contains the answers to all the questions posed at the end of the lessons in this book. To ensure you have understood everything, try to refrain from checking these answers until you have attempted to answer all the questions in a lesson.

If you don't know an answer, try to find it in the book before you look here if you can, because this will help you to remember it next time.

Lesson 1 Answers

1. PHP is available for Windows, Mac OS X, and Linux/Unix computers.

2. PHP is compiled only at runtime, effectively making it a scripted language.

3. You can include as many sections of PHP as you like in an HTML document.

4. You must place a $ character in front of all PHP variables.

5. PHP supports both procedural and object-oriented programming (OOP).

6. You should give PHP documents the file extension .php (although servers can be configured to use PHP with any file extension).

7. The five main browsers with which you should test your PHP programs are Microsoft Internet Explorer, Apple Safari, Google Chrome, Mozilla Firefox, and Opera. You should also test your programs on tablets and mobile devices, too, if your target market uses them.

8. You can write and edit PHP programs using a plain text editor, but for better control and handy development tools you may prefer to use a program editor, or an integrated development environment (IDE).

9. There are several PHP server suites (also known as *stacks*) on the Internet. I recommend XAMPP, which is easy to download, install, and use right away.

10. After installing a web server such as Apache (included with XAMPP), your PHP files should be placed in its document root folder, whose location will vary according to operating system.

Lesson 2 Answers

1. You can place sections of PHP code anywhere in a document, but generally will do so in either the body or head (or you can make an entire document PHP, which then uses commands to output HTML).

2. To include a file of PHP instructions into a document, you can use an `include`, `require`, `include_once`, or `require_once` statement (for example: `include 'header.php';`).

3. To prevent an external PHP file from being included multiple times, you can use the `include_once` or `require_once` statement (for example, `include_once 'header.php';`). Any additional attempts to load the file will be ignored.

4. To ensure that a PHP file gets included in a document, you can use the `require` statement (for example: `require 'header.php';`). If the file cannot be loaded, an error will be thrown.

5. To ensure that a PHP file is included *and* that it doesn't get included more than once, you can use the `require_once` statement (for example: `require_once 'heading.php';`). If the file cannot be loaded, an error will be thrown, and any additional attempts to load the file will be ignored.

6. To create a single-line comment in PHP, start it with the `//` comment marker (for example, `// This is a comment`). All text after the comment marker to the end of the line is ignored.

7. To create a multiline comment in PHP, you start it with `/*` and end it with `*/` (for example, `/* The contents between and including these two comment markers is completely ignored by PHP */`).

8. To indicate that a PHP instruction is complete, you must place a semicolon character (`;`) after it (for example, `echo "Hello world";`). Failure to do this is one of the most common causes of errors for beginners.

9. The code `$items = 120; $selection = 7;` is legal PHP because multiple statements are allowed on a line, due to requiring semicolons after each instruction.

10. The code `$items = 120 $selection = 7;` will cause PHP to throw a parse error because there is no semicolon after the number 120 to separate the statements.

Lesson 3 Answers

1. PHP is case-sensitive. This means that the combination of uppercase and lowercase characters used in variables, objects, and function names is important (for example, `$todaysdate` is a different variable to `$TodaysDate`).

2. Any combination of spaces, tabs, linefeeds, and some other non-alphanumeric or punctuation characters is known as *whitespace*.

3. PHP generally ignores whitespace characters that appear outside of strings—whitespace within strings is stored and acted upon, though.

4. A numeric variable is a container for a number, which allows you to address the value using a name (for example, `$age = 32;`).

5. A string variable is a container for a sequence of characters, which can be addressed using a name (for example: `$name = 'Albert Einstein';`).

6. You can include quotation marks within a string (regardless of whether or not the same type is used to contain the string) by escaping them with the `\` escape character, which can also be used to insert special characters (for example, `$mystring = "He said, \"Hello\"\n";`—which also includes a linefeed at the end).

7. A heredoc string is one that is not enclosed in any type of quotation mark. Instead, a token is used to denote the string's start and end, and it is commonly used in conjunction with an `echo` statement or string assignment. The tokens are generally given a preceding underline character to help them stand out (although not required), and the closing token must appear at the very start of a new line (with no indentation and no spaces or tabs before or after the semicolon).

8. PHP variables do not necessarily retain the type they are initially assigned, because if an operation is performed on them that makes better sense if the content were of a different type, then PHP will change the type. Therefore, a string containing all digits is turned into a number by PHP if a mathematical operation is performed on it—for example, the following will output the number 1235, even though `$n` is initially a string: `$n = '1234'; $n = $n + 1; echo $n;`.

9. To force PHP to store a certain type of value in a variable, you can use a casting keyword such as `(int)` or `(string)`. An example would be `$n = (int) '1234';` or `$s = (string) (12 * 34);`.

10. In PHP, to display the values of variables within a string, you do not need to break the string into smaller parts and then use the concatenation operator to splice the parts and variables together (as you must in some languages). Instead, just enclose the string in double quotation marks (not single quotes) and then drop the variable names right in where they are needed (for example, `echo "Hello $name, you have previously visited on $times occasions.";`).

Lesson 4 Answers

1. A constant is similar to a variable in that it stores a value that becomes accessible by name (but without the preceding $ character that is used to access variables). However, unlike a variable, once a value is assigned to a constant, it can never be changed.

2. You define constants using the `define()` function, passing it a name and a value (for example, `define('MAX_USERS', 128);`).

3. Predefined constants are those that PHP has already defined for you to provide information you can access such as the path and filename of the current file (for example, `echo __FILE__;`).

4. The `print` and `echo` commands are very similar to each other in that they both display values provided to them. The differences are that `print` accepts only a single argument but has a return value of 1, so it can be used in some places where `echo` cannot, but `echo` is a little faster and also supports multiple arguments separated by commas (which `print` does not).

5. The statement `($var == TRUE) ? echo "true" : echo "false";` is not valid PHP because echo doesn't return a value and therefore cannot be used within expressions. In such instances, `print` can be used instead (for example, `($var == TRUE) ? print "true" : print "false";`).

6. The superglobal arrays that handle information sent to a PHP program via forms sent using Get and Post methods are `$_GET[]` and `$_POST[]`.

7. The `$_COOKIE[]` superglobal array contains cookie data.

8. You can display the URL of a page from which a user was referred to the current one (if available) with a statement such as `echo $_SERVER[ 'HTTP_REFERER'];`.

9. To sanitize input and other data by replacing any HTML tags with entities that only display the tag names, you can run them through the `htmlentities()` function (for example, `echo htmlentities($_POST['bio']);`).

10. You can get PHP to display its configuration information and the current environment and script with the `phpinfo()` function—for example, `phpinfo(32);` will display the PHP predefined variables.

Lesson 5 Answers

1. The four main mathematical operators (and their symbols in PHP) are plus (+), minus (-), multiply (*), and divide (/).

2. To increment or decrement a variable, you use the increment (++) or decrement (--) operator, respectively.

3. The difference between pre- and post-incrementing and pre- and post-decrementing is the position in which you place the operator. To pre-increment a variable, you place the increment operator in front of it (for example, ++$a). To post-increment, you place it afterwards (for example, $a++). Pre- and post-decrementing are similar (for example, --$a and $a--). Pre-incremented and pre-decremented variables have their value changed *before* it is accessed for use in an expression, whereas post-incremented and post-decremented variables first have their value used in an expression, and only *after* that is it changed.

4. The modulus operator symbol is %, and it returns the integer remainder after a division.

5. To return a number as a non-negative value, regardless of whether it is positive or negative, pass it through the abs() function (for example, $absvalue = abs($myvalue);).

6. In this question, the task is to not allow $v to be negative; therefore, you should use the max() function (even though at first sight it appears that min() should be the answer, because we want a minimum value), like this: $v = max(0, $v);. If $v is less than 0, then the 0 argument will pull it up to 0, because 0 is the maximum of the two values. But if $v is greater than 0, then the argument of $v itself will be the maximum value, and so the same positive value will be assigned back to the variable.

7. To obtain a pseudo-random number between 1 and 100, inclusive, you call the rand() function, passing the minimum and maximum values (for example, $randnum = rand(1, 100);).

8. Using the assignment += operator, you can shorten expressions such as $a = $a + 23; to $a += 23;.

9. If $a has the value 58, the expression $a /= 2; will evaluate to 29.

10. To set the variable $n to contain the remainder after dividing it by 11, you can use the expression $n %= 11;.

Lesson 6 Answers

1. You can compare two values for equality with the == comparison operator (for example, if ($a == 23) ...).

2. To test whether two values are the same *and* of the same type, you use the === identity operator (for example, if ($b === '23') ...).

3. The results of the expressions are a) FALSE, b) TRUE, c) TRUE, and d) FALSE.

4. The result of !(23 === '23') is TRUE, because 23 is not identical to '23' (they have the same numeric value, but one is a number and one is a string), so the inner part evaluates to FALSE, and the ! (not) operator negates this, turning the final value into TRUE.

5. To set the variable $bulb to the value 1 when the variable $daypart has the value 'night', and 0 when it doesn't, you can use the ternary expression: $bulb = ($daypart == 'night') ? 1 : 0;.

6. PHP will evaluate the expression 5 * 4 + 3 / 2 + 1 using precedence, with * and / having greater precedence than +. The result will be 5 * 4 (which is 20) plus 3 / 2 (which is 1.5) plus 1, making 22.5, the same as (5 * 4) + (3 / 2) + 1.

7. To force PHP to evaluate the expression 1 + 2 / 3 * 4 – 5 from left to right, you need to place parentheses in appropriate places. There are different ways to do this, including (1 + 2) / 3 * (4 – 5), which increases the precedence of the + and – operators to that of / and *, but requires a human to determine where to place the parentheses. Alternatively, you can systematically parenthesize each pair of operands and their operator in turn, like this (with the final pair not requiring any parentheses): (((1 + 2) / 3) * 4) – 5.

8. The math operators have left-to-right associativity because the value on the left is being applied to the value on the right, by the operator.

9. The assignment operators have right-to-left associativity because the value on the right is being assigned to the item on the left.

10. It is a good idea to place the most likely to be TRUE expression on the left of the || operator because it has left-to-right associativity. This means that the left-hand expression is tested first, and if it evaluates to TRUE, the right-hand expression will not be tested (thus saving processor cycles). The right-hand expression will only be tested if the left-hand one evaluates to FALSE.

Lesson 7 Answers

1. PHP array names must begin with a $ character and then be followed by any upper- or lowercase letter or the underline character, followed by any sequence of upper- or lowercase letters, digits, or the underline character.

2. Array elements can store strings, numbers, and even other arrays.

3. To create an unpopulated array, use the array() function (for example, $ThisArray = array();).

4. To assign a value to a specific element in a numeric array, reference the array with an index value, starting from 0 (for example, $Food[7] = 'Doughnuts';).

5. To create and populate an array with a single instruction, pass the initial element values as arguments to the array() function (for example, $Tools = array('Hammer', 'Screwdriver', 'Pliers');).

6. To add elements to a numeric array without specifying an index location, use an empty index—for example, use $Shopping[] = 'Bread'; to insert the value at the end of the array.

7. To retrieve a value from a numeric array, supply an index value between the square brackets (for example, echo $Tools[2];).

8. To reference a numeric array element using a variable, use the variable in place of a numeric value—for example, use echo $Shopping[$index]; to display the contents of the element referenced by whatever numeric value is stored in $index.

9. A new associative array to hold the names and phone numbers of three contacts could be created in this way: $Contacts = array('Albert' => '123-456-7890', 'Becky' => '111-222-3333', 'Charles' => '098-765-4321');.

10. To retrieve a value from an associative array, supply the key of the key/value pair between the square brackets—for example, this displays Becky's number from the preceding question: echo $Contacts['Becky'];.

Lesson 8 Answers

1. Although PHP doesn't natively support arrays of more than one dimension, it allows entire arrays to be assigned to array elements, resulting in a structure that can be addressed like a multidimensional array.

2. To hold the contents of a 3×3 Tic-Tac-Toe board, you can create an array of three elements, and assign each element another three-element array. For example, you could do this: $oxo = array(array(' ', ' ', ' '), array(' ', ' ', ' '), array(' ', ' ', ' '));.

3. To reference the top-left element in a 3×3 array called $oxo, you could use a statement such as echo $oxo[0][0];, or for the bottom-right corner you could use echo $oxo[2][2];.

4. To pre-increment a numeric value stored in an associative array at $PageClicks['homepage'], you could use a statement such as the following: ++$PageClicks['homepage'];.

5. You can post-decrement a numeric value stored in an associative array at $PageClicks['homepage']['menu'] with a statement such as this: $PageClicks['homepage']['menu']--;.

6. To populate an associative array called $marbles with three sizes of marbles in 17, 23, and 21 bags, you could use a statement such as $marbles = array('small' => 17, 'medium' => 23, 'large' => 21);.

7. You could create an array called $marbles with the three sizes of marbles, and a sub-array in each element, like this: $marbles = array('small' => array(), 'medium' => array(), 'large' => array());.

8. You could assign colors and quantities to the second level of the array in Question 7, like this: $marbles ['small'] ['red'] = 11;.

9. Assuming all the elements for the array in Question 7 have been assigned values for the three sizes, three colors, and stock quantities, you could determine the stock level of medium bags of blue marbles like this: echo $marbles ['medium'] ['blue'];.

10. You can increment the value in $marbles ['large'] ['red'] by 10 with a single statement, such as $marbles ['large'] ['red'] += 10;.

Lesson 9 Answers

1. You can use the foreach() function to iterate through a numeric array and extract the values, like this: foreach ($Array as $Value) { /* do something with $Value */ }.

2. You can use the foreach() function to iterate through an associative array and extract the key/value pairs, like this: foreach ($Array as $Key => $Value) { /* do something with $Key and $Value */ }.

3. You can merge together the arrays $Cars and $Trucks into a new array called $Vehicles using a statement such as $Vehicles = array_merge ($Cars, $Trucks);.

4. You can combine all the elements of the array $Itinerary into a string with the separator string ', ', using a statement such as $ToDo = implode (', ', $Itinerary);.

5. You can call the function process() on all elements of the array $info[] like this: array_walk ($info, 'process');.

6. You can add a new value to the end of an array using the array_push() function. For example, you could use array_push($Chores, 'Sweep the yard');, which is equivalent to $Chores [sizeof ($Chores)] = 'Sweep the yard';.

7. You can read and remove the last item in an array using the array_pop() function (for example, $Chore = array_pop ($Chores);).

8. When you call the array_push() function, the supplied value is placed at the end of the array.

9. When you call the array_pop() function, the value at the end of the supplied array is removed and returned.

10. To switch all the keys in an array with their associated values, you can call the array_flip() function in the following manner: $Presidents = array_flip($Presidents);.

Lesson 10 Answers

1. The term FILO stands for *First In, Last Out*. It is the kind of storage and retrieval that happens when `array_push()` and `array_pop()` are used together. This kind of array is more commonly known as a *stack*.

2. The term FIFO stands for *First In, First Out*. It is the kind of storage and retrieval that happens when `array_unshift()` and `array_pop()` are used together. This kind of array is more commonly known as a *buffer*.

3. You can "push" a value to the start of an array using the `array_unshift()` function.

4. You can "pop" a value from the start of an array using the `array_shift()` function.

5. To sort the array `$Recipes[]` alphabetically, you can issue the command `sort($Recipes);`.

6. To numerically sort the array `$Temps[]`, add the argument SORT_NUMERIC to the `sort()` function (for example, `sort($Temps, SORT_NUMERIC);`).

7. If you need to have access to the original order of an array after it has been sorted, you must make a copy of the array before sorting (for example, `$CopyOfRecipes = $Recipes; sort($Recipes);`).

8. To remove the elements at indexes 4 and 5 from the array `$URLs[]`, you could use the statement `array_splice($URLs, 4, 2);`.

9. You can insert the string google.com into the array `$URLs[]` at index 6, with the statement `array_splice($URLs, 6, 0, 'google.com');`.

10. To overwrite the existing value at index 3 in the array `$URLs[]` with the string google.com, you can use the statement `array_splice($URLs, 3, 1, 'google.com');`.

Lesson 11 Answers

1. The basic PHP construct for testing whether an expression evaluates to TRUE is the `if()` construct. Here's an example: `if ($NewScore > $HighScore) $HighScore = $NewScore;`.

2. When more than one statement is to be executed following an `if()` condition, you must enclose them all in curly braces; otherwise, only the first will be executed as a result of the condition, and the remaining ones will always be executed.

3. If you wish to execute one or more statements when an if() condition is FALSE, you can follow the if() section with an else section. Here's an example: if ($Today == $Birthday) echo 'Happy Birthday!'; else echo 'Welcome back';.

4. When an if() expression evaluates to FALSE, you can continue testing further expressions using elseif(). Here's an example: if ($Today == $Birthday) echo 'Happy Birthday!'; elseif ($Yesterday == $Birthday) echo 'How is your head?';.

5. In a sequence of conditions using if(), elseif(), and else statements, there should be only one if() statement, followed by one else statement (or none), and there can be as many elseif() statements as you like (or none) in between.

6. Because editing complex condition structures without the braces in place is a common source of program flow errors, if any part of an if() ... elseif() ... else construct contains more than one statement (and thus requires encapsulating in curly braces), then it is a good idea to also enclose all accompanying sets of statements in curly braces too, even if they are single statements.

7. When there is more than one elseif() statement in a sequence of conditions, it can make sense to convert the code to using a switch() statement.

8. To test each individual condition in a switch() statement, you use the case keyword (for example, case 'Rebecca': echo 'Hi Becky';).

9. To signify the end of a sequence of statements following a case keyword, you use a break keyword (for example, case 'Andrew': echo 'Hi Andy'; break;).

10. In a switch() statement, the default case is equivalent to an else section in an if() construct, supplying a default set of statements for all unmatched cases (for example, default: echo 'Hi Guest'; $DoLogin(); break;).

Lesson 12 Answers

1. The type of PHP loop that is not entered unless an expression evaluates to TRUE, and then continues looping until the expression is FALSE, is a while() loop. Here's an example: while ($count < 10) { ++$count; }.

2. Curly braces are required around loop statements if there is more than one statement. Where there is a single statement, the braces are optional. Here's an example: while ($count < 10) ++$count;.

3. A do ... while() loop will always execute at least once, because the condition test occurs after the body of statements. Here's an example: do $count -= 2; while ($count > 0);.

4. With a for () loop, you can initialize variables, test for conditions, and modify variables after each iteration, all in a single statement.

5. You separate the three sections of a for () loop with a semicolon character. Here's an example: for ($count = 0 ; $count < 10 ; ++$count) echo $count;.

6. You can include additional variable initializations and post-iteration assignments in a for () loop by placing them in the relevant sections, separated with commas. Here's an example: for ($count = 0, $c2 = 20 ; $count < 10 ; ++$count, $c2 -= 2) echo $count, $c2;.

7. To cease execution of a loop, and move program flow to the following statement after the loop, you can issue a break statement.

8. You can break out of the current loop, as well as another loop that contains it, by adding an extra argument along with the break keyword, indicating the number of levels to break out from, like this: break 2;.

9. You can skip the current iteration of a loop, and move onto the next iteration, by issuing a continue statement.

10. To drop out of a loop *and* skip an iteration in the enclosing loop structure, you can supply an additional parameter along with the continue keyword, like this: continue 2;.

Lesson 13 Answers

1. Functions are sections of code that you call from any other part of the code, and which perform one or more actions before returning, with an optional value.

2. Curly braces are required around the statements in a function, even if there is only one. Here's an example: function SquareRoot ($n) { return pow ($n, 0.5); }.

3. To call a function, you use its name, followed by parentheses, within which you place the arguments to the function (for example, echo SquareRoot (81) ;).

4. A function receives the values on which it will work via the arguments passed to it within parentheses.

5. To assign default values to the arguments passed to a function, assign the default value to the variable within the function parentheses. Here's an example: function MyFunc ($a = 1) { /* Code goes here */ }.

6. You can handle variable numbers of arguments for a function by calling func_num_args () to determine how many arguments have been passed and func_get_arg (n), where n is the index of the argument to access (starting from 0). Here's an example: for ($j = 0 ; $j < func_num_args () ; ++$j) echo func_get_arg ($j);.

7. A function returns to the calling code, either when the closing curly brace is reached or when a `return` statement is encountered.

8. The difference between local and global scope in PHP is that by default all variables in functions have a value local only to that function, unless the `global` keyword has been used to indicate that the variable is global.

9. To access a global variable from a PHP function, use the `global` keyword (for example, `global $contents;`).

10. You can access global variables in a function with the superglobal `$GLOBALS[]` array (for example, `echo $GLOBALS['contents'];`).

Lesson 14 Answers

1. In OOP (Object-Oriented Programming), the combination of code and the data it manipulates is called a *class*.

2. To declare a class in PHP, use the `class` keyword (for example, `class MyClass { ... }`).

3. To create an object from a class, use the `new` keyword (for example, `$MyObject = new MyClass;`).

4. You can modify properties of an object with the `->` operator (for example, `$MyObject->property = 'Property Value';`).

5. The recommended way to create a constructor method for a class is to define a `__construct()` function, like this: `function __construct($arg1, $arg2) { ... }`.

6. It is a good idea to include a `__destruct()` method in your classes to enable PHP to release its resources back to the system in the manner you specify.

7. To copy an object, use the `clone` operator (for example, `$ThisObj = clone $ThatObj;`).

8. To access a method in the parent of a subclass, you will need to use both the `parent` keyword and the scope resolution operator (`::`). Here's an example: `parent::ParentMethod();`.

9. To create a new class that inherits the properties and methods of an existing one, use the `extends` keyword. Here's an example: `class NewClass extends OldClass { ... }`.

10. The three types of visibility you can apply to properties and methods are `public` (the default), `protected` (accessible only by an object's class and subclass methods), and `private` (accessible only in the same class).

Lesson 15 Answers

1. You can add your own error handler to PHP with the `set_error_handler()` function, to which you pass the name of a function (or the function itself) for processing the error. The function you supply will be passed four values: the error number, the error message, the file containing the error, and the line number within the file.

2. To disable your own error handler, call the `restore_error_handler()` function to revert to the previous error handler.

3. You can search for occurrences of a string using the `preg_match()` function. For example, `$result = preg_match('/search/', $haystack, $match);` will return the result in the array `$match[]`.

4. Search strings must be formatted as regular expressions, starting and ending with a / character (for example, `$search = '/LookForMe/';`).

5. To set a regular expression to match regardless of case, add the pattern modifier `i` (for insensitive) at the end of the expression (for example, `$search = '/find/i';`).

6. To match all occurrences of a search string, you use the `preg_match_all()` function. Here's an example: `$result = preg_match_all('/search/', $haystack, $matches);`.

7. You must pass two arguments to the `preg_match()` and `preg_match_all()` functions: a regular expression string and a string to search in. The third argument is optional and is an array in which results will be saved.

8. To replace any matches with a replacement string, call the `preg_replace()` function, which requires the following: a regular expression, a replacement string, and a string to be searched and replaced in. To count the number of replacements, you can add an optional fifth argument. Here's an example: `preg_replace('/pin/i', 'needle', $haystack, -1, $count);`.

9. To search for any occurrences of either `car` or `automobile`, you could use either of the following regular expressions: `'/car|automobile/'` or `'/(car)|(automobile)/'`.

10. Here is one way you can case-insensitively find all six-letter words in a string: `preg_match_all('/\b[\w]{6}\b/', $string, $matches);`. The `\b` metacharacters require a word boundary both before and after each word, and `[\w]{6}` will return only those words within those word boundaries that are six letters long. The `i` pattern modifier is not required to make this search insensitive, because the `\w` metacharacter matches both lower- and uppercase characters (as well as digits and the underline character). The file *sixletters.php* in the accompanying archive illustrates this in action.

Lesson 16 Answers

1. A Post request sends form data to a program in the form of headers, which are transmitted separately from the HTML, whereas a Get request sends this data in the form of a query string, which is attached to the tail of the requested URL.

2. In a Get request, the ? character indicates the start of a query string. The = character is used to separate keys and values, and the & character separates key/value pairs, like this: `http://site.com?key1=one&key2=two`.

3. To access form data sent to PHP via a Post request, look for expected keys in the `$_POST[]` array and, if they exist, load the values from that array, like this: `if (isset($_POST['mykey'])) $mykey = $_POST['mykey'];`.

4. To access form data sent to PHP via a Get request, look for expected keys in the `$_GET[]` array and, if they exist, load the values from that array, like this: `if (isset($_GET['mykey'])) $mykey = $_GET['mykey'];`.

5. To ensure that your PHP program doesn't throw an error if no submitted data can be retrieved, you should initialize all variables that are to be used for retrieving submitted data with default values such as the empty string. Then, if no data is retrieved, they will still have an initialized value that can be tested without error.

6. To enable users to resubmit a form with a problem in one of its inputs, without requiring them to reenter all the data, you assign values to the `value` attributes of the `<input>` elements, based on the data posted to PHP. Here's an example (assuming there is a string already in $username): `echo "<input type='text' name='username' value='$username'>";`.

7. To submit a collection of checkbox inputs, the name attribute of each `<input type='checkbox' ...>` element should be given the same name, which must end with `[]` (square brackets, which indicate that array data is desired). Here's an example: `<input type='checkbox' name='choices[]' value='item1'>`.

8. To submit a collection of options from a `<select>` element that uses the `multiple` attribute, the name attribute of the `<select>` element must end with `[]` (square brackets, which indicate that array data is desired). Here's an example: `<select name='options[]' multiple> ... </select>`.

9. To access array data submitted from a web page using PHP, you read it from either the `$_GET[]` or `$_POST[]` array (according to how it was sent to the program), in the normal way. The only difference is that the retrieved data will be an array, which you can iterate through or retrieve individual elements from, just like any other array.

10. You can store data in a form without showing it to the user by placing it in an `<input>` element that uses the type of hidden. Here's an example: `<input name='secret' type='hidden' value='terceSpoT'>`.

Lesson 17 Answers

1. You can sanitize user input so that no HTML tags get through by passing it through the `htmlentities()` function.

2. In order to be able to upload files to a web server, a `<form>` element should use the encoding type of `multipart/form-data`. Here's an example: `<form method='post' action='form.php' enctype='multipart/form-data'>`.

3. In order to allow a file to be selected for uploading via a form, `<input>` elements must use a `type` of `file` (for example, `<input type='file' name='file'>`).

4. After a form has uploaded a file to a web server, all the details about the file will be in the superglobal `$_FILES[]` array, using the value supplied to the name attribute of the `<input>` element as a key. If the value in name is `file` (for example), the array to process will be `$_FILES['file'][]`.

5. After a file upload, you can retrieve the following pieces of information from the `$_FILES[]` array using these keys for the second level of the array: name, type, size, tmp_name, and error. For example (if the value given to the name attribute of the `<input>` element is `file`), `$_FILES['file']['size']` returns the size of the uploaded file.

6. The three main image MIME types you are likely to encounter are `image/gif`, `image/jpeg`, and `image/png`, but there are several other image types, too.

7. To ensure that an uploaded file will not compromise your web server, you can strip out all / characters and other file system control characters from the filename using a regular expression such as `'/[^\w.-]/'`. You can also ensure that the file is never allowed to be executed as a program by ensuring that (if it is an image, for example) only the file extensions .gif, .jpg, and .png in the filename supplied are allowed, and by refusing to handle any others. Some web servers also virus-check files as soon as they are uploaded, and may also scan them for other malicious intent.

8. Once you have received a file and sanitized its filename, you are ready to move the file from temporary storage to its permanent location, which you do with the `move_uploaded_file()` function. For example (assuming the value given to the name attribute of the `<input>` element is `file`, and $name contains the sanitized filename), you can use the following: `move_uploaded_file ($_FILES['file']['tmp_name'], "/usr/home/robin/$name");`.

9. To lessen the possibility that "bots" are accessing your websites instead of humans, you can add a CAPTCHA procedure to your web forms, and only allow processing of the form if the test for a human succeeds.

10. If your program might have to run on different platforms, there may be differences between the case-sensitivity or otherwise of filenames. Therefore, it's best to remove any doubt and filter all filenames to all upper- or lowercase before you save them, like this: `$file = strtolower($file);`.

Lesson 18 Answers

1. To set a cookie with the name `cookie`, a value of `choc-chip`, and an expiry date of 30 days time, you could use a statement such as `setcookie('cookie', 'choc-chip', time() + 60 * 60 * 24 * 30);` (or you could replace the calculation of `60 * 60 * 24 * 30` with the predetermined value `2592000`). The `setcookie()` statement must be executed before any body data is sent to the browser; otherwise, the cookie header cannot be sent.

2. To read the value (if there is one) of a cookie named `cookie`, you can use an expression such as `if (isset($_COOKIE['cookie'])) $cookie = $_COOKIE['cookie'];`.

3. To delete a cookie, you assign it an expiry date in the past—for example, `setcookie('cookie', '', time() - 500);`—and you can leave the cookie value blank when doing so, because the cookie is going to be erased anyway. The `setcookie()` statement must be executed before any body data is sent to the browser; otherwise, the cookie header cannot be sent.

4. You can generally determine the make of browser and the platform it is running on by interrogating the browser's User Agent string, referring to `$_SERVER['HTTP_USER_AGENT']`. You can then look for words or phrases that indicate particular browsers and platforms.

5. To test for the preexistence of a file on your web server, you can call the `file_exists()` function, passing the filename (including path if required). Here's an example: `if (file_exists('log.txt')) echo 'The file exists';`.

6. To open a file for writing to, you can call the `fopen()` function, passing the name of the file and a string specifying the file mode of `w`, also making a note of the file handle that the call returns for using with later write operations. Here's an example: `$handle = fopen('log.txt', 'w');`.

7. You can write the string `'This is a sentence'` to a file opened in write mode with the following statement: `fwrite($handle, 'This is a sentence');`.

8. To open a file for reading, use a statement such as `$handle = fopen('log .txt', 'r');`.

9. With a file opened in read mode, you can read in a string of up to a maximum of 100 characters, or the next newline or file end (whatever comes first), with a statement such as `$string = fgets($handle, 101);`.

10. With a file opened in read mode, you can read in exactly 1,000 bytes (or up to the file end if sooner) using a statement such as `$data = fread($handle, 1000);`.

Lesson 19 Answers

1. When calling a function, you can prevent PHP from displaying its own error messages by prefacing the function name with an @ symbol—for example: `@fwrite($handle, $string);`.

2. To determine the length of a file, you can call the `filesize()` function (for example, `$length = filesize('myfile.txt');`).

3. You can insert newline characters when writing to a file using the \n escape sequence (for example, `fwrite($handle, "Line1\n Line2\n");`).

4. You can read in an entire file using the `file_get_contents()` function. Here's an example: `$contents = file_get_contents('document.txt');`.

5. You can save an entire file using the `file_put_contents()` function. Here's an example: `file_put_contents('document.txt', $contents);`.

6. To read in a web document or object from a URL, you can call the `file_get_contents()` function, passing it the URL to retrieve. Here's an example: `$image = file_get_contents('http://webserver.com/ pic.gif');`.

7. You can create a copy of a file using the `copy()` function (for example, `copy('this.file', 'that.file');`).

8. You can delete a file using the `unlink()` function (for example, `unlink('unwanted.file');`).

9. You can move the pointer into an open file using the `fseek()` function (for example, `fseek($handle, 123);`).

10. You can prevent file accesses by one user conflicting with those by another by using the `flock()` function. Here's an example: `if (flock($handle, LOCK_ EX)) { fwrite($handle, $contents); flock($handle, LOCK_UN); }`.

Lesson 20 Answers

1. To initiate HTTP authentication, you must send a pair of headers to the browser requesting the authentication, like this: `header('WWW-Authenticate: Basic realm="Restricted Section"'); header('HTTP/1.0 401 Unauthorized');`. Once these headers have been sent, you can optionally output some text telling the user what is expected of them in order to log in. Here's an example: `echo 'Please enter your username and password';`.

2. To verify the credentials (username and password) that a user enters in response to an authentication request, you must test the `PHP_AUTH_USER` and `PHP_AUTH_PW` elements in the superglobal array `$_SERVER[]` to determine whether they match any of the allowed username/password pairs. Here's an example: `if ($_SERVER['PHP_AUTH_USER'] != $username || $_SERVER['PHP_AUTH_PW'] != $password) die("Sorry, Invalid details");`.

3. To initiate a PHP session, before any HTML has been sent to the browser you must call the `session_start()` function.

4. To save values into a session, assign them to the `$_SESSION[]` superglobal array (for example, `$_SESSION['username'] = $username;`).

5. To read a value from a session, fetch it from the `$_SESSION[]` superglobal array (for example, `$password = $_SESSION['password'];`).

6. To close a PHP session, you can quickly clear the `$_SESSION[]` array by assigning it the value `array()`, and you should also delete the session cookie if there is one (you can look up its name with the `session_name()` function). Finally, you should call the `session_destroy()` function to close the session.

7. Without enforcing the use of cookies, you can prevent sessions from being hijacked maliciously by saving each user's IP address and User Agent string in the `$_SESSION[]` array when the session is first initiated, and then comparing it with the current IP address and User Agent on each subsequent page load. If they don't match, terminate the session and ask the user to login again.

8. To force a session to only use cookies, you can issue this statement at the start of your PHP script: `ini_set('session.use_only_cookies', 1);`. Remember that you may have to comply with laws such as the cookie opt-out requirement in European Community countries, for this and any other cookie use.

9. To conduct Ajax background communications with a web server, you first need to create an Ajax object in JavaScript, and then make a Get or Post request to a PHP program (or other URL), requesting some data. The accompanying archive of examples includes the file *ajaxfunctions.js* to handle this for you.

10. A simple PHP statement that receives an Ajax Post request with a key named `ajax`, whose value is the name of a file in the local folder, and then returns the contents of the file to the calling web page, could look like the following: `if (isset($_POST['ajax'])) echo file_get_contents($_POST['ajax']);`.

Index

33164005236059